PHILOSOPHY OF SCIENCE, COGNITIVE PSYCHOLOGY, AND EDUCATIONAL THEORY AND PRACTICE

SUNY Series in Science Education
Robert E. Yager, Editor

PHILOSOPHY OF SCIENCE, COGNITIVE PSYCHOLOGY, AND EDUCATIONAL THEORY AND PRACTICE

Richard A. Duschl
and
Richard J. Hamilton,
Editors

STATE UNIVERSITY OF NEW YORK PRESS

Published by
State University of New York Press, Albany

© 1992 State University of New York

For information, address State University of New York
Press, State University Plaza, Albany, N.Y., 12246

Production by E. Moore
Marketing by Bernadette LaManna

Library of Congress Cataloging-in-Publication Data

Philosophy of science, cognitive psychology, and educational theory
    and practice / Richard A. Duschl and Richard J. Hamilton, editors.
        p.   cm. — (SUNY series in science education)
    Includes bibliographical references (p.   ) and index.
    ISBN 0-7914-1053-6 (alk. paper). — ISBN 0-7914-1054-4 (pbk. :
alk. paper)
        1. Science—Study and teaching (Elementary)—United States.
    2. Cognition in children—United States. 3. Science—United States-
    -Philosophy. I. Duschl, Richard A. (Richard Allan), 1951-
    II. Hamilton, Richard J., 1952-   . III. Series.
    LB1585.3.P47 1992
    372.3'5044—dc20   91-22633
                                                                      CIP

10 9 8 7 6 5 4 3 2 1

To the memory of my mother, Marcelle Hamilton.

To my parents Herman and Elizabeth Duschl,
who have been so supportive in so many ways.

Contents

Preface

The preparation of this edited volume represents a culmination of many years of inquiry by the editors into the complex set of issues and questions surrounding the teaching and the learning of science. It began in 1987 as an informal reading group of University of Houston and Rice University faculty and students interested in exploring the idea of adopting "schema" as the cognitive unit for representing an individual's theoretical knowledge. Early on, it became apparent that the domain of the topic cut across numerous fields of scholarly inquiry. In the ensuing years, the scientific theory/cognitive schema theme was developed in papers presented at a variety of national and international psychological, educational, science teaching, and philosophy of science conventions. At each of these venues, reactions from those in attendance indicated a keen interest in the topic embraced by this edited volume.

As the title of the volume suggests, we have sought to merge perspectives from the fields of philosophy of science and cognitive psychology. All too often scholars can be unaware of research on education that falls outside their own discipline—even when such work offers exciting insights directly relevant to their own inquiries. One general purpose of this volume, then, is to foster cross-discipline communication on emerging issues in science teaching and learning. By design we have brought together into one volume philosophers, cognitive psychologists, and educational theorists and researchers.

We have carefully selected authors who we feel are attempting to "revolutionize" current thought and research on the design, implementation, and assessment of science instruction. Our intent in putting together this edited volume is threefold. We hope to introduce established researchers, curriculum writers, supervisors and/or policy makers in science education to new and diverse ideas. We hope to introduce individuals new to these areas of education to broader and richer perspectives of science education and science education research. We hope to stimulate the interest of all readers in becoming active participants in the interfield dialog of philosophers of science, cognitive psychologists, and educational researchers.

Over the last ten to fifteen years, the underlying assumptions about what it means to learn and to teach science have changed dramatically. And such changes, it is safe to say, principally have come about due to changes in perspectives on (1) the nature and structure of the growth of scientific knowledge as defined by philosophers and (2) the cognitive tasks associated with the development of science knowledge as defined by cognitive psychologists. The effect of these changes has begun to blur the lines which have traditionally separated philosophical and psychological inquiry into the nature and development of scientific knowledge. However, of particular interest to us is, even with the considerable overlap in inquiry between domains, the fact that instructional prescriptions derived from each domain differ significantly. Hence, there exists certain tensions that will be alleviated only through continued dialog and research on the usefulness of each set of prescriptions.

This volume reflects, then, an attempt to bring together perspectives which share a similar purpose and focus, but which suggest different methods for fulfilling their shared purpose. From this interchange, we hope to alter beliefs and standards about what count as effective curriculum designs, instructional sequences, and assessment strategies, that is, as components of an effective science learning environment. Also, we hope to motivate you to contribute to and/or learn more about this emerging area of educational research.

Acknowledgments

This book was made possible because of the spirit of collegiality shared by Richard, Dick, and Rick, who, in spite of the names, could never keep it straight who was who. One a psychologist, one a philosopher, and one a science educator, but all are perpetual students.

The excitement of being a part of something as special as the collaboration leading up to preparation of this edited volume is hard to explain. It involved the complex task each of us faced in coming to grips with new terms, new theories, and new schema. It involved a lot of compromise, some harmless and yet some crucially important and hurtful. It was reading and writing of the sort that one got excited about performing. It was stimulating discussion that owed a great deal to each individual's wanting to grow and to truly understand the perspective of the others. And, in the end, it was a collaboration that has been forced to fit in with many other competing agendas, both professional and personal. Let's all hope it sustains itself—it has made a significant difference in more ways than anyone of us can know. Let us hope, too, that others seek to form such interdisciplinary collaborations.

I, Richard Hamilton, would like to acknowledge the never ending support and encouragement of my wife, Leslie Hamilton. Also, I would like to thank my children, Marcus and Megan Hamilton, who came into my life at about the same time as this edited volume, and Leslie for helping me maintain a balanced perspective on the relative importance of work and play.

RICHARD A. DUSCHL
RICHARD J. HAMILTON

Introduction: Viewing the Domain of Science Education[1]

OUTLINE

I. Introduction
  A. Intended, implemented, and learned curriculum
    1. Nature of science
    2. Nature of learning
    3. Nature of teaching
  B. Teacher conceptions, nature of science, learning, and teaching
  C. Student conceptions, nature of science and learning
II. An Emerging Domain
III. Overview of Chapters
IV. Summary

ABSTRACT

We find ourselves at a critical and exciting time in science education. It is critical because scholars from distinct disciplines are working on similar types of problems that have relevance for science education research and practice. Separate disciplines that explore a common ground of inquiry, that seek solutions to the same problem, that ask related questions, that draw from a related literature, and that share knowledge claims are referred to as "domains." Since the 1950s, advances in philosophy of science, cognitive psychology, and science education have led to the development of an "emerging domain" that seeks to understand the dynamics of the growth of scientific knowledge. The first part of this chapter describes how important ideas drawn from the different disciplines of the emerging domain have contributed to our knowledge of curriculum development and implementation of science curriculum. The second part presents an overview of the following chapters and outlines how each chapter contributes to our understanding of the dynamics of knowledge growth and the teaching and learning of science.

INTRODUCTION

Given the present demand for change in science instructional practices and science curriculum frameworks—e.g., NSTA's scope and sequence, AAAS's Project 2061—we must ask to what extent teacher educators, teachers, and curriculum writers are being provided with the necessary background knowledge to implement curricula that embrace the intentions of educational researchers and curriculum developers. An important lesson learned from the early attempts at teacher training and curriculum development in science education is the various ways in which teachers can change developers' intended curricula (NSF 1955-1975). Connelley (1972), in a review of science education research, reports that curriculum developers intentions are often lost in the transmission of the curriculum to teachers and thence to students.[2] Research that examines teachers' beliefs about teaching, about students and learning, and about subject matter (i.e., the nature of scientific inquiry) demonstrates that classrooms are extremely complex settings (Tobin & Gallagher 1987; Duschl & Wright 1989; Borko & Shavelson 990). Furthermore, this research suggests that teachers' beliefs do effect the type of instructional activities and tasks that make up the cognitive and psychosocial learning environment of the classroom (Doyle 1986; Tobin & Fraser 1990).

Thus, it is possible, and educationally sound, to differentiate between the intended, implemented, and learned curriculum. Roberts (1980/1986) calls changes across this continuum "the modulation of the curriculum." Attempts to develop an effective curriculum framework must, according to Roberts, allow teachers to see the developer's intentions embodied in curriculum materials. An important element of educational practice, and the one emphasized in this volume, is the role teachers play in making decisions about curriculum and instructional activities and tasks.

If it is important to allow teachers to understand a developer's curricula intentions, then it is equally important to clearly represent to curriculum developers teachers' conceptions of both the developers' intentions and the subject matter embodied within the intended curriculum. Current approaches to knowledge representation may be helpful in this regard. Research on expert knowers suggests that they employ two types of knowledge: declarative or domain—specific knowledge and procedural/general strategic knowledge (Perkins & Salomon 1989). The importance of this division of knowledge for understanding teachers' beliefs and curriculum writers' intentions is twofold. At the curriculum development level, attempts to develop science curricula should focus on the strategic knowledge required to adequately use domain specific scientific knowledge. This would entail the identification of general procedures that allow for the acquisition and use of scientific knowledge. At the implementation level, a critical goal of teacher training and student learning should be the acquisition and use of both domain—specific knowledge and generic strategic knowledge (cf, Borko & Shavelson 1990; Alexander & Judy 1988; Derry 1990; Wittrock 1986). A major theme of the current volume is the development and examination of conceptual frameworks that outline the nature of strategic or procedural knowledge within and across scientific domains. Our goal is that these frameworks will establish criteria for teachers and curriculum writers that influence the modulation-of-the-curriculum problem in positive ways.

Current instructional approaches for teaching traditional school subjects to students view learners as active agents in the process of constructing meaning (Resnick & Klofper 1989). The explanatory statements of science—theories—are conceived as having a developmental history which is characterized by continual and ongoing restructuring, modification, and adaptation of knowledge claims as well as investigative methods and aims. Examples of new approaches in science that employ learning frameworks and subject matter frameworks that emphasize knowledge restructuring include:

1. learning cycle[3] (Champagne 1988)
2. the conceptual change teaching model (West & Pines 1985; Anderson & Smith 1986; Roth 1990)
3. the generative learning model (Osborne & Wittrock 1983; Osborne & Freyberg 1985)

These models of conceptual change teaching make specific assumptions, often unarticulated, about the role of the teacher and the dynamics of classroom instruction. Research that looks at classrooms (Doyle 1983, 1986; Lampert 1984; Leinhardt and Greeno 1986; Sanford 1987, 1984; Tobin & Fraser 1990) indicates that when we examine the dynamics of meaning-making instructional strategies at the level of the classroom we find that very complex cognitive tasks confront both teachers and learners.

Doyle (1986, 1983), for example, in his studies on academic work, has found that teachers' definitions of academic work and students' perceptions of instructional tasks can transform the curriculum in ways that have implications for what students learn in classrooms. Such transformations were particularly common when instructional tasks sought to engage students in higher cognitive tasks involving meaning-making activities. Thus, distinguishing between the intended, the implemented, and the learned curriculum would be helpful in capturing the transformations that occur as students and teachers renegotiate instructional tasks.

New images of the complexity of exemplary teaching are emerging. Tobin and Fraser's (1990) study of exemplary teachers' practices found that the lack of teachers' content knowledge result in an emphasis on learning facts and the development or reinforcement of students' misconceptions. Lampert's (1984, 1986) efforts have examined the way in which teachers can use student intuitive knowledge frameworks as stepping stones to learning the formal knowledge of the curriculum. Here, again the complexity of the cognitive tasks for students and for teachers is apparent. Sanford (1987) found that elaborate instructional devices she refers to as "safety nets" are employed by exemplary teachers to encourage and support higher-level thinking instructional activities and tasks.

Leinhardt and Greeno (1986) have also studied exemplary teacher practice, and their findings indicate that elaborate and complex cognitive tasks are characteristic of instructional moves made by these teachers. It is our opinion that the elusive nature of teaching for conceptual change or the restructuring of students' knowledge is embedded in an underestimation of the cognitive and psychosocial dynamics of classroom environments that teach students to understand both scientific knowledge (what we know) and knowledge about science (how we know). Research by Lampert (1990), Tobin and Gallagher (1987), Duschl and Wright (1989), and Mitman et al. (1987) support this opinion. A serious practical problem, however, is that contemporary reform recommendations (i.e., Project 2061 and the National Science Teachers

Associations Scope and Sequence Report) that suggest science curricula ought to consider the inclusion of topics that foster meaning-making among students have yet to fully explore the specific procedures and dynamics for implementing a curriculum of this type.

A rapidly emerging consensus among science and math educators holds that education ought to concentrate on fundamental principles that underlie a domain rather than on the numerous facts and procedures that have made up the curriculum for the majority of students (e.g., Duschl 1990a; Lampert 1986; Resnick 1989; Charles & Silver 1988). Duschl (1990a) has argued for the extension of the notion of "principled knowledge" (Lampert 1986) to science, based on the similarity between the structure of scientific theories and the structure of cognitive schemata. The essence of the argument is that epistemological criteria for guiding the testing of theories and for describing the development of theories do exist and, in turn, can be used to format science instruction (Duschl 1990b). Hodson (1988) also endorses the use of philosophy of science to guide the design and implementation of science instruction toward a more philosophically valid curriculum.

The implications for teaching that are consistent with this view are threefold. First, curricular objectives and lesson plans must focus on fundamental principles of scientific understanding. Second, teaching activities that encourage the development of principled understanding need to be developed. Finally, student work should be considered or assessed in terms consistent with this view.

The process of science is one of developing and testing theories to explain phenomena. Students, current science instruction notwithstanding, are natural theory builders. Of course, these theories are often incomplete (e.g., White & Frederiksen 1987), incoherent (e.g., Ranney & Thagard 1988), and misguided (e.g. Caramazza, McCloskey & Green 1981). Science curricula need to be built around the development, testing, and restructuring of scientific theories if students are to "do science," and not simply learn "about science."

A curriculum should foster theory building at the same time that it respects belief systems that are currently held by the student. Often, these theories recapitulate the historical development of scientific thought (e.g., Nersessian 1989; Nussbaum 1983; Thagard 1990). Instructional activities can provide the opportunities whereby students' current conceptions are confronted and challenged, and, through a set of teacher-guided interactions, theories are restructured. Linn (1986), Novak (1977), Novak and Gowin (1984), Resnick (1983), Finley (1983), Anderson and Smith (1986), and Krupa et al. (1985), among others, each speak to the effect a learner's prior knowledge has on subsequent learning. The collective body of this research implies that learners, as Carey (1986) asserts, develop their cognitive abilities through the process of progressively changing conceptual schemes.

Scientific thinking, of course, must be grounded in the particulars of a domain. Thus, declarative or domain-specific knowledge related to principles, laws, theories, and generalizations must be taught, along with the procedural/generic strategic knowledge and the conditions of its applicability. Within the context of normal scientific developments or weak restructurings there is a small amount of procedural knowledge to be acquired about the fine tuning of theories and the adjustment of conceptual relations. But if we are to produce radical restructuring of concepts, the personal correlate of revolutionary science, then it seems that we must also teach the procedural knowledge involved in evaluation of theory and data. Duschl, Hamilton, and Grandy (this volume) posit that the nature of such procedural knowledge has been little studied and not at all agreed upon. Moreover, they contend it may well vary greatly from one scientific domain (and epoch) to another! The instructional strategy and design that are employed to teach a unit on the Theory of Evolution or Theory of Plate Tectonics might require a very different set of procedural knowledge guidelines than a unit on biological or mineralogical identification and classification.

The challenge, then, for teachers and curriculum writers is how best to integrate both the declarative knowledge structures and the procedural or strategic knowledge structures of a discipline into the framework of curriculums and into the cognitive and psychosocial characteristics of classroom learning environments. Thus, science teachers and curriculum writers need to consider how teachers' conceptions of subject matter and of learners can assist in making the intended curriculum the implemented curriculum and, in turn, the learned curriculum. A promising strategy to employ is one that draws from both cognitive psychological and epistemological principles. Concomitant with the developments of NSF science curriculum projects (1955-1975) were the equally dynamic developments in the fields of cognitive science, computer science, and history and philosophy of science (Duschl 1985). Today, there is a growing consensus among psychologists (e.g., Carey 1986), philosophers (e.g., Giere 1988; Nersessian 1989), and science educators (e.g., Duschl, Hamilton & Grandy this volume; Hodson 1988) that there exist interfield relationships between history and philosophy of science and cognitive science that can inform science education research and practice. Hodson (1988) describes this symbiotic type relationship as follows:

The view that scientific concepts and theories are subject to modification and growth has a direct counterpart in the assumption . . . that children's conceptual frameworks are continuously modified, refined, and made more precise as they gain in experience and understanding. Thus, acceptance of this view of progressive conceptual differentiation in science and of constructivist views of the nature of learning ensures *harmony* between the philosophical and psychological principles underpinning the curriculum. (P. 28, emphasis added)

AN EMERGING DOMAIN

We find ourselves, then, at a critical and exciting time in science education. It is critical because scholars from distinct disciplines are working at similar types of problems that have relevance for science education research and practice. Separate disciplines that explore a common ground of inquiry, that seek solutions to the same problem, that ask related questions, that draw from a related literature and that share knowledge claims are referred to as "domains." "A domain . . . is not *merely* a body of related information; it is a body of related information about which there is a problem, well defined usually and raised on the basis of specific considerations" (Shapere 1977). The history of science during the twentieth century is one in which the generation of new domains of science has been a commonplace event. Biophysics, fluid dynamics, artificial intelligence, geochemistry, and geophysics are examples of the subfield domains that represent a unified subject matter for scientists trained in separate disciplines.

The spawning of interfield relationships among scholars is certainly not restricted to the above sciences. As mentioned above, since the 1950s advances in philosophy of science, cognitive psychology, and science education have led to the development of a domain that, for lack of any specific label, seeks to understand the dynamics of the growth of scientific knowledge. It is the quest for richer analyses of what constitutes scientific knowledge that has spawned domains relevant to science education researchers and practitioners.

Our edited volume has two purposes. The first is to inform those persons unfamiliar with the "growth of scientific knowledge" domain about the domain and thereby hopefully extend the community of participants. The second is to embellish the dialog among teachers and science education researchers interested in participating in research and practice activities that draw upon epistemological and psychological principles of scientific knowledge growth.

OVERVIEW OF CHAPTERS

This edited volume draws upon the expertise of scholars in philosophy of science, cognitive psychology, and science education, scholars who share an interest in understanding the dynamics of knowledge growth, to outline the elements of this important emerging domain for educational researchers. It begins with an article by Richard Duschl, Richard Hamilton, and Richard Grandy, a synthesis of views from science education, cognitive psychology, and philosophy of science, respectively. This lead article was prepared to stimulate the interfield developments cited above and to do so by pointing out where the fields of cognitive psychology and philosophy of science were at odds with one another. It is hoped that by drawing attention to the tensions within the domain, progress will be made.

Each of the contributors to this volume was given a copy of the lead article and asked to react to the ideas presented in the lead article within the context of their respective chapters. Care was taken to invite contributors who would represent the breadth as well as the depth of analysis and inquiry taking place in the emerging domain. As indicated in the introduction, a theme that runs throughout chapters within this volume is the importance of the procedures or strategic knowledge required for the acquisition, appropriate use, and modification of scientific knowledge. Instructional implications related to the nature of procedures for knowledge acquisition in the sciences and the factors which influence the use and development of these procedures are presented in the following chapters. A predominantly psychological or epistemological perspective dominates most chapters; however, each chapter represents a blend of these perspectives. As a collection, we feel the volume represents a strong synthesis of relevant research issues and trends.

The task environment of philosophers of science since the 1950s has been to accurately characterize the dynamics of theory change. This scholarly environment has been informed by historians of science and subsequently shaped by the symbiotic relationship between historians of science and philosophers of science. The efforts by philosophers to establish precise normative guidelines for what it is that "counts" as a theory of science—a task of the logical positivists'—have, along with the observational/theoretical distinction, been rejected. What has emerged, in its place, is a commitment to describing actual science as it is practiced, or reported to have been practiced by historians of science, at a level of detail that embraces the dynamics of theory restructuring.

We have chosen to follow the introductory chapters with an innovative work by a philosopher of science who employs history of science to increase our understanding of the dynamics of theory restructuring. Nancy Nersessian's research and her chapter here, "Constructing and Instructing: The Role of 'Abstraction Techniques' in Creating and Learning Physics," represent a synthesis of history of science, philosophy of science, and cognitive science. What makes her effort different from previous efforts to integrate history of science into science education (e.g., Conant's 1957 Harvard Case Histories in Experimental Science.) is the inclusion of contemporary philosophical and psychological perspectives that focus on knowledge development and restructuring. In this chapter, she argues that the cognitive activities (i.e., "abstraction techniques") of scientists who have constructed new conceptual structures are directly relevant to learning and that understanding these practices will assist us in our efforts to help students construct representations of extant scientific knowledge. That is, we need to investigate (via the history of science) the kinds of procedures employed in the initial construction of conceptual structure and attempt to teach students how to construct these representations for themselves using the same procedures. Students would then not only be made aware of discrepancies in their scientific knowledge, but also be given tools to either restructure their knowledge structures or create new structures.

The next chapter, by Greg Nowak and Paul Thagard is entitled "Newton, Descartes, and Explanatory Coherence" and also represents a synthesis of history of science, philosophy of science. and cognitive science. The authors, however, take a very different approach to the investigation of the history of science. In there chapter, a computational theory of explanatory coherence is applied (via "ECHO" a connectionist computer program) to the conflict between Newtonian mechanics and the Cartesian system of the world. The authors attempt to assess the global coherence of each explanatory system. "Explanatory coherence" can be described as the degree to which propositions of theories are consistent or are interrelated. The successful application of the computational theory to this and other important scientific "revolutions" of the past (cf. Nowak & Thagard in press; Thagard & Nowak 1990, 1988) underscores its usefulness as an efficient means of selecting the best set of explanatory hypotheses and relations within current and past scientific theories. The underlying principles of "explanatory coherence" may be useful in aiding students and teachers to evaluate and compare theories. In this way, students and teachers would have another set of tools by which to evaluate and, perhaps, reconstruct their knowledge of scientific theories.

Richard Kitchener's contribution to the volume—"Piaget's Genetic Epistemology: Epistemological Implications for Science Education"— focuses on the role of the epistemic subject in the process of knowledge growth. His research over the years has shed new light on the proper interpretation of research derived from Piagetian Theory. Within the epistemic subject we see specific ways in which the principles of cognitive psychology join with epistemological principles. A major implication for science education derived from this chapter is the need to focus on *epistemological* change as well as conceptual change. This requires both the monitoring and development of students' theories of knowledge as well as their ability to reason epistemically. Science curricula should induce students to move from an absolutism view of science to a falibilism (probabilititistic) view of science. The author suggests that a historical approach to science may be the best source for the development of science curriculum with the above aims. Again, we see that the history of science is a valuable source for the development of science education curriculum. It is clear that teachers' theory of knowledge and ability to reason epistemically also need to be monitored and modified. How can we ask science teachers to improve students' ability to reason epistemically if they themselves are at a similar stage or a lower stage of epistemic reasoning (cf., Kitchener & King 1981)?

Those familiar with the literature on conceptual change know that the seminal article on the theoretical foundations of conceptual change is that by Posner et al. (1982). But as with science, change is inevitable and we are pleased to include a chapter by Kenneth A. Strike and George J. Posner—"A Revisionist Theory of Conceptual Change"— which represents a revision of their thoughts about what it is that is necessary to foster conceptual change within learners. It also represents an attempt on their part to address some of the criticisms brought against the model of conceptual change advocated in the 1982 article. Their position is a strong step forward in the scholarly dialog surrounding conceptual change teaching. A central construct in the original theory of conceptual change is a learner's "conceptual ecology." Learners' conceptual ecology consists of their knowledge of anomalies, analogies, metaphors, epistemological beliefs, metaphysical beliefs, and knowledge from other areas of inquiry and knowledge of competing conceptions. The difficulty of changing a learner's misconceptions is partially a function of the degree to which these misconceptions are supported by a learner's conceptual ecology. One suggested change presented in the Revisionist Theory is a proposal to broaden our definition of the range of factors which comprise the learner's conceptual ecology to include psychological factors, that is, learner motives and goals. This represents a blending of psychological influences with epistemological factors within a learner's conceptual ecology. An important element of the chapter is the presentation of empirical data in support of the authors' proposed revisions of the original conceptual change framework.

The next chapter, "Contexts of Meaning and Conceptual Integration: How Children Understand and Learn" by Jeffrey Bloom, fits nicely with the Revisionist Theory proposed above, for it is Dr. Bloom's contention that we have underestimated the complexity of children's conceptions about the constructed meanings of science. The research discussed in this chapter sets out the extensiveness of the task science education must undertake, at times in directions not previously considered. Children are viewed as interdisciplinary thinkers, their constructed meanings influenced by a mix of factors, that is, emotions, values, aesthetics, interpretive frameworks, metaphors, and formal and experiential knowledge. To attempt to separate science in a formal way from these multiple contexts of meaning is to ignore the varied nature of childrens' constructed view of the world. The "contexts of meaning" described in this chapter overlap considerably with the extensions of conceptual ecologies proposed in the Revisionist Theory of Conceptual Change. In both cases, a predominantly epistemological view of scientific knowledge is modified in order to incorporate psychological factors and dimensions.

The task environment of cognitive psychologists has increasingly become one that is concerned with learning domain-specific knowledge. The adoption of a view of knowledge and learning that recognizes differences in the declarative knowledge and procedural knowledge employed by individuals working in distinct subject areas has significant implications for others concerned with the structure of knowledge and knowledge restructuring. It isn't surprising, then, to find philosophers examining and integrating the social dimensions and cognitive psychological dimensions into their philosophies of science. The chapter by Stephen P. Norris—"Practical Reasoning in the Production of Scientific Knowledge"—extends the dimensions of this discussion into the area of practical reasoning based on values about what ought to be done. Dr. Norris outlines aspects of scientific knowledge production as well as scientific knowledge acquisition toward the argument that a focus on practical reasoning is central to the epistemic and inquiry frames of understanding. Again, the suggested instructional approach is one that "mines" the history of science and describes the processes and influences on the reasoning (in this context—the practical reasoning) involved in the production of past and current scientific theories.

The final two chapters of the volume are perhaps the most "psychological" and "applied" treatments of the blending of epistemology, psychology, and science education. Richard Mayer's contribution—"Knowledge and Thought: Mental Models that Support Scientific Reasoning"—examines the epistemological, psychological, and educational aspects of science explanations. According to the author, scientific explanations are best represented within the context of the invention of explicit systems models. The models include a description of the main components of the system, the possible states of each component, the causal relations among state changes in the components, and the principles underlying the causal relations. Illustrations of these models (when presented to learners) provide information that supports scientific reasoning and allows for problem-solving transfer including explanation, prediction, and control. The positions taken in this manuscript are derived from a decade-long research program that has had as its goal the development of insights into how students acquire the explanative knowledge they need to achieve scientific understanding.

Continuing with the practical, the chapter by Robert Sherwood and his colleagues at Vanderbilt University's Cognition and Technology Group—"Anchored Instruction in Science and Mathematics: Theoretical Basis, Developmental Projects, and Initial Research Findings"—puts theory into practice. It is very appropriate that we finish this volume with a chapter that contains the most explicit prescriptions for the development of science curriculum. Over the past several years, the authors of this chapter have been developing the concept of "anchored instruction." Outlined here is their model of anchored instruction which situates science and mathematics in meaningful and authentic contexts.

One of the major goals of anchored instruction is to create shared environments that permit sustained exploration by students and teachers and enable them to understand the kinds of problems and opportunities that experts in various areas encounter and the knowledge these experts use as tools. Students and teachers are exposed to situations which require both problem formulation and problem solving. Participants experience the value of exploring the same setting from multiple perspectives and are encouraged to explore the complex settings from their own perspectives. Embedded in the anchored instruction approach are many of the procedures identified and discussed in early chapters of this volume, for example, analogies, imagistic representation, coherence and consistency, cognitive conflict, importance of motives and goals, illustrative models, and so forth. The research described in this last chapter, then, is a preliminary evaluation of the usefulness of both anchored instruction *and* the procedures outlined by the other authors.

SUMMARY

Norwood Hanson in his classic book *Patterns of Discovery* (1958) distinguishes between two ways of seeing. The first, "seeing as," is observation that occurs without the benefit of the appropriate background knowledge. The second, "seeing that," involves observations with the appropriate background knowledge. In a sense, the task science educators face is to take individuals who are "seeing as" observers and help them become "seeing that" observers. This is a simplistic but nonetheless accurate version of what it means to engage in conceptual change teaching.

Sounds simple enough—but anyone who has attempted to restructure a learner's knowledge base knows how difficult the task really is. Educators are fortunate, then, that many cognitive psychologists and philosophers of science have involved themselves in activities which seek to understand the procedural and developmental steps aligned with knowledge growth and restructuring. For psychologists the task is one of documenting the dynamics of reasoning. For philosophers the task is one of accurately characterizing the processes of knowledge growth. The former are principally concerned with the activities of individuals, while the latter are concerned with the activities of individuals within communities. But each discipline has a mutual concern for what it is that counts as prototypical evidence (exemplars) and counter evidence (anomalous data) for an individual.

We hope that this volume will bring about a type of "seeing that" conceptual change among science educators in ways that serve to positively affect instructional decision making. Each chapter is organized structurally to facilitate readers' understanding of the implications for science education theory and practice. There is an abstract and an outline at the beginning of each chapter, which provide an overview of the central concepts. But most importantly each author has been asked to generate a summary section that specifically addresses the implications their ideas have for science education researchers and practitioners. We are convinced that individuals who work through the set of readings in this volume will "see that" science education has evolved a great deal over the last thirty years.

NOTES

1. The editors would like to acknowledge Dr. Drew Gitomer, Educational Testing Service, Princeton, NJ, for the contribution he made to the preparation of the overview of science education research section of this chapter.

2. These results are consistent with the results of research on curriculum implementation in other fields of education as well (See Fullan & Pomfret 1977; Berman & McLaughlin 1976; Waugh & Punch 1987).

3. Champagne's learning cycle, while similar in name to the instructional model developed by Robert Karplus and extended by John Renner, Anthony Lawson, and others, is nonetheless quite different in its intent. Champagne's learning cycle is based on the psychological theories of Vygotsky and Ausubel. The Karplus learning cycle is based on Piagetian Stage Theories of Development.

REFERENCES

Alexander, P., & Judy, J. (1988). The interaction of domain-specific and strategic knowledge in academic performance. *Review of Educational Research, 58,* 375-404.

Anderson, C. A., & Smith, E. (1986). Teaching science. In V. Koehler (Ed.), *The Educator's Handbook: A research perspective.* New York: Longman.

Berman, P., & McLaughlin, M. W. (1976). Implementation of educational innovation. *Educational Forum, 40,* 345-70.

Borko, H., & Shavelson, R. J. (1990). Teacher decision making. In B. F. Jones & L. Idol (Eds.) *Dimensions of thinking and cognitive instruction.* Hillsdale, NJ: Lawrence Erlbaum.

Caramazza, A., McCloskey, M., & Green, B. (1981). Naive beliefs in "sophisticated" subjects: Misconceptions about trajectories of objects. *Cognition, 9,* 117-23.

Carey, S. (1986) Cognitive science and science education. *American Psychologist, 41,* 1123-30.

Champagne, A. (1988, April). *A psychological model for science education.* Paper presented at the meeting of the American Educational Research Association, New Orleans.

Charles, R. I., & Silver, E. A. (Eds.) (1988). *The teaching and assessing of mathematical problem solving.* Hillsdale, NJ/Reston, VA: Lawrence Erlbaum and National Council of Teachers of Mathematics.

Conant, J. B. (1957) *Harvard case histories in experimental science* (Vols. 1 & 2). Cambridge, MA: Harvard University Press.

Connelly, F. M. (1972). The functions of curriculum development. *Interchange 3,* (nos. 2-3), 161-77.

Derry, S. (1990). Learning strategies for acquiring useful knowledge. In B. F.

Jones & L. Idol (Eds.) *Dimensions of thinking and cognitive instruction*. Hillsdale, NJ: Lawrence Erlbaum.

Doyle, W. (1986). Content representation in teachers' definitions of academic work. *Journal of Curriculum Studies, 18*, 365-79.

Doyle, W. (1983). Academic Work. *Review of Educational Research, 53* (2), 159-99.

Duschl, R. (1990a) Guiding science instruction: The use of historical analyses. Paper presented at the annual meeting of the American Educational Research Association, Boston.

Duschl, R. (1990b). *Restructuring science education: The importance of theories and their development*. New York: Teachers College Press.

Duschl, R. (1985). Science education and philosophy of science: Twenty-five years of mutually exclusive development. *School Science and Mathematics, 85*, 541-55.

Duschl, R., & Wright, E. (1989). A case study of high school teachers' decision making models for planning and teaching science. *Journal of Research in Science Teaching, 26* (6) 467-501.

Finley, F. (1983). Scientific processes. *Journal of Research in Science Teaching, 20*, 47-54.

Fullan, M., & Pomfret, A. (1977). Research on curriculum and instructional implementation. *Review of Educational Research, 47* (1), 335-97.

Giere, R. (1988). *Explaining science: A cognitive approach*. Chicago: University of Chicago Press

Hanson, N. (1958). *Patterns of discovery*. Cambridge: Cambridge University Press.

Hodson, D (1988). Toward a philosophically more valid science curriculum. *Science Education, 72* (1), 19-40.

Kitchener, K. S., & King, P. M. (1981). Reflective judgment: Concepts of justification and their relationship to age and education. *Journal of Applied Developmental Psychology, 2*, 89-116.

Krupa, M., Selman, R., & Jaquette, D. (1985). The development of science explanations in children and adolescents: A structural approach. In S. Chipman, J. Segal, & R. Glaser (Eds.), *Thinking and learning skills, Vol. 2*. Hillsdale, NJ: Lawrence Erlbaum.

Lampert, M. (1990). When the problem is not the question and the solution is not the answer: Mathematical knowing and teaching. *American Educational Research Journal, 27*, 1, 29-63.

Lampert, M. (1986). Knowing, doing, and teaching multiplication. *Cognition and Instruction, 3,* 305-42.

Lampert, M. (1984). Teaching about thinking and thinking about teaching. *Journal of Curriculum Studies, 16,* 1-18.

Leinhardt, G., & Greeno, J. G. (1986). The cognitive skill of teaching. *Journal of Educational Psychology, 78,* 75-95.

Linn, M. (1986). Science. In R. Dillon & R. Sternberg (Eds.), *Cognition and instruction* pp. 155-204. New York: Academic Press.

Mitman, A. L., Mergendoller, J. R., Marchman, V. A., & Packer, M. J. (1987). Instruction addressing the components of scientific literacy and its relations to student outcomes. *American Educational Research Journal, 24,* 611-33.

Nersessian, N. (1989). Conceptual change in science and in science education. *Synthese, 80,* 163-83.

Novak, J. (1977). *A theory of education.* Ithaca, NY: Cornell University Press.

Novak, J., & Gowin, R. (1984). *Learning how to learn.* New York: Cambridge University Press.

Nowak, G., & Thagard, P. (in press). Copernicus, Ptolemy, and explanatory coherence. In R. Giere (Ed.), *Cognitive Models of Science* (Minnesota Studies in the Philosophy of Science Vol. 15). Minneapolis: University of Minnesota Press.

Nussbaum, J. (1983). Classroom conceptual change: The lesson to be learned from the history of science. In H. Helm & J. Novak (Eds.), *Proceedings of the International Seminar on Misconceptions in Science and Mathematics* (pp. 272-81). Ithaca, NY: Cornell University, Department of Education.

Osborne, R., & Freyberg, P. (Eds.). (1985). *Learning in science: The implications of children's science.* London: Heinemann.

Osborne, R., & Wittrock, M. (1983). Learning Science: A generative process. *Science Education, 67,* 489-508.

Perkins, D. N. & Salomon, G. (1989). Are cognitive skills context-bound? *Educational Researcher, 18*(1), 16-25.

Posner, G., Strike, K., Hewson P., & Gertzog, W. (1982). Accommodation of scientific conception: Toward a theory of conceptual change. *Science Education, 66*(2), 211-27.

Ranney M., & Thagard, P. (1988). *Explanatory coherence and belief revision in naive physics. Proceedings of the Tenth Annual Conference of the Cognitive Science Society.* Hillsdale, NJ: Lawrence Erlbaum. 426-67

Resnick, L. (1989, September). *Developing thinking abilities in arithmetic class.* Paper presented at the Third European conference for Research on learning and Instruction, Madrid.

Resnick, L. (1983). Mathematics and science learning: A new conception. *Science, 220,* 477-78.

Resnick, L., & Klopfer, L. (Eds.). (1989). *Toward the thinking curriculum: Current cognitive research. 1989 Yearbook of the Assoc. for Supervision and Curriculum Development.* Reston, VA: ASCD.

Roberts, D. (1986). Theory, curriculum development, and the unique events of practice. In H. Munby, G. Orpwood, & T. Russell (Eds.). *Seeing Curriculum in a New Light: Essays from science education.* Lanham, MD: University Press of America. (Reprint of 1980 copyright held by OISE)

Roth, K. (1990, Winter). Science Education: It's Not Enough to 'Do' or 'Relate'. *American Educator,* 16-22, 46-48.

Sanford, J. P. (1987). Management of science classroom tasks and effects on students' learning opportunities. *Journal of Research in Science Teaching, 24,* 249-65.

Sanford, J. P. (1984). Management and organization in science classrooms. *Journal of Research in Science Teaching, 21,* 575-87.

Shapere, D. (1977). Scientific theories and their domains. In F. Suppe (Ed.), *The structure of scientific theories* (2nd ed.). (pp. 518-65). Champagne-Urbana, IL: University of Illinois Press.

Thagard, P. (1990). The conceptual structure of the chemical revolution. *Philosophy of Science, 57,* 183-209.

Thagard, P., & Nowak, G. (1988). The explanatory coherence of continental drift. In A. Fine & J. Leplin (Eds.), *PSA 1988, Vol. 1.* East Lansing, MI: Philosophy of Science Association, 118-26.

Thagard, P., & Nowak, G. (1990). The conceptual structure of the geological revolution. In J. Shrager & P. Langley (Eds.), *Computational models of discovery and theory formulation* (pp. 27-72). San Mateo, CA: Morgan Kaufman.

Tobin, K., & Fraser, B. (1990). What does it mean to be an exemplary science teacher? *Journal of Research in Science Teaching, 27,* 3-26.

Tobin, K., & Gallagher, J. (1987). What happens in high school science classrooms? *Journal of Curriculum Studies, 19,* 549-60.

Waugh, R. F, & Punch K. F. (1987). Teacher receptivity to system-wide change in the implementation stage. *Review of Educational Research, 57*(3), 237-59.

West, L., & Pines, A. (Eds.). (1985). *Cognitive structure and conceptual change*. New York: Academic Press.

White, B., & Frederiksen, J. (1987). Progressions of qualitative models as a foundation for intelligent learning environments. (BBN Report No. 6277). Cambridge, MA.: Bolt, Beranek and Newman Inc.

Wittrock, M. (1986). Students' thought processes. In M. Wittrock (Ed.), *Handbook of research on teaching* (pp. 297-314). New York: Macmillan.

RICHARD A. DUSCHL[1]
RICHARD J. HAMILTON
RICHARD E. GRANDY

1

Psychology and Epistemology: Match or Mismatch When Applied to Science Education?*

OUTLINE

I. Introduction
    A. Cognitive schemata
    B. Theories
    C. Joining schemata and theories
    D. Tensions
II. The perspective of cognitive psychology
    A. Schemata
        1. Acquisition and retrieval of knowledge
        2. Nature of schematic knowledge
    B. Implication for science education
        1. Context of future use
III. The perspective of epistemology
    A. Theories
        1. Nature of theory change
        2. Mechanisms for theory change
    B. Implications for science education
        1. Context of justification
        2. Context of development
IV. Implications for implementation and research
    A. For teachers and teaching

B. For learners and learning
C. For historians and philosophers of science

ABSTRACT

Cognitive psychology's descriptions of an individual's knowledge resemble those philosophers offer of scientific theory. Both offer resources for conceptual change teaching. Yet the similarities mask tensions—philosophers stress rationality and psychologists focus on causal structures. Both domains distinguish two kinds of change in knowledge structures—one common and cumulative, the other rare and noncumulative. The structures facilitate incrementation but resist major revisions. Unless instruction actively induces restructuring, students' knowledge will be confused and incomplete.

Knowledge is largely organized by schemata, representing the significant concepts and relations in a domain. But using knowledge also requires procedures for recalling, applying, and revising schemata.

Questions discussed include:

- When should we present a theory in the context of justification—where knowledge claims are systematically but ahistorically delineated—and when in the context of development—where knowledge claims are initially developed?
- How can prototypical examples facilitate schema acquisition and appropriate retrieval?
- How can individuals be made active participants in the restructuring process?
- How can the need for restructuring be motivated?
- To what extent should we stress the historical and rational *development* of modern science?
- Are educators prepared to employ complex teaching strategies identified by researchers?
- To what extent do students' naive theories parallel early stages of science?

INTRODUCTION

The process of theory development by scientists has often been compared to an individual's acquisition of knowledge of the world (Piaget 1970; Kitchener 1987; Krupa, Selman & Jaquette 1985). Scientists assimilate new information to their existing theories and accommodate these theories when presented with contradictory information. This comparison raises the question of how the processes responsible for theory development and justification and the structure of theoretical knowledge influence each other. The answer to this question has profound implications for the design and development of science instruction which are based on both psychological and epistemological principles.

Philosophy of science and cognitive psychology appear to be making similar discoveries and using similar terminology in describing the acquisition and modification of knowledge. It would seem foolish not to use the resources of one or both in improving science teaching. Yet the similarities mask differences that raise serious problems about the combination of the two, and if they conflict in their advice we must consider which to use as our guide in curriculum revision. While we remain optimistic about the ultimate fruitfulness of the combined resources of the two fields, we are more cautious about the immediate fruits than some (Nersessian 1989).

We will examine the difficulties which develop when epistemological and cognitive psychological guidelines are applied together to address educational problems and practice. More exactly, our discussion will focus on how the new ideas in cognitive psychology and in epistemology, when applied together, may confound the acts of learning and teaching science. We offer a word of caution for those researchers and scholars willing to apply principles of philosophy and cognitive psychology in an educational context (Carey 1986; Dillon & Sternberg 1986; Chipman, Segal & Glaser 1985). We also address the inherent difficulties associated with a teacher decision-making model which partitions curriculum and instruction between knowledge justification frameworks and knowledge development frameworks. Thus, the focus is the tensions between the two fields when these are applied to education. By examining the anomalies between the domains of philosophy of science and educational psychology, we hope that new interfield relationships may be spawned.

Cognitive Schemata

A first step in dealing with the above issues is to adopt "schema" as the cognitive unit for representing an individual's theoretical knowledge. Schemata are considered by many to be the building blocks of cognition (Rumelhart 1980). As units of knowledge the schemata are joined together with rules and associations about how this knowledge is to be used.

A schema, then, is a data structure representing the generic concepts stored in memory. A schema contains, as part of its specification, the network of interrelationships that is believed to normally hold among the constituents of the concept in question. That is, inasmuch as a schema underlying a concept stored in memory corresponds to the meaning of that concept, meanings are encoded in terms of the typical or normal situations or events that instantiate that concept. (Rumelhart 1980, p. 34)

Thus, a schema is a unit of knowledge with thematic content. For example, we possess unitary knowledge concerning our expectations of what occurs in certain settings, for example, restaurants. That is, the schema for restaurant would consist of the typical sequence of events which occur in going out to a restaurant, procedures for ordering, paying for the meal, and so forth and related knowledge such as types of restaurants and typical foods available at these restaurants. Schema consist of: (1) an organized set of prototypical concepts related to a theme, (2) the strategies and rules that allow the individual to evaluate new facts and events as viable additions or alternatives to existing knowledge subsumed within the relevant schema, and (3) the procedures for using and justifying this knowledge (Rumelhart 1980; Thorndyke 1984). The concepts, strategies, rules, and procedures are all instances of procedural knowledge—an active dynamic knowledge which is responsible for all our internal and external activities. The verbal facts and descriptions of events subsumed within schemata are instances of declarative knowledge—a static knowledge. Although declarative knowledge may include cues which are helpful for gaining access to relevant knowledge, it is procedural knowledge that is primarily responsible for our ability to apply schemata to appropriate situations.

Rumelhart (1980) describes how schemata aid the process of comprehension:

> . . . just as the activity surrounding a theory is often focused on the evaluation of the theory and the comparison of the theory with observations we have made so it is that the primary activity associated with a schema is the determination of whether it gives an adequate account for some aspect of our current situation. Just as the determination that a particular theory accounts for some observed results involves the determination of the parameters of the theory, so the determination that a particular configuration of schemata accounts for the data presently available to our senses

requires the determination of the values of the variables of the schema. If a promising schema fails to account for some aspect of a situation, one has the options of accepting the schema as adequate in spite of its flawed account or of rejecting the schema as inadequate and looking for another possibility. Therefore, the fundamental processes of comprehension are taken to be analogous to hypothesis testing, evaluation of goodness of fit, and parameter estimation. (Pp. 37-38)

As you can see, schemata possess functions which are analogous to the functions of theories and seem to be well suited for representing our knowledge of the content and use of scientific theories.

Cognitive psychology has made considerable progress in describing the nature of an individual's knowledge, and these descriptions appear to be similar to those offered by philosophers of science for scientific theory. Studies in both domains distinguish two kinds of change in knowledge structures—one frequent, steady, cumulative type of change and the other a rarer, less continuous, and noncumulative type. Vosniadou and Brewer (1987) characterize the first type of change as "weak restructuring" and the second type of change as "radical restructuring." Weak restructuring results in the accumulation of new facts and the formation of new relations between existing concepts. In contrast, radical restructuring consists of a change in core concepts, structure and phenomena to be explained. The rarity of the latter type may be due to characteristics of knowledge and knowledge acquisition systems, that is, the systems facilitate incremental addition of factual information but are resistant to wholesale abandonment of information. In effect, there is a strong inertial component that resists radical knowledge restructuring.

A review of the literature on cognitive psychology reveals that researchers and scholars are willing to join psychological concepts focusing on schema theory with philosophical concepts addressing theory development (Carey 1985a, 1985b; Rissland 1985). Certainly at an intuitive level it is possible to appreciate how each of these domains is concerned with the growth of knowledge. Contemporary developments in history and philosophy of science and cognitive psychology suggest the growth of knowledge in a field of study (theory development) and in individuals (schema building) have much in common and can be described by a common language.

Educational researchers have discovered that the schemata employed by learners are often not well grounded by sound rules or relevant associations of concepts. The research of students' alternative frameworks (Osborne & Freyberg 1985), for example, has found that young learners frequently have schemata that are, when taken together, inconsistent. Such results have led Carey (1985a) to argue that the task of understanding the cognitive development of children can no longer be divorced from the task of understanding the processes associated with how learners change schema. Simply stated, "cognitive development involves conceptual change" (Carey 1986, p. 1127).

Theories

As indicated earlier, researchers have compared the structure and function of "schemata" to "theories" (Gibson 1985; Rumelhart 1980; Thorndyke 1984). Both are concerned with the construction of an interpretation of an event, object, or situation as well as a source of predictions about unobserved events. Until fairly recently the predominant view of theories in philosophy of science was that theories were direct descriptions of the world or a part thereof. Copernicus's theory of the solar system was a paradigmatic example. More recently, though, an alternative conception has gained currency according to which theories provide a schematic, often mathematicized description, which then requires application to a specific part of the world before any predictions or descriptions are forthcoming. Newton's laws can be thought of as specifying the relevant parameters for describing any mechanical system—the Newtonian description of the solar system is an application of the general theory. The theory tells us explicitly that forces, masses, positions, and velocities are relevant and how they matter; it tells us implicitly that color, material composition, and place of origin do not matter. In this respect the new conception of theory bears a much greater resemblance to the schema of everyday reasoning than did the previous conception.

Nonetheless, some differences remain. Theories are explicitly formulated, even if many features of their application and assessment are not, and they are explicitly taught. Schemata are not. Theories are often mathematically formulated. These differences are probably quite important to bear in mind in applying cognitive psychology precepts about schemata to designing a curriculum for science. Another difference that may or may not ultimately prove important is that schemata tell us about the behavior of normal or typical objects, whereas theories tells us about the behavior of ideal objects—frictionless planes, dimensionless points, perfectly elastic spheres. In this respect the application of scientific theories may be less immediate than the application of schemata. Indeed according to the newer philosophy of science, something like theories/schemata is needed to apply the explicit theories (Suppes 1967; Giere 1988).

In general, theories are developed to explain and predict events. As such they represent a synthesis of knowledge claims which seek to account for past, present, and future events. Historians and philosophers of science investigate the growth of knowledge among communities of scientists seeking explanations for data, patterns, and facts derived from many modes of inquiry. The process of knowledge restructuring occurs through activities involving both the development and justification of theories (Nickles 1980; Kuhn 1970; Laudan 1977).

Although the theories are quite explicitly developed and taught, the procedures for modifying them are not. They are implicit and taught by example and textbook versions of history. In spite of the attempts by Carnap (1950), Hempel (1945), Reichenbach (1938), and others, the rules for theory evaluation never yielded to formalization. This led many writers (e.g., Kuhn, Toulmin, Hanson) to challenge the then prevailing viewpoints concerning both the structure and development of scientific theories (See Suppe 1977 and 1989 for two reviews of changes in philosophy of science on the topic of scientific theories). By focusing on the writings of the history of science, these philosophers of science asserted that a type of conceptual change was occurring with the restructuring of scientific knowledge. Not only are there times when scientists engage in activities which seek to refine their understanding of known scientific theories—Kuhn's normal science—but there are times when scientists introduce novel conceptual frameworks—Kuhn's revolutionary science. Then we find the guiding conceptions of a domain of knowledge, for example, causes of earthquakes, prove inadequate and are replaced by newer guiding conceptions, for example, The Plate Tectonic Theory.

Thus conceptual change is the most significant idea the recent philosophy of science contributes to science education. It is especially significant because the principles of conceptual change are generally recognized to be implicit. They are not only not formally articulated but may elude complete future formal study. This possibility has led some philosophers, especially Feyerabend, to claim that science is governed by no principles, and ought not to be! Opponents of this point of view have advanced suggestions as to how restructuring of scientific knowledge could also be subsumed under a logic of development. More recently, philosophers of science (Giere 1988; Gibson 1985; Freedman & Smith 1985) have argued for applying the principles of cognitive psychology to philosophy of science to account for the nature of the conceptual changes that occur.

Joining Schemata and Theories

The treatment of scientific theories as cognitive schema raises questions about the consequences for educational policy and practices. More exactly, what effect would a position which seeks to join epistemological and psychological principles have on curriculum planning, implementation, and evaluation?

Carey (1986), a cognitive psychologist, calls for educational researchers to consider the contributions principles and concepts from the history and philosophy of science can make to researchers attempting to understand the conceptual development of young learners. In essays addressing how children's schemata change in the course of acquiring new knowledge, she writes:

> If my diagnosis of the problem that developmental psychologists face is correct, then at least we know what we are up against—the fundamental problems of induction, epistemology, and philosophy of science. We ignore the work in these fields at our peril. (Carey 1985b, p. 514)

> I hope to provide a feel for the complexity of the issues, to show that progress is being made, and to suggest that success will require the collaboration of cognitive scientists and science educators, who together must be aware of the understanding of science provided by both historians and philosophers of science. (Carey 1986, p. 1125)

Yet another example of the symbiotic relationship between cognitive psychology and philosophy of science can be found in the fundamental premises for a leading theory of conceptual change learning (Posner et al. 1982). In this theory, instructional ideas are adapted from philosophical positions on theory change and development as described by Thomas Kuhn (1970) and Imre Lakatos (1970).

The degree to which the principles of cognitive psychology and the principles of epistemology are held to be quite similar when applied to tasks associated with knowledge growth is perhaps best demonstrated with the science education research literature. Linn (1986), Novak (1977), Novak and Gowin (1984), Resnick (1983), Finley (1983), Anderson and Smith (1986), and Krupa, Selman and Jaquette (1985), among others, each speak to the effect a learner's prior knowledge has on subsequent learning. Furthermore, the collective body of this research implies that learners, as Carey (1986) asserts, develop their cognitive abilities through the process of changing conceptual schemes. In fact, the literature (Nussbaum 1983) states the position that the growth of knowledge in the individual can be understood or interpreted in terms outlined by historians of science.

Thus, one finds Linn (1986) employing Lakatos's (1970) concepts of a theory's hardcore and softcore to explain resistance to change in learners. Or Novak (1977) developing Hanson's (1958) "seeing as"/"seeing that" position as a basis for establishing how prior knowledge alters the learning of subsequent knowledge. That such applications are indeed becoming a part of the mainstream of education and education research is perhaps best demonstrated by the presence of counterposition statements which warn us of the inherent pitfalls associated with such applications (Phillips 1982; Haroutunian 1982).

But the path between cognitive psychology and philosophy of science is turning out to be a two-way street. That is, recently philosophers of science have argued for epistemologies which employ concepts from cognitive psychology. Giere (1988), Freedman and Smith (1985), and Gibson (1985) are examples of philosophers who take the position that individuals who attempt to develop a better understanding of theory change in science ought to consider applying concepts from cognitive psychology about knowledge restructuring. Referred to by Giere as "naturalized realism" the position seeks to apply psychological models of schema and schema change to the interpretation of the growth of knowledge in science as such knowledge is represented by scientific theories. In this way, theory change has both a developmental aspect—"constructive"—and a justification aspect—"realism." Freedman and Smith put forth the same sentiment when they write:

> In varying degrees, the evidence from cognitive psychology poses anomalies, or to borrow a phrase from Laudan (1977), cognitive threat for the extant approaches to the philosophy of science. It can therefore be argued that philosophers of science need to respond by acknowledging that science is influenced by cognitive mechanisms that may produce systematic biases and errors. The philosophy of science must also recognize that these processes influence all aspects of scientific activity, not merely those decision that are considered nonprogressive or degenerating. With the recent emphasis on cognitive processes involved in scientific theory choice, future philosophical analyses of science can be expected to go grounded substantially on the framework of modem cognitive psychology. (p. 8)

Evoking the language of philosophy of science in the study of scientific theories and the language of cognitive psychology in the study of conceptual schema, an argument can be made that the nature of theory change described in philosophy and the nature of schema change described in cognitive psychology have much in common. However, tensions arise from attempts to marry epistemology with psychology.

Tensions

The framework of common terms—schema, theory, conceptual change—suggests a more unified view of conceptual development between philosophy and psychology than actually exists. Some of the dichotomies are closely related—the Kuhnian distinction between normal and revolutionary periods in science parallels at the level of the scientific community the distinction between weak and radical restructuring of knowledge that Vosniadou and Brewer (1987) describe at the personal level.

Another important distinction for philosophers is that between the context of justification—the situation in which knowledge claims are systematically presented in relation to the data—and the context of development—the situation in which knowledge claims are created and initially developed. One decision that must be made when choosing how to present a theory in the classroom is whether it will be presented in the ahistorical context of justification (without regard to predecessor theories) or in the historical context of development (considering the alternative predecessor theories). A suggestion would be to use the context of justification whenever the development was within normal science and the context of development whenever it was a bit of revolutionary science. Another suggestion would be to use the context of justification whenever new theory requires only weak restructuring on the part of the student and the context of development when it requires radical restructuring. Perhaps these two suggestions converge, and any historically revolutionary episode corresponds to a radical restructuring on the part of the student, but this remains to be demonstrated.

A second tension arises from the fact that epistemology is concerned with the rational evaluation of theory choice, regardless of the actual historical developments or of human frailties and the causal structures that may produce them. Epistemology is concerned with *knowledge*, which must be true and justified. The fact that a certain conceptual structure is internally represented does not make it knowledge for the epistemologist. Cognitive psychology, on the other hand, is concerned with understanding the nature, causes, and dynamics of internal representations of conceptual structures and has no concern with rationality, truth, or justification. This difference is often obscured because cognitive psychologists use *knowledge* but they mean by it what an epistemologist means by *belief,* and which philosophers contrast with knowledge. The researcher and teacher may have to choose whether to emphasize rationality or effectiveness in changing concepts.

A third tension concerns the appropriate domain of procedural knowledge to be inculcated. It is agreed that the declarative knowledge related to principles, laws, theories, and generalizations must be taught, and that in the appropriate laboratory settings the procedural knowledge to apply these must be developed. Within the context of normal scientific developments or weak restructurings there is a small amount of procedural knowledge to be acquired about the fine tuning of theories and the adjustment of conceptual relations. But if we are to effect radical restructuring of concepts, the personal correlate of revolutionary science, then it seems that we must also teach the procedural knowledge involved in wholesale reevaluation of theory and data. The nature of such procedural knowledge has been little studied and not at all agreed upon. Moreover it may well vary greatly from one scientific domain (and epoch) to another! Perhaps the teaching and learning of science entails more complex procedural knowledge than we have yet recognized. The instructional strategy and design that are employed to teach a unit on the Theory of Evolution or Theory of Plate Tectonics might require a very different set of procedural knowledge guidelines than a unit on biological or mineralogical identification and classification.

What is being suggested has significant implications for the training of science teachers and for the designing and writing of science curricula. Consequently, the appropriate procedural knowledge to invoke when teaching a given science unit might vary with either the epistemological characteristics of that science unit (i.e., normal science or revolutionary science), the cognitive characteristics of the learners (i.e., weak restructuring or radical restructuring of conceptual schema), or both.

This proposal for varying procedures stands in sharp contrast to the view that the growth and development of scientific knowledge are always of a single cumulative kind. Our proposal is more sympathetic to philosophical accounts which recognize the important role substitution and replacement of knowledge claims, methods, and cognitive aims have in the growth or restructuring of scientific knowledge.

It is our contention that unless science instruction integrates activities that aim at inducing various types of restructuring, students' knowledge of science will be confused and incomplete. Cognitive psychology may be used to induce more effectively in students the schemata and heuristics associated with testing and justifying new information of particular scientific domains. But this type of knowledge appears to be domain specific and does not impart a more holistic sense of the nature of science or of its historical development.

On the other hand an appreciation of the historical development of scientific theories requires the study of a succession of conceptual structures. This course of study may produce an appreciation of the overall nature of science and scientific development without producing an adequate understanding of any particular scientific domain.

Moreover, from an educational perspective, the general grasp of the principles governing scientific development themselves give no domain-specific knowledge, except to psychology and history of science. One of the important lessons to be learned from both cognitive psychology and history of science is that the rules by which scientists apply theories to experimental situations and the rules by which they evaluate modifications of theory are quite deeply implicit. The rules are internalized in the process of learning the domain-specific knowledge of the science but are not explicit. The process of articulating them is unnecessary even if it is possible.

Given the constraints of classroom time that already limit the amount of science education that can be provided at most levels, this seems to pose a difficult choice between, on the one hand, imparting the knowledge requisite to moving toward a scientific career and, on the other hand, the culturally important appreciation of the power of science as a cognitive enterprise, including its continually evolving character and its dependence on diverse internal and external factors. Consequently, attainment of a "Science for All" curriculum (Fensham 1986) will need to address issues outlined in this paper if such a curriculum is to be compatible with modern theories of learning.

The tension alluded to above affects educational decisions concerning *what* and *how* to teach and reflect the philosophical argument about the relative importance of the context of justification and the context of development. Whereas the psychological perspective argues for teaching knowledge structures based on the assimilation to current theory, the epistemological perspective suggests teaching how the new data undermines previous theories and leads to their revision. There is a fundamental tension in this interdisciplinary dialogue and it has important consequences for educational policy! If we have limited time and resources we must choose what is to be the focus of science education curricula.

THE PERSPECTIVE OF COGNITIVE PSYCHOLOGY

One of the major concerns of cognitive psychology has been the nature of knowledge representation. Although there is still some question as to the descriptive adequacy of proposed theoretical formats (i.e., psychological reality of the different formats), one particular theory has been useful for the organization of existing research and the development of principles of application, that is, schema theory. As indicated earlier, a schema is a unit of knowledge with thematic content which includes knowledge related to the theme, strategies to evaluate new related information, and procedures for using this knowledge.

The adoption of a "schema" representational format has been useful in summarizing the effects of schematic knowledge on the *encoding* of related information and knowledge and the *retrieval* of this knowledge. In terms of encoding, schemata have been found to be helpful for the preservation of incoming information as well as for the integration of new information with old knowledge (Bransford & Johnson 1972; Brewer & Treyens 1981; Chi, Feltovich & Glaser 1981; Dooling & Lachman 1971; Dooling & Mullet 1973; Thorndyke 1977; Thorndyke & Hayes-Roth 1979). Schemata are said to give individuals appropriate frameworks, themes, and/or prototypes which help preserve and integrate new knowledge. In terms of retrieval, schemata have been found to be helpful as guides for searching for schema-related information and knowledge and eventual retrieval of this information (Anderson & Pichert 1978; Anderson et al. 1977; Bower, Black & Turner 1979; Kintsch & Green 1978; Mandler 1978; Pichert & Anderson 1977).

The above set of results point to two characteristics of schemata which it may be helpful to remember in the design and development of science instruction. The first is the prototypicality of concepts subsumed within the schemata, and the second is the encoding of contextual attributes during schema acquisition and the instantiation of these attributes during retrieval. As indicated earlier, a schema consists of a set of generalizations which summarize the theme of that particular schema. These generalizations describe the thematic characteristics that will tend to be true of most instances to which the schema can be applied. In this way, these generalizations are "prototypical" of schema related events or instances. This suggests that the integration of "prototypical" instances of concepts, scenarios, and so forth, within instructional materials will aid learners to develop appropriate schema to be applied in future situations (cf., Tennyson & Cocchiarella 1986). Research in the area of concept learning has found that presenting students with prototypes of mathematical and social science concepts produced higher levels of concept acquisition than presenting students with definitions and descriptions of critical attributes of the target concepts (Tennyson, Youngers & Suebsonthi 1983; Park 1984; Dunn 1983).

The prototypicality of core concepts subsumed within schemata should help in the encoding and retrieval of appropriate knowledge. That is, the core concepts share many characteristics with most relevant and related information/concepts and may facilitate the process of encoding and retrieval of this new information. In essence, these prototypes would make available appropriate contexts within which to encode related information and gain access to this information at the time of retrieval.

As indicated earlier, a second important aspect of schemata that may influence the success of instructional materials is the degree to which the materials integrate relevant contextual variables. That is, one needs to identify the context within which the learners will be required to use the knowledge and build both the attributes of the future tasks (e.g., experimentation with materials), and future processing requirements, (e.g., scientific method, into instructional materials). A variety of experiments have found that often, relevant knowledge (e.g., list of words, study strategies, problem-solving strategies) is not spontaneously accessed when appropriate (Brown et al. 1983; Simon & Hayes 1977). That is, even though the individuals possess relevant knowledge, it is not accessed when appropriate. This inaccessible knowledge is described as 'inert knowledge' (Whitehead 1929).

Bransford, Franks, Vye & Sherwood (1986) and Sherwood et al. (1987) emphasize the importance of teacher's integrating *problem-oriented activities* into instructional materials in order to insure appropriate transfer by making knowledge accessible. Problem-oriented activities involve: (1) information presented within the context of future use (e.g., laboratories, real life) and which includes the processing requirements of the future use of this information and (2) information presented as close to the medium within which students will be required to use this new information (e.g., video presentation of problem scenarios). Matching the encoding context with the retrieval context takes advantage of the schema-based format of knowledge.

When applied to the area of theory development and justification, two specific types of knowledge can be described: one type is schematic and consists of facts and descriptions of events that relate to a theory (i.e., declarative knowledge), as well as a coordinated set of concepts and rules which make up the core of a theory (i.e., procedural knowledge). The second type of knowledge contains procedures that relate to the use and development of scientific theories or schemata. This second type of schema is responsible for theory development and for theory justification. As suggested earlier, it is unclear whether instruction could be developed which can explicitly induce this latter type of knowledge.

Considerable research has been done on expert/novice differences and how the schemata of these two populations within the expert's domain differ in terms of the misconceptions, the level of abstraction, and the availability of appropriate problem-solving procedures that exist as part of the expert's and novice's schema (cf., Perkins & Salomon 1989). Within the area of science education, as outlined above, there has been an impetus to use ideas from both cognitive psychology and epistemology to help induce learners to acquire a new conceptual structure or induce "conceptual change" and to increase the level of abstractions which exist within the schema (Anderson & Smith 1986; Carey 1986; Otero 1985). The instructional prescriptions have been aimed at overcoming misconceptions and presenting appropriate contextual information to make this possible.

Although this blends the notion of context of development from epistemology with the notions of schema/knowledge structure from cognitive psychology, it fails to address the basic psychological processes involved in the retrieval of this knowledge. From a psychological perspective, the above focuses primarily on encoding issues. Presenting the context of development should be very useful for the development of appropriate scientific theory schemata but contribute little to the development of methods to gain access to this knowledge. By presenting the historical context and problems that were responsible for the initial development of a scientific theory, one is focusing primarily on the acquisition of facts, events, and a conceptual structure that relates to the target theory or theories. However, unless this context is similar to the context within which this knowledge is to be used, this approach may result in knowledge which is inaccessible.

Without the use of techniques aimed at making information/schema accessible, we will run into the problem of learners who possess "inert knowledge" (Bransford, Franks, Vye & Sherwood 1986; Bransford, Sherwood, Vye & Rieser 1986). The context of development notion may be the best vehicle to bring about conceptual changes; however, it may not be helpful in insuring retrieval of appropriate information. The distinction here is a simple one, that between those procedures that are useful for encoding and those that are useful for retrieval. Traditional psychological learning research has supported the notion that contextual cues that are present during encoding are most successful at inducing retrieval of the encoding information. Thus, there are questions concerning how procedural knowledge ought to be a part of instruction and learning. Are the procedural cues associated with the context of development those which will be most useful for:

1. applying one's "scientific knowledge" to future problem situations;
2. developing an understanding of the revisionary nature of scientific inquiry—a "knowledge about scientific development"?

The focus in integrating epistemological and cognitive psychology notions in the teaching of science should be to evaluate how the epistemological notions (e.g., context of development and justification) influence not only students' acquiring their understanding of where scientific theories come from and how they might work, but also their ability to use these theories and their knowledge of theories in future scientific situations. There is a need for educators to identify the best techniques to ensure both the acquisition and the application of scientific knowledge.

THE PERSPECTIVE OF EPISTEMOLOGY

Arguments that the structures of scientific theories and cognitive schema have much in common (Carey 1986; Gibson 1985; Giere 1988) must consider both the structural characteristics and the developmental characteristics of these conceptual frameworks. From a structural perspective, scientific theories and cognitive schema may indeed have much in common. Theories can be thought of as composed of facts, principles, lawlike statements which are molded together by accepted methodological and axiological practices. Cognitive schemata, from a structural perspective, can also be thought of as being made up of concepts and propositional statements governed by rules and values which guide synthesis.

A problem occurs though when it is necessary to describe the mechanisms for change in the structure of theories (Kuhn 1970; Rumelhart 1980). Educational psychology research and research in history of science both speak clearly to the changing character of a person's individual knowledge and of a scientific community's scientific knowledge, respectively. Given the revisionary character of scientific methodology, focusing on the development of theories as well as their structure will show that a much wider range of procedural knowledge is significant.

Cognitive psychological models of learning maintain that individuals ought to be active participants in the learning process. One important element of this process is for the learners to become aware of the need to restructure their knowledge and thereby engage in tasks which bring about a conceptual change. Of course the need and subsequent

tasks can be and often are identified by the teacher. A problem, though, is that the knowledge bases of science become increasingly more sophisticated and complicated as students progress through school. In turn, then, it becomes increasingly more difficult to establish a rational basis for knowledge restructuring. The complicated dynamics of knowledge restructuring can be justified and made comprehensible when epistemological criteria that emphasize developmental characteristics of scientific theories are addressed. One example is the important role anomalous data have in the genesis of scientific knowledge. The concept of *anomalous data* is an important and subtle epistemological one. There is considerable tension in accepting as *data* facts which are perceived as *anomalous*. The other is the importance of establishing a rational mechanism for explaining the never-ending replacement and substitution of knowledge claims, methods, and cognitive aims in science.

A central issue here is the extent to which a very important goal of science education is being addressed by teachers and curriculum writers. That goal is an understanding or at least an awareness of the nature of scientific inquiry. Duschl (1988) has argued that in order to achieve such an awareness, the instructional tasks must embrace those characteristics of science which are part of the context of development. In other words, the science activities employed in the classroom will, through the sequence in which they are placed, address the historical and rational development of the modern claims of science. A curriculum so designed would emphasize different concepts in conceptual change teaching.

Consider a recent example from geology. Employing a context of development approach to the study of Plate Tectonics requires attention be given to the important role British physicists played in the revival of the idea of continental drift during the 1950s. These scientists found that the magnetometer—an instrument initially designed to test theories about the dynamics of the magnetic core of the Earth—could be used to measure the remnant magnetism of rocks. Their subsequent studies of continental rocks in England, India, and America produced a set of data which indicated that the remnant magnetism directions differed with the age of the rocks. Employing a context of development point of view we find that a change in method (using the magnetometer to measure rocks) led to a change in cognitive aim (physicists turning their resources and efforts away from a classical problem of magnetism to the problem of whether the differences in rock magnetism were due to wandering poles or drifting continents) which in turn led to a restructuring of our knowledge of the earth. Shifts in commitments to method and to aims preceded shifts in commitment to scientific theories.

A context of justification approach, on the other hand, to the teaching of Plate Tectonics would need only to cite magnetic reversals in ocean floor rocks as a reliable source of evidence for proposing the theory of sea-floor spreading. How we came to learn about magnetic reversals and how that knowledge contributed to a revival of the idea of continental drift are not relevant to the encoding and retrieval of our contemporary knowledge. In the end, an incomplete picture of the restructuring of knowledge is provided.

The context of development approach is concerned with the way restructuring of knowledge has taken place and with establishing a basis for understanding the generation of new scientific evidence and the shift in commitment from one theory to another theory. Thus, changes in knowledge, in method, and in aims are equal partners in the restructuring of scientific knowledge. The context of justification, however, stresses the final form of the restructured knowledge and places changes in commitment to knowledge claims above all other influences to knowledge restructuring, that is, historical and sociological criteria and changes in methodological commitments.

The relevance of including epistemological criteria that focus on the development of scientific knowledge is supported by a leading theory of conceptual change learning advanced by Posner et al. (1982). We have already cited how their theory of conceptual change is taken from Kuhn's (1962) and Lakatos's (1970) epistemological arguments that the growth of scientific knowledge develops through cyclic periods of consensus and dissentation among practitioners. Supported by studies in the history of science, Posner et al. suggest that this conceptual change view of the growth of scientific knowledge can be applied to education. Their position suggests that if children are to change their commitments to scientific ideas, then four conditions must be met:

1. existing ideas must be found to be unsatisfactory;
2. the new idea must be intelligible; it must appear to be both coherent and internally consistent;
3. the new idea is plausible; and,
4. the new idea is fruitful; it is preferable to the old viewpoint on the grounds of perceived elegance, parsimony, and/or usefulness.

Inasmuch as the consensus/dissentation activities of science are involved in the process of theory change, it is an issue that focuses on establishing a context of development in science. Scientific knowledge, while seemingly a story of success when painted by broad strokes, is, when examined more carefully, a story of many false starts and misdirections. At issue is whether the growth of knowledge in science, or in the learning of science, is perceived as involving not only continual revision but also complex revision. Our classroom teachers need better mechanisms for describing and prescribing changes in knowledge structures. Epistemological criteria which embrace a context of knowledge development can be used by teachers to outline the complexity of the revision at hand.

Consider the concerns of the science teacher in the classroom. In presenting instruction which seeks to model and bring about a restructuring of knowledge, the teacher is faced with the difficult task of demonstrating that the growth of knowledge in science, with its periods of consensus and dissentation, is, nonetheless, a rational activity. If the process of change within science is viewed by learners as an irrational process, then one of the fundamental criteria for conceptual change teaching—plausibility—is threatened. While the philosophical issue is whether changes in scientists' central commitments involve holistic changes or piecemeal changes (Laudan 1984), the educational issue is which view of the nature of knowledge change provides a better model for the development of a curriculum that seeks to bring about conceptual changes in learners. The position taken here is that the problem of plausibility is best addressed if the central commitments of science are parcelled out to the distinct categories of knowledge, method, and cognitive aim.

Precollege science education curricula should address not only *what* is known by science, but should also include *how* science has come to arrive at such knowledge. To teach what is known in science is to stress declarative scientific knowledge. To teach how the scientific enterprise has arrived at its knowledge claims is to develop declarative and procedural knowledge of scientific developments. Knowledge of scientific development, as opposed to scientific knowledge, then, is knowledge of both why science believes what it does and how science has come to think that way. The distinction being drawn between scientific knowledge as a curricular objective and knowledge about scientific development as a curricular objective is that the latter is more inclusive.

Similarly, in establishing criteria for what will be important procedural knowledge to teach students, epistemological perspectives of a context of development would also be more inclusive. It is through an understanding of the procedures of knowledge restructuring in science, as such change relates to commitments to evidence, observation, method, goals, and theory from a developmental perspective, that teachers of science shall gain a perspective on how and what declarative and procedural knowledge ought to be included in the planning, implementation, and evaluation of the science curriculum.

IMPLICATIONS FOR IMPLEMENTATION AND RESEARCH

The adoption of a curriculum and an instructional perspective which joins together constructivist views of educational psychology with new views from the history and philosophy of science has deep implications for teachers of science, students of science, and researchers investigating science education questions. For example, partitioning learning processes into encoding/retrieval categories, scientific knowledge into declarative/procedural components, and processes of scientific knowledge growth into development and testing contexts represents a more accurate description of what occurs in the growth of knowledge. But when we consider that each of these paired sets of terms would be applied differently depending on the science content or context being employed, then and only then do we truly begin to grasp the complexity of the task we face. In this last section we do not intend to offer solutions to these complex problems and issues. Rather, we hope to offer comments and questions which will direct the efforts of those developing interfield relationships between philosophy of science and educational psychology within the areas of instructional implementation and research.

The synthesis of cognitive psychology with history and philosophy of science requires that we consider how domain specific guidelines would affect educational practice. This recommendation is not that different from Resnick's (1983) call for a better qualitative understanding of the academic work of our classrooms. Thus, procedural guidelines for learning biology concepts are different from guidelines for learning chemistry, and the key foundational concepts for understanding the Theory of Plate Tectonics owe more to an understanding of physics than to an understanding of chemistry.

An important issue here is the extent to which educators are prepared to explore, define, and employ teaching and learning strategies identified by researchers. We have proposed that a science-for-scientist curriculum design would be very different from a science-for-all design. Given the constraints of classroom time that already limit the amount of science education that can be provided at most levels, this seems to pose a difficult choice between imparting, on the one hand, the knowledge requisite to moving toward a scientific career and, on the other hand, the culturally important appreciation of the power of science as a cognitive enterprise, including its continually evolving character and its dependence on diverse internal and external factors. It poses a difficult challenge for those working in science education, either as educators of teachers or researchers.

For Teachers and Teaching

Research on teaching (Clark 1988; Peterson & Walberg 1979) has found that teachers' beliefs about subject matter knowledge, teaching, and learning influence the academic work of the classroom. More to the point, it seems teachers' knowledge of science and pedagogy and beliefs about teaching and learning alter the intended curriculum (Doyle 1984; Duschl & Wright 1989; Tobin & Gallagher 1987). There is a significant difference, then, between what is actually being taught by teachers and what is intended to be taught. Questions which emerge include: How should teacher decision making be guided to insure that their translated curriculum reflects the intended curriculum? What are their decision-making strategies which emerge from our synthesis of epistemology and psychology? How might these be integrated effectively into the repertoire of the classroom teacher?

If teachers' conceptions of the subject matter and the goals teachers set for the instructional tasks they employ alter the ways teachers implement instruction (Clark 1988; Shavelson & Stern 1981), then teachers need to have a richer understanding of content developed from the study of epistemology. Speaking to the foundations of a teacher's knowledge base, Shulman (1986) argues that one element of teachers' knowledge of content must necessarily include an understanding of what we know—the declarative knowledge of science. But, and he stresses this point, teachers' pedagogical knowledge content base must also include an understanding of the rules of the discipline—rules which explain why we have come to believe what we believe to be our scientific view of the world. We agree. This second element of teacher knowledge stresses knowledge of procedure and focuses on why we believe what we do. Relevant questions include: What combination of the contribution of cognitive science and epistemological frameworks is best in helping students learn science and, therefore, teachers teach science? Should this combination vary with each change in specific content domain of knowledge or should it remain invariant? Are teachers capable of using multiple and complex sets of instructional heuristics?

For Learners and Learning

A significant amount of research has revealed that students are quite reluctant to change conceptions even in the face of instruction which seeks such change. A recent review of this research on the learning of science by Gunstone, White, and Fensham (1988) laments that attempts to change students' conceptions are frequently unsuccessful and usually quite time consuming. Perhaps we have underestimated what must be considered in bringing about restructuring of knowledge. It would seem plausible to suggest that changes in the declarative knowledge structures might need to be accompanied by concomitant changes in procedural knowledge structures. We have also given arguments that the context of development is likely to be more effective. However, it is unclear what the most appropriate combination of declarative and procedural knowledge would be, given the nature of the restructuring, the scientific domain, and the context of instruction.

There is also the question of to what extent the naive theories of students parallel those of early stages of science. Parallels have been demonstrated between medieval theories of dynamics and those of young students. But in other cases the psychological and historical records may not converge so readily. The naive astronomical theories of students are certainly not so complex and observationally accurate as the Ptolemaic theories that Copernicus confronted. And the current naive astronomical theories certainly do not include assumptions about the immutability of the heavens or the existence of crystalline spheres surrounding the earth. Thus, a case by case study needs to be made of the dominant naive theories in various domains and of how much individual variation there is.

A final concern for research on student learning and knowledge change is the identification of characteristics of future tasks and situations within which they will employ their restructured knowledge. In order for knowledge to be accessible, it must consist of appropriate cues related to the contexts of future use (cf., Bransford, Franks, Vye & Sherwood 1986; Sherwood et al. 1987). Given this, there is a need to identify appropriate heuristics and strategies that would allow students to access and employ their knowledge in appropriate situations. How will these procedures differ for contexts of development and justification? Can these procedures be invariant across knowledge domains? The discoveries of "alternative frameworks" in learners and the effect these have on subsequent learning, of limited capacities for processing knowledge, and of a constructivist active character to learning (Driver & Easley 1978; Resnick 1983; Wittrock 1978) suggest that instructional strategies in science ought to be dynamically altered from extant models of instruction (Champagne 1988; Wittrock 1974; West & Pines 1985).

For Historians and Philosophers of Science

For historians and philosophers of science, there are two important areas of research. One is to develop more cognitively oriented accounts of the development of the many scientific theories that have not yet been investigated in this mode. If we are right that teaching methodology must vary with the content and context of theory, then we need a large amount of such information. Even to test our claims that such variation is desirable, considerable amount of work must be done in order to design a satisfactory experimental test.

A larger and more difficult issue is that if we are to have teachers employ epistemological rules in teaching science, then philosophers of science must come to considerably more agreement than currently exists as to what those rules are. There is a serious danger that if we attempt to implement the complex and varied methodological approach that we have discussed we will only succeed in conveying the impression that science is an arbitrary hodge-podge of unrelated theories. The last thirty-five years of the philosophy of science illustrate how difficult it is to overthrow the dogma that science has a single, unified methodology and that scientific knowledge is totally cumulative and unrevisable with a newer more realistic and complex account without falling into what is perceived as an antiscientific position arguing that science is only a matter of social construction. If it is difficult to maintain the proper balance in detached scholarly discussion, it is certainly more difficult to convey that balance to teachers and for them to maintain it in the classroom under public scrutiny.

NOTES

*A much shortened version of this paper was published in the *International Journal of Science Education* as part of the proceedings of the First International Conference on The History and Philosophy of Science and Science Teaching, Florida State University, Tallahassee, November 5-9, 1989.

1. All three authors have contributed equally to the development and writing of this paper.

REFERENCES

Anderson, C. A. & Smith, E. (1986). Teaching science. In V. Koehler (Ed.), *The educator's handbook: A research perspective*. New York: Longman.

Anderson, J. (1983). *The architecture of cognition*. Cambridge, MA: Harvard University Press.

Anderson, R., & Pichert, J. (1978). Recall of previously unrecallable information following a shift in perspective. *Journal of Verbal Language Learning and Verbal Behavior, 17*, 1-12.

Anderson, R., Reynolds, R., Schallert, D., & Goetz, E. (1977). In A. Lesgold, J. Pelligrino, S. Folkema, & R. Glaser (Eds.), *Cognitive psychology and instruction.* New York: Plenum.

Bower, G., Black, J., & Turner, T. (1979). Scripts in memory for text. *Cognitive Psychology, 11,* 177-220.

Bransford, J., Franks, J., Vye, N., & Sherwood, R. (1986, June). *New approaches to instruction: Because wisdom can't be told.* Paper presented at a Conference on Similarity & Analogy, University of Illinois.

Bransford, J., & Johnson, M. (1972). Contextual prerequisites for understanding: Some investigations of comprehension and recall. *Journal of Verbal Learning and Verbal Behavior, 11,* 717-26.

Bransford, J., Sherwood, R., Vye, N., & Rieser, J. (1986). Teaching thinking and problem solving: Research Foundations. *American Psychologist, 41*(10), 1078-89.

Brewer, W., & Nakamura, G. (1984). The nature and functions of schemas. In R. Wyer & T. Skull (Eds.), *Handbook of social cognition.* New York: Academic Press.

Brewer, W., & Treyens, J. 1981, Role of schemata in memory for places. *Cognitive Psychology, 13,* 207-30.

Brown, A., Bransford, J., Ferrara, R., & Campione, J. (1983). Learning, remembering and understanding. In J. Flavell & E. Markman (Eds.), *Carmichael's manual of child psychology (Vol. 1),* pp. 77-166. New York: Wiley.

Carey, S. (1985a). *Conceptual change in childhood.* Cambridge, MA: MIT Press.

———. (1985b). Are children fundamentally different kinds of thinkers and learners than adults? In S. Chipman, J. Segal, & R. Glaser (Eds.), *Thinking and learning skills, Vol. 2.* Hillsdale, NJ: Lawrence Erlbaum.

———. (1986). Cognitive science and science education. *American Psychologist, 41,* 1123-30.

Carnap, R. (1950). *The logical foundations of probability.* Chicago: University of Chicago Press.

Champagne, A. (1988, April). *A psychological model for science education.* Paper presented at the meeting of the American Educational Research Association, New Orleans.

Chi, M., Feltovich, P., & Glaser, R. 1981, Categorization and representation of physics problems by experts and novices. *Cognitive Science, 5,* 121-52.

Chipman, S., Segal, J., & Glaser, R. (Eds.). (1985). *Thinking and learning skills, Vol. 2. Research and open questions.* Hillsdale, NJ: Lawrence Erlbaum.

Clark, C. (1988). Asking the right questions about teacher preparation: Contributions of research on teacher thinking. *Educational Researcher, 17*, 5-12.

Dillon, R. & Sternberg, R. (Eds.) (1986). *Cognition and Instruction.* New York: Academic Press.

Dooling, D., & Lachman, R. (1971). Effects of comprehension on retention of prose. *Journal of Experimental Psychology, 88*, 216-22.

Dooling, D., & Mullet, R. (1973). Locus of thematic effects in retention of prose. *Journal of Experimental Psychology, 97*, 404-6.

Doyle, W. (1983). Academic work. *Review of Educational Research, 53*(2), 159-99.

Driver, R., & Easley, J. (1978). Pupils and paradigms: A review of literature related to concept development in adolescent science students. *Studies in Science Education, 5*, 61-84.

Dunn, C. (1983). The influence of instructional methods on concept learning. *Science Education, 67*, 647-56.

Duschl, R. (1988). Abandoning the scientific legacy of science education. *Science Education, 72*(1), 51-62.

Duschl, R., & Wright, E. (1989). A case study of high school teachers' decision making models for planning and teaching science. *Journal of Research in Science Teaching, 26*(6), 467-501.

Fensham, P. (1986, September). Science for all. *AERA Division B—The Newsletter from Division B*, no. 5.

Finley, F. (1983). Scientific processes. *Journal of Research in Science Teaching, 20*, 47-54.

Freedman, E., & Smith, L. (1985, August). *Implications from cognitive psychology for the philosophy of science.* Paper presented at the 93rd annual convention of the American Psychological Association, Los Angeles.

Gibson, B. S. (1985). The convergence of Kuhn and cognitive psychology. *New Ideas in Psychology, 3*, 211-21.

Giere, R. (1988). *Explaining science: A cognitive approach.* Chicago: University of Chicago Press.

Grandy, R. (forthcoming). The semantic conception of theories. In J. Earman (Ed.), *Inference, Explanation and other Philosophical Frustrations.* Berkeley: University of California Press.

Gunstone, R., White, R., & Fensham, P. (1988). Developments in style and purpose of research on the learning of science. *Journal of Research in Science Teaching, 25*(7), 513-30.

Hanson, N. (1958). *Patterns of discovery*. Cambridge, MA: Cambridge University Press.

Haroutunian, S. (1982). Conceptual change: The nativist-constructivist debate. In D. DeNicola (Ed.), *Proceedings of the 37th annual meeting of the Philosophy of Education Society*. Normal, IL: Philosophy of Education Society.

Hempel, C. G. & Oppenheim, P. (1965). Studies in the logic of confirmation. In C. G. Hempel, *Aspects of scientific explanation and other essays in the philosophy of science* (pp. 3-46). New York: Free Press. (Original work published 1945)

Kintsch, W., & Greene, E. (1978). The role of culture-specific schemata in the comprehension and recall of stories. *Discourse Processes, 1,* 1-13.

Kitchener, R. (1987). Genetic epistemology: Equilibration and the rationality of scientific change. *Studies in the History and Philosophy of Science, 18,* 339-66.

Krupa, M., Selman, R., & Jaquette, D. (1985). The development of science explanations in children and adolescents: A structural approach. In S. Chipman, J. Segal, & R. Glaser (Eds.), *Thinking and learning skills, Vol. 2. Research and open question*. Hillsdale, NJ: Lawrence Erlbaum.

Kuhn, T. S. (1970). *The structure of scientific revolutions* (2nd ed.). Chicago: University of Chicago Press.

Lakatos, I. (1970). Falsification and the methodology of scientific research programs. In I. Lakatos & A. Musgrave (Eds.), *Criticism and the growth of knowledge* (pp. 91-196). Cambridge: Cambridge University Press.

Laudan, L. (1984). *Science and values: The aims of science and their role in scientific debate*. Berkeley and Los Angeles: University of California Press.

Laudan, L. (1977). *Progress and its problems*. Berkeley and Los Angeles: University of California Press.

Linn, M. (1986). Science. In R. Dillon & R. Sternberg (Eds.), *Cognition and instruction* (pp. 155-204). New York: Academic Press.

Mandler, J. (1978). A code in the node: The use of story schema in retrieval, *Discourse Processes, 1,* 14-35.

Nersessian, N. (1989). Conceptual change in science and in science education. *Synthese, 80,* 163-83.

Nickles, T. (Ed.). (1980). *Scientific discovery, logic, and rationality*. Dordrecht, The Netherlands: Reidel.

Novak, J. (1977). *A theory of education*. Ithaca, NY: Cornell University Press.

Novak, J., & Gowin, R. (1984). *Learning how to learn*. New York: Cambridge University Press.

Nussbaum, J. (1983). Classroom conceptual change: The lesson to be learned from the history of science. In H. Helm and J. Novak (Eds.), *Proceedings of the International Seminar on Misconceptions in Science and Mathematics* (pp. 272-81). Ithaca, NY: Cornell University, Department of Education.

Osborne, R., & Freyberg, P. (Eds.). (1985). *Learning in science: The implications of childrens' science*. London: Heinemann.

Otero, J. (1985). Assimilation problems in traditional representations of scientific knowledge. *European Journal of Science Education, 7*(4), 361-69.

Park, O. (1984). Example comparison strategy versus attribute identification strategy in concept learning. *American Educational Research Journal, 21*, 145-62.

Perkins, D. N., & Salomon, G. (1989). Are cognitive skills context-bound? *Educational Researcher, 18*(1), 16-25.

Peterson, P., & Walberg, H. (Eds.). (1979). *Research on Teaching*. Berkeley: McCutchan Press.

Phillips, D. (1982). Conceptual change: Muddying the conceptual waters—research on cognitive change. In D. DeNicola (Ed.), *Proceedings of the 37th annual meeting of the Philosophy of Education Society*. Normal, IL: Philosophy of Education Society.

Piaget, J. (1970). *Six psychological studies* (A. Tenzer, Trans.). New York: Vintage Books. (Original work published 1964).

Pichert, J., & Anderson, R. (1977). Taking different perspectives on a story. *Journal of Educational Psychology, 69*, 309-15.

Posner, G., Strike, K., Hewson, P., & Gertzog, W. (1982). Accommodation of a scientific conception: Toward a theory of conceptual change. *Science Education, 66*(2), 211-27.

Reichenbach, H. 1938, *Experience and Prediction*. University of Chicago Press.

Resnick, L. (1983). Mathematics and science learning: A new conception. *Science, 220*, 477-78.

Rissland, E. (1985). The structure of knowledge in complex domains. In S. Chipman, J. Segal, & R. Glaser (Eds.), *Thinking and learning skills, Vol. 2*. Hillsdale, NJ: Lawrence Erlbaum.

Rumelhart, D. E. (1980). Schemata: The building blocks of cognition. In R. Spiro, B. Bruce, & W. Brewer (Eds.), *Theoretical issues in reading comprehension*. Hillsdale, NJ: Lawrence Erlbaum.

Shapere, D. (1984). *Reason and the search for knowledge: Investigations in the philosophy of science*. Dordrecht, The Netherlands: Reidel.

Shavelson, R., & Stern, P. (1981). Research on teachers' pedagogical thought, judgments, decisions, and behavior. *Review of Educational Research, 51,* 455-98.

Sherwood, R., Kinzer, C., Bransford, J., & Franks, J. (1987). Some benefits of creating macro-contexts for science instruction: Initial findings. *Journal of Research in Science Teaching, 24*(5), 417-35.

Shuell, T. (1987). Cognitive psychology and conceptual change: Implications for teaching science. *Science Education, 71,* 239-50.

Shulman, L. (1986). Those who understand: Knowledge growth in teaching. *Educational Researcher, 15,* 4-14.

Simon, H., & Hayes, J. (1977). Psychological differences among problem isomorphs. In M. Castelan, D. Pisoni, & G. Potts (Eds.), *Cognitive theory, Vol. 2.* Hillsdale, NJ: Lawrence Erlbaum.

Stein, N., & Nezworski, T. (1976). The effects of organization and instructional set on story memory. *Discourse Processes, 1,* 177-94.

Suppe, F. (1989). *The semantic conception of theories and scientific realism.* Champaign-Urbana, IL: University of Illinois Press.

Suppe, F. (1977). *The structure of scientific theories* (2nd ed.). Champaign-Urbana, IL: University of Illinois Press.

Suppes, P. (1967). What is a scientific theory? In S. Morgenbesser (Ed.). *Philosophy of Science Today.* New York: Basil Books.

Tennyson, R., & Cocchiarella, M. (1986). An empirically based instructional design theory for teaching concepts. *Review of Educational Research, 56,* 40-71.

Tennyson, R., Youngers, J., & Suebsonthi, P. (1983). Acquisition of mathematics concepts by children using prototype and skill presentation forms. *Journal of Educational Psychology, 75,* 280-91.

Thorndyke, P. (1977). Cognitive structures in comprehension and memory for narrative discourse. *Cognitive Psychology, 9,* 77-110.

Thorndyke, P., & Hayes-Roth, F. (1979). The use of schemata in the acquisition and transfer of knowledge. *Cognitive Psychology, 11,* 82-106.

Thorndyke, P. (1984). Application of schema theory in cognitive research. In J. R. Anderson & S. M. Kosslyn (Eds.), *Tutorials in learning and memory.* San Francisco: WH Freeman & Co.

Tobin, K., & Gallagher, J. (1987). What happens in high school science classrooms? *Journal of Curriculum Studies, 19,* 549-60.

Van Patten, J., Chao, C., & Reigeluth, C. (1986). A review of strategies for sequencing and synthesizing instruction. *Review of Educational Research, 56*, 437-71.

Vosniadou, S., & Brewer, W. F. (1987). Theories of knowledge restructuring in development. *Review of Educational Research, 57*(1), 51-67.

West, L., & Pines, A. (Eds.). (1985). *Cognitive structure and conceptual change.* New York: Academic Press.

Whitehead, A. (1929). *The aims of education.* New York: Macmillan.

Wittrock, M. (1974). Learning as a generative process. *Educational Psychologist, 11*, 87-95.

Wittrock, M. (1978). The cognitive movement in instruction. *Educational Psychologist, 13*, 15-29.

2

Constructing and Instructing:
The Role of "Abstraction Techniques" in
Creating and Learning Physics*

OUTLINE

ABSTRACT

There is growing interest in how philosophy and history of science, cognitive science, and science education might interface on the problem of how to teach science more effectively. A central problem has been how to get students to learn the conceptual structure of a sci-

ence. This paper argues that the cognitive activities of scientists who
have constructed new conceptual structures are directly relevant to
learning, and that understanding these practices will assist us in our
efforts to help students construct representations of extant scientific
knowledge. It proposes that, for these purposes, we view the history of
scientific change as a repository of strategic knowledge about how to go
about constructing, changing, and communicating new scientific conceptual structures. Throughout the history of science "abstraction techniques," such as analogy, imagery, thought experiment, and limiting
cases analysis, have played a central role in both the construction of
new scientific representations and the communication of these to others
in the scientific community. Constructive practices of Galileo, Faraday,
and Maxwell are examined.

INTRODUCTION

A substantial body of literature establishes quite conclusively that
even after training in physics large numbers of students, including those
who have learned to perform the requisite calculations, have not
learned the scientific conceptual structure of the domain (Clement 1982;
Champagne, Klopfer & Gunstone 1982; Driver & Easley 1978; Halloun
& Hestenes 1985; McCloskey 1983; McDermott 1984; Viennot 1979). The
evidence for this is that the qualitative explanations students give for
various phenomena are at odds with those given by physics. The source
of the difficulty is widely held to be the fact that students come to their
physics classes with preconceptions about the nature and processes of
such phenomena as motion which, while not fully developed and integrated, interfere with learning scientific conceptions. Thus, students
are thought to have to undergo a major conceptual "restructuring" in
order to learn a physical theory fully.

Much of the recent literature in science education and in the psychology of learning has been addressing the problem of what the nature
of the requisite restructuring is and how best to get students to undergo
the process (See, Ranney 1987 for a survey). While there is limited
understanding and some disagreement as to just what the intuitive representations in a given domain are and whether or how they are or are
not structured, there is a widespread belief that the restructuring
required to learn a science is much like that which takes place in major
"scientific revolutions." In fact, some researchers who hold this position
hypothesize that both cognitive development and learning ensue not
from the unfolding of predetermined "stages" but from active con-

struction of new conceptualizations (Carey 1985; Keil 1989). This opens the possibility that, learning abstract scientific concepts may not depend as much on a student's maturational level as we previously thought. In other words, the perceived inability of young students to learn Newtonian mechanics may be less a matter of their not having the cognitive resources, that is, of not having attained their developmental stage a la Piaget, than a function of our not having developed appropriate teaching methods.

What learning researchers mean by "restructuring" is best seen by an example. I will use one that I have discussed in some detail in previous work (Nersessian 1989; Nersessian & Resnick, 1989). From what we know thus far, in learning Newtonian mechanics students must change from believing that "motion implies force" to believing that "accelerated motion implies force." However, examination of student protocols reveals that their concepts of 'motion' and 'force' are not the same as the Newtonian concepts. In Newtonian mechanics 'motion' is a state in which bodies remain unless acted upon by a force. 'Rest' and 'motion' have the same ontological status: they are both states. Like rest, motion per se does not need to be explained, only changes of motion. 'Force' is a functional quantity that explains changes in motion. Newtonian forces are relations between two or more bodies. Students, however, conceive of 'motion' as a process that bodies undergo and believe that *all* motion needs an explanation. They conceive of 'force' as some kind of power imparted to a body by an agent or another body. This makes 'force' ontologically a property or perhaps even an entity, but not a relationship. On the whole, the student understanding of how objects move resembles more the Aristotelian/medieval conception than the Newtonian understanding we wish them to acquire.

We can see from the example that changing a student's beliefs will take more than just introducing them to the new relations among existing concepts. Teachers need to be aware that when they use scientific language, students may already have different representations associated with the same words, as we saw for *motion* and *force*. Changing existing representations requires that they be taught how to construct the new concepts and work these into a quite different representation of the phenomena. We can also see that calling this process "restructuring" is potentially quite misleading. It makes it seem like the elements of the conceptual structure are fixed and all that is required is to rearrange these elements, as one would the furniture in a room. However, *learning a scientific conceptual structure requires more than rearranging existing elements and also more than fitting new facts into an existing framework: As discussed above, it requires constructing new concepts and working them into a new framework.* I, thus, prefer to refer to this process as "conceptual change."

The main support for the hypothesis that conceptual change in learning resembles that in scientific revolutions comes from research that describes the initial states of learners and compares them with the desired final states. These end-state comparisons, such as in the motion-and-force example, do give a sense that the kinds of cognitive changes students must make in order to learn new concepts may be like those in what philosophers and historians of science have characterized as "scientific revolutions." However, even if the *kinds* of changes are strikingly similar, this does not mean that the *processes* of change will in any way be alike. We appreciate the force of this point most clearly when we realize that the work on conceptual change both in learning and in development, while descriptive of the states of a conceptual change, by and large has not investigated the nature of the processes or "mechanisms" through which we get from one state to the next. For the claim that these kinds of changes are "like scientific revolutions" to have a real payoff for instruction, though, the question of the mechanisms of change has to be addressed in a rigorous way.

Likening these changes and processes to those of scientific revolutions does not, of course, solve the problem; it just displaces it. Science educators and psychologists should be aware that we in the history and philosophy of science are as far from having an understanding of how scientific revolutions take place as they are from understanding the mechanisms of change in learning and development. The characterization by Kuhn of a scientific revolution as a gestalt switch has been fairly uncritically adopted by psychologists and education researchers. He likens conceptual change to a gestalt switch: first we have the duck (e.g., Newtonian mechanics) and then the rabbit (relativistic mechanics), with no analyzable procedures leading from one to the other. He also maintains that learning the conceptual structure of an extant scientific theory is something that just suddenly happens to one, as was the case in his own learning of Aristotelian physics (Kuhn 1987). However, his characterization has received heavy criticism from philosophers and historians of science (see, e.g., Shapere 1984, Suppe 1977). My own position is that the metaphor of a gestalt switch has led us astray in ways that have had deep and lasting consequences. The metaphor does not support the extended nature of the conceptual changes that have actually taken place in science. It blocks the possibility of investigating how precisely the new gestalt is related to its predecessors and it reinforces the widespread view that the processes of change are mysterious and unanalyzable. So, those who would import characterizations of conceptual change from philosophy and history of science into other domains should do so with caution.

Nonetheless, I am one of those who does think we should explore and take seriously the hypothesis that conceptual change in learning and conceptual change in science may involve much the same processes. Those who assume a priori that understanding conceptual change as it occurs in science will not shed light on learning science usually are working with a narrow conception of scientific method that stems from traditional epistemology. In traditional epistemology the processes of knowledge development are conceived of in terms of what is required for justification of knowledge claims. This view is reflected in the lead article in this volume. The question that is asked in traditional epistemology is "What must the origin of scientific knowledge claims be in order for them to be maximally warranted?" In order to answer this question, "The Scientific Method" is portrayed by means of rationally reconstructed processes having little to do with the actual constructive practices of scientists. The real processes of "discovery" are held to be mysterious, and this fosters the belief that whatever procedures "discovery" may employ can, at most, be transmitted tacitly. Thus, traditional epistemology defines the "context of discovery" out of the analysis of scientific change.

Recent work in philosophy of science, based either on detailed examination of historical cases or examination of contemporary scientists at work, takes issue with this traditional conception (See, e.g., Giere 1988; Nersessian 1984, in press; Shapere 1984). What will here be called a "constructivist" view of scientific discovery emerges from this research. As used traditionally within philosophy and history of science, a "logic of discovery" would comprise a set of algorithmic procedures for generating scientific knowledge. While constructivists agree that there is no "logic of discovery" in this sense, they also agree that scientists construct new representations through reasoned processes that do constitute a set of methods that can be analyzed and evaluated. To eliminate confusion, we should say these methods comprise the "processes of invention" rather than a "logic of discovery."

The literature on scientific discovery abounds with portrayals of genius flashes of insight, such as Archimedean eureka-experiences and Kekulean dreams, as the road to discovery. What is omitted from such renderings are the periods of intense and often arduous thinking and, in some cases, experimental activity, that precede such "instantaneous" discoveries. However, there is no *inherent* conflict between the view that discovery processes are creative and the view that they are reasoned. To have a more realistic depiction of scientific discovery we need to give up the notion that creativity is an *act* and try to fathom it as a *process*.

Historical case studies of scientific discovery show it to be an extended process in which scientists actively construct representations by employing problem-solving procedures. New conceptual structures do not emerge fully grown from the heads of scientists but are constructed in response to specific problems using systematic procedures. The underlying presupposition of my own method of analysis—which I call a "cognitive-historical" method—is that the problem-solving strategies scientists have invented and the representational practices they have developed over the course of the history of science are very sophisticated and refined outgrowths of ordinary reasoning and representational processes. Creative scientists are not only exceptionally gifted human beings—they are also human beings with a biological and social makeup like the rest of us. Understood in this way, the cognitive activity of scientists becomes potentially quite relevant to learning.

Looking at things from the perspective of learning research, much of it has been focused on the point that students need to become dissatisfied with their representations in order to learn the scientific ones (see, e.g., Posner et al. 1982); the nature of the processes through which students could construct the alternative representation they are supposed to consider has not received much attention. Even if instruction were to shift from what the lead article in this volume calls the "psychological perspective" (teaching based on assimilation to current theory) to the "epistemological perspective" (teaching how data undermine previous theories and "lead" to revision), students would still not be taught how to go about *constructing* the new theory. *Learning a new conceptual structure involves more than creating dissatisfaction with existing representations.* It includes this *and* active construction of new representations.

The essence of my point is that in order to make a choice, *both* the student and the scientific representations need to be "on the table." For this to happen, students have to build a scientific representation they can manipulate and apply in thinking about diverse situations, for example, a pendulum, a projectile, and a balance arm. As Toulmin (1982, p. 110) notes, the scientific questions, problems, and explanations make sense only relative to a scientific conceptual structure. Students require access to both in order to mount a comparison and make the choice the "epistemological perspective" calls for. We need, thus, to devise strategies for helping them to construct the new conceptual structures as well as for evaluating them and for discerning their fertility. As

I will demonstrate further on in this paper, building a conceptual structure requires a different set of heuristic strategies than those evaluation calls for. What we need first to consider is in what ways the history of scientific change can assist us in getting students to construct scientific representations.

MINING THE HISTORY OF SCIENCE

The interface I envisage for the history of science and science education is different from that customarily proposed. The traditional position—taken by Dewey, Bruner, and Conant, among others—is that developing an appreciation for the historical roots of scientific ideas in students will provide motivation and a context for understanding these ideas. While there are good reasons for teaching science students some history of science, just knowing the history will not assist them in learning the actual content of a scientific theory. Even understanding the scientific problems and how scientists resolved them at that time will not, of itself, show them how to construct a scientific representation. What I suggest is that *the historical processes provide a model for the learning activity itself.*

This proposal differs significantly from the customary "recapitulation" theories with which it might be compared. While there are interesting parallels between historical prescientific conceptions in some domains and untutored conceptions, "recapitulating" the historical process is not possible, feasible, or desirable. Rather, my proposal calls for a *fundamental recasting* of how we view the role of the history of science in the science education context. I suggest that, for the purposes we have been discussing here, the history of science be viewed as *a repository of knowledge of how to go about constructing, changing, and communicating scientific representations.*

In coming to understand the constructive practices of scientists, educators will be in a better position to devise explicit strategies for leading students through their own constructions of extant scientific representations. Examinations of the history of scientific change will enable us to discern the specific processes that generate new scientific conceptual structures and the means by which those who have created these structures communicate them to others, that is, *instruct* other scientists how to construct them for themselves. The recommendation is, thus, that we "mine" the historical data—publications, diaries, notebooks, and correspondence—for these practices and then integrate into our instructional procedures what we learn about how scientists have brought about conceptual change.

My own investigations of the periods of transition before major conceptual "revolutions" in physics find repeated use of specific heuristic procedures: analogy, thought experiment, limiting case analysis, and reasoning from imagistic representations (Nersessian, 1984, in press). I have been calling these "abstraction techniques" because they are ways in which scientists have abstracted from existing conceptual structures to create genuinely novel ones. While our present understanding of these procedures is limited, we know enough about how they function to see that they are not mere "guides" to thinking, but actually generate conceptual change in science. We cannot, of course, formalize this kind of knowledge, but it is possible to make it explicit for teachers and to communicate it to students.

The remainder of this paper will be devoted to examining and interpreting, briefly, how these abstraction techniques have functioned in specific historical instances (For a fuller analysis see, Nersessian in press). The cases to be discussed are Galileo's use of thought experiments and limiting case analysis and Faraday's and Maxwell's use of analogical reasoning and reasoning from imagistic representations.

GALILEO AND THE "MATHEMATIZATION" OF THE MOTION OF BODIES

Determining the nature of the fit between mathematics and the physical world was a central conceptual issue of the Scientific Revolution of the sixteenth and seventeenth centuries. The historian Koyré has called this problem the "mathematization of nature." What this means is most clearly seen in the construction of the concept of inertial motion. As Koyré says, "what it involves, strictly speaking, is the explanation of that which *exists* by reference to that which *does not exist*, which never exists, by reference even to that which *never could exist*" (Koyré 1978). That is, *inventing the concept of inertia required figuring out how to construct idealized entities defined in terms of mathematical relations from real-world phenomena and working out how that idealized representation maps back onto the natural world.* By the end of the Scientific Revolution the objects of the scientific representation are completely quantifiable and interact according to mathematical laws in a purely geometrical space. And we also know how these laws apply to the real-world phenomena they represent: the objects with mass moving in a world full of friction and other forces.

Galileo's importance as a pivotal figure in the transition from the qualitative categories of Aristotelian and medieval theories of motion to the quantitative representation of motion provided by Newtonian mechanics is widely recognized. Although Galileo did not formulate the modern principle of inertia himself, he did make significant progress on the problem of how to go about constructing a mathematical representation of the phenomena of motion. His primary techniques for constructing idealized representations are thought experiment and limiting case analysis. We will take as an example part of his analysis of falling bodies.

According to the Aristotelian theory, heavier bodies fall faster than lighter ones. This belief rests on purely qualitative thinking about the 'essence' of the notions of 'heaviness' and 'lightness'. Galileo argues against this believe and constructs a new, quantifiable representation through a sustained analysis using several thought experiments and limiting case analyses. The outlines of his use of these procedures is as follows. He asks us to suppose we drop a heavy body and a light one at the same time. We would then say that the heavy body falls faster and the light body more slowly. Now suppose we tie the two bodies together. The combined body should both fall faster and more slowly. It should fall faster because a combined body should be heavier than two separate bodies and should fall more slowly because the slower body should retard the motion of the faster one. Clearly something has gone amiss in the thinking here.

Galileo then demonstrates how it is mistaken to extrapolate from what is true of bodies at rest to what happens when bodies are in motion. That is, when the two bodies are at rest, the lighter will press on the heavier, and therefore the combined body is heavier. But, when the two bodies are in motion, the lighter does not press on the heavier and thus does not increase its weight. What Galileo has done to this point is use the thought experiment to reveal the inconsistencies in the medieval belief, the ambiguities in the concepts of 'heaviness' and 'lightness', and the need to separate the heaviness of a body from its speed in order to analyze free fall. He then goes on, using the methods of thought experiment and limiting case analysis in tandem, to show that the apparent difference in the speed of falling bodies is due to the effect of the medium and not the difference in heaviness between bodies.

As the historian Clavelin has pointed out in his analysis of this case, it is crucial for quantifying the motion of falling bodies that 'heaviness' not be the cause of the difference in speed, because then we could not be sure that "motion" would be the same for all bodies (Clavelin 1983). Galileo demonstrates, again by thought experiment, that the observed differences in speed are caused by the unequal way media lift bodies. He asks us to suppose, for example, that the density of air is one, that of water 800, of wood 600, and of lead 10,000. In water the wood would be deprived of 800/600th of its weight, while lead would be deprived of 800/10,000ths. Thus, the wood would actually not fall (i.e., would float) and the lead would fall more slowly than it would in a less dense medium, such as air. If we extrapolate to a less dense medium, such as air, we see that the differential lifting effect is much less significant (e.g., 1/600 to 1/10,000 in air). The next move is to consider what would happen in the case of no medium, that is, in extrapolating to the limiting case. With this move, Galileo says "I came to the opinion that if one were to remove entirely the resistance of the medium, all materials would descend with equal speed" (Galilei 1638, p. 75). Having performed the extrapolation in this way, we are now in a position to quantify the idealized representation of the motion of a falling body and know that it is relevant to actual physical situations; we need only add back in the effects of a medium.

Galileo repeatedly uses thought experiments and limiting case analyses in the way shown by this example both in constructing a quantifiable representation of bodies in motion and in attempting to convey this new representation to others. In general terms, a thought experiment embodies specific assumptions—either tacit or explicit—of the representation under investigation. Depending on the circumstances, this can be either a theoretical or a commonsense representation. Thought experiments usually expose inconsistencies or exhibit paradoxes that arise from our assumptions. These can take the form either of contradictions in our representation or of things not physically possible. But we also use thought experiments to reason about situations for which it is impractical to carry out a real experiment. We could tie two stones together and clock how fast they fall, but obtaining a precise measure is quite difficult and the thought experiment simplifies the task. Even where it is possible to carry out the experiment, the thought experiment is usually so compelling that we do not feel the need to make the empirical investigation.

I propose we understand the methods of thought experiment and limiting case analysis in the following way. The cognitive function of thought experiments and limiting case analyses is much the same. They facilitate the construction of a mental model that enables manipulation of a representable but actually or practically physically unrealizable situation. What we do is construct a simulation of a prototypical situation and "run" it. It is the simulative aspect of the experiment that gives it its empirical force. Although it is not well understood yet just how the simulation process takes place in thought, it does seem that it is the constructing and developmental aspects of a thought experiment that gives it applicability to the real world. The constructed situation is abstracted from our assumptions about and activities in the world and thereby inherits their empirical force. No matter how bizarre the situation depicted may seem, the simulation unfolds in ways to which we are accustomed by experience, for example, rocks fall as they do in real-world sequences. In these ways, at the very least, the data of the thought experiment, while constructed, are also empirically relevant. These empirical consequences are often used in conjunction with those from real experiments in developing each new representation.

In limiting case analysis, a mental model is created by abstracting a specific physical dimension to create an idealized representation. This process of isolating aspects of the physical system reveals what is and is not integral to understanding the system and provides idealized data to be quantified. The idealized representation is rooted in and relevant to the real world because it has been created by controlled extrapolation from the real-world phenomena. We get that world back by adding in some of the dimensions we have abstracted, again in a controlled process.

To bring things briefly back to the learning problem, we should keep in mind that a problem quite similar to that which Galileo and his followers faced is faced by students in learning Newtonian mechanics: they must learn how to construct an abstract, mathematical representation of phenomena for the first time and come to understand the fit between that representation and the world. Consequently, the constructive practices of scientists in this period may be especially pertinent to instructional development in this area. What we have seen here is that, to a significant degree, Galileo worked out the nature of that fit by the method of constructing thought experiments and limiting case analyses.

FARADAY, MAXWELL, AND THE
FIELD REPRESENTATION OF FORCES

Our first case outlined above showed the use of certain abstraction techniques in constructing a scientific representation for the first time; that is, in the transition from a prescientific conceptualization of a domain to a scientific one. Our second case will discuss a conceptual change that took place within science in the attempt to incorporate electricity and magnetism into Newtonian mechanics. During the nineteenth century, a radically new way of understanding the nature and transmission of forces was constructed: the concept of the electromagnetic field. The development of this concept was central in the 'scientific revolution' of the early twentieth century.

In this period, Ampère and others were developing conceptions of electric and magnetic actions as Newtonian actions at a distance. In opposition to these ideas Faraday hypothesized that the lines of force that form when iron filings are sprinkled around magnets and charge matter indicate that some real physical process is going on in the space surrounding these objects and that this process is part of the transmission of the actions. Figure 2-1(a) shows the actual lines as they form around a magnet and figure 2-1(b) shows the abstraction that represented them in geometrical and dynamical form for Faraday. That the visual representation played a central role in the construction of his field conception of electric and magnetic phenomena can be seen in the many "line-like" features that are incorporated into his descriptions of the actions and that guided his attempts to detect them experimentally. For our purposes, it is most notable that the only quantitative measure he introduced is between the number of lines cut and the intensity of the

Figure 2-1
(a) Actual pattern of lines of force surrounding a bar magnet
(from Faraday (1839-55), vol. 3);
(b) Schematic representation of lines of force surrounding a bar magnet.

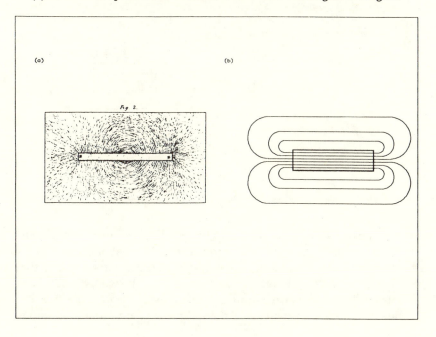

induced force. This relationship is incorrect, because "number of" is an integer, while "field intensity" is a continuous function. The mistake occurs because in the abstracted representation the lines appear discrete, while they actually spiral indefinitely in a closed volume.

Near the end of his research, Faraday introduced a imagistic representation of the dynamical balance between electricity and magnetism (fig. 2-2[a]). We can see from figure 2-2(b) that this picture of interlocking curves has itself been abstracted from the earlier "lines of force" representation. For example, a lateral repulsion of the magnetic lines

Figure 2-2
(a) Faraday's representation of the interconnectedness of electric currents and magnetic force from Faraday (1839-55), vol. 3);
(b) Schematic representation of the reciprocal relationship between magnetic lines of force and electric current lines.

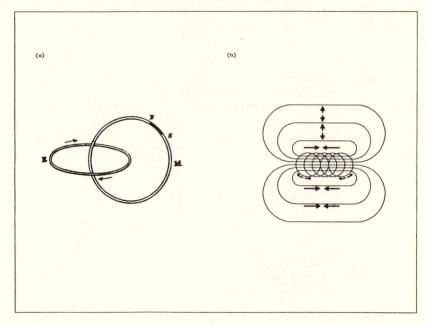

(outer lines) has the same effect as a longitudinal expansion of the current lines (inner lines). Maxwell used both of Faraday's imagistic representations in his first attempt to mathematize electromagnetism, that is, to derive the electromagnetic field equations (Maxwell, pp. 155-229). In this analysis he replaced Faraday's relationship between the number of lines cut and the intensity of the induced force with a continuous measure by representing the lines of force as the flow of an incompressible fluid through fine tube of variable section, filling all space. The interlocking curves, called "mutually embracing curves" by Maxwell, formed the basis of his reciprocal dynamics. The effect of this visual representation on his thinking can be seen most directly in his complicated use of two fields—one for a longitudinal measure of force and one for a lateral measure—where we would now only use one (fig. 2-2[b]).

These visual representations were useful primarily in Maxwell's kinematical analysis. A dynamical analysis of the underlying forces that could produce the lines involved the construction of a quite different representation: one that embodied the causal relationships between electric and magnetic forces. For this case, Maxwell constructed an analogy between electromagnetism and continuum mechanics (fluids, elastic media, etc.). He first retrieved a crude source consistent with a set of four constraints. This is a fluid medium composed of vortices and under stress, as represented in figure 2-3[a]. With this form of the analogy he was able to provide a mathematical representation for various magnetic phenomena. Analyzing the relationships between current and magnetism required alteration of the analogy. We can see in figure 2-3(a) that all the vortices are rotating in the same direction, which means that if they were to touch, they would stop. Mechanical consistency, thus, requires the introduction of "idle wheels" surrounding the vortices, and Maxwell argued that their translational motion could be used to represent electricity. Figure 2-3(b) shows a cross section of Maxwell's visual representation of this altered analogy. For the purposes of calculation, Maxwell had now to make the elastic vortices into rigid pseudospheres. He next formulated the mathematical relationships between currents and magnetism. It then took him nine months to figure out how to represent the final—and most critical—piece of the problem: electrostatic actions. He found that if he gave the vortices elasticity and identified electrostatic polarization with elastic displacement, it was possible to calculate the wave of distortion produced by polarization. That is, enhancing the source with elasticity enabled him to show that electromagnetic actions are propagated with a time delay, that is, they are field actions and not Newtonian actions at a distance. At this point we have a viable quantitative representation of the electromagnetic field, from which testable consequences, such as that electromagnetic actions are transmitted at approximately the speed of light, follow.

There is much to be learned from this case study about the use of analogical and imagistic models in creating new conceptual structures.

Figure 2-3
(a) Schematic representation of initial crude source retrieved by Maxwell;
(b) Maxwell's representation of his fully elaborated "physical analogy"
(from Maxwell (1861-2).

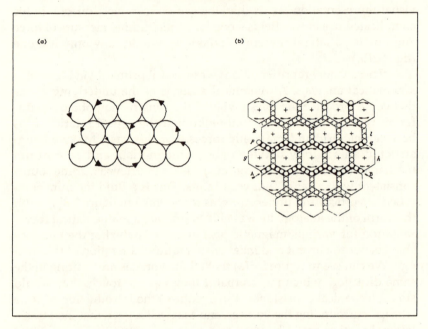

The most salient points for the instructional problem are as follows. First, it is important to underscore that Maxwell, on his route to "mathematization" of the field representation of forces, did not just take an existing physical system and plug the electromagnetic parameters into the equations for that system. Rather, he used various aspects of continuum mechanics *to put together a system* that in its entirety even he maintained did not exist—*possibly could not exist*—in nature; and *by drawing inferences from this abstracted model* he formulated the laws of a *non-Newtonian* dynamical system.

Second, in line with current computational theories of analogical reasoning, I agree that the process of analogical reasoning involves the abstraction and mapping of systems of causal and formal relationships known to hold in the source domain and hypothesized to hold in the target domain. However, as exemplified by this case, the productivity of the analogy stems from being able to repeatedly change the abstracted model to fit the constraints of the new domain, rather than from simply matching the relational structures of the two domains. Current computational theories do not capture this constructive and dynamical aspect of analogical reasoning.

Finally, how are we to understand the function of the imagistic representations used by both Faraday and Maxwell? Their power in the mathematization process may lie in their providing an intermediate level of abstraction between phenomena and mathematical forms of representation. By embodying structural relations thought to underlie phenomena, they facilitate access to quantifiable aspects of phenomena. (For recent work on this subject see, Larkin & Simon 1987; Nersessian & Greeno 1990; Roschelle & Greeno 1987). A great deal of mathematical information is implicit in such representations. By making visual a chain of interconnected inferences, they support a large number of immediate perceptual inferences, which are easy for humans to make. A major drawback, however, is that with inadequate constraints too many features specific to the picture and not to the phenomena under investigation may be incorporated into the new representation, as was the case with Faraday's field concept expressed in terms of the image of lines of force. That is, they can be taken as too nearly identical with what they are representing and, coupled with the ease with which we make perceptual inferences, they may be too generative.

Additionally, we can see that such imagistic representations could play an important role in communicating new concepts by providing a stable embodiment that is public. For example, Maxwell did not comprehend all the subtleties of the field concept Faraday articulated, but he did grasp the mathematics inherent in the way Faraday used the lines of force and in the dynamical balance embodied in the interlocking curves. Maxwell, in trying to communicate his new field concept to his colleagues, felt it necessary to provide them with a physical, that is, embodied, analogy, as well as extensive commentary on how to understand the method and the image. He did this in addition to leading them through the reasoning and in lieu of just presenting the mathematical arguments.

IMPLICATIONS FOR INSTRUCTION

We have been examining how it is that three scientists went about constructing radically new conceptions in periods of "scientific revolution." The depiction of their methods for generating conceptual change is quite different from the characterization of "The Scientific Method" by traditional epistemology, with which most science educators are familiar. The very procedures that I have been discussing, heuristics such as thought experiment and analogy, have customarily been dismissed by philosophers as at most guides to thinking and ruled out as "methods" by fiat. To be a "method" the procedure must be formalizable. Traditional psychology has also equated "reasoning" with algorithmic thinking, namely, the propositional calculus. But, as we have seen there is a good case to be made that "reasoning" comprises more than formal algorithms.

How do the constructive procedures we have been discussing compare with the procedures customarily assumed for learning? The derivation of the electromagnetic field equations provides a particularly salient case study for pedagogical purposes. The standard electrodynamics textbook accounts at both the undergraduate and graduate levels (cf. Jackson 1962; Feynman, Leighton & Sands 1963; Panofsky & Phillips 1962) all present Maxwell as *starting* from a set of field equations for closed circuits plus the equation for continuity of charge. Maxwell's problem is portrayed as that of reconciling these equations for the case of open circuits. It is said that considerations of formal consistency required that he add a term to Ampère's Law to represent the contribution of electrostatic polarization to current. As we have seen, it was through a process of embodying the structural relationships between electric and magnetic actions in a series of abstracted models and reasoning about these and manipulating them in various ways that Maxwell constructed a quantitative field concept. Considerations of formal consistency played but a small role in the initial construction. This should raise the question: Why do we think that students can learn a new concept though such considerations of formal consistency?

By and large, traditional textbook arguments are concerned with justification. That is, they present the student with reconstructed arguments that try to establish and persuade them of the correctness of the theory. But such arguments are most useful only *after* the conceptual structure of a science has been learned and we want to show why, for example, a particular law holds. As this paper has argued, what students need to do initially is learn the conceptual framework in which these arguments hold. The usual expectation is that students will learn the concepts of a theory as they do the words of a language—by rote; and the "vocabulary" of a physics text is often larger than the vocabulary that must be mastered in a language course (Tweney 1987). But learning the concepts of scientific theory is not the same as learning a language. What I have been suggesting is that we take a new approach: we investigate the kinds of procedures employed in the initial construction of a conceptual structure and attempt to teach students how to construct extant scientific representations for themselves using the same procedures. In fact there is precedent for this approach. When the scientists who have constructed the new representations attempt to communicate them to others in the scientific community, they often employ the very same constructive procedures to help their colleagues learn the new framework. This is, itself, a form of instruction, and we may have much to learn from how it has been—and is—done by scientists.

The examples provided above demonstrate that the constructive practices of scientists include constructing mental simulations, creating external pictorial representations, and constructing and manipulating analogical models. These techniques all involve a process of abstracting from phenomena or existing representations and creating a schematic or idealized model to reason with and quantify. These procedures are not formalizable, but as the examples given above show, they are techniques that can be made explicit and specific applications can be evaluated as good or bad. From my perspective the best way to go about transferring these insights into the pedagogical realm is to start with giving teachers a more realistic sense of the constructive practices of scientists. As a philosopher and historian of science I cannot speak with any confidence about specific ways to go about incorporating the knowledge we gain from the historical cases into pedagogical techniques. I do hope my discussion will persuade some science educators to take up the task.

AREAS FOR FUTURE RESEARCH

The editors of this volume have requested that we conclude our papers with a list of what we believe to be pressing research problem areas for science educators. I offer three for the domain of physics education:

1. What do students mean by the scientific words they commonly use in ordinary discourse, such as *gravity*? While there has been considerable research into "naive" beliefs about motion, these studies have offered little understanding of the meanings students attach to the words they use. In the research that I have been undertaking with Lauren Resnick, we found that while it is possible to glean meanings for *force* and *motion* from the existing studies, we were continually frustrated by wanting to know what students meant when they used other common words, such as *gravity* and *energy*. Knowing what students mean by these words is not only important for theoretical considerations about the nature of their representations, but, as we

saw in the force-and-motion example, teachers could be more effective if they knew how different the meanings students attach to their
words is from the scientific usage.

2. To what extent are the heuristic procedures employed by scientists in
creating new conceptual structures already in the cognitive repertoire of students? We know, for example, from the extensive literature on analogical problem solving, that this heuristic is available to
and employed by students of all ages. Do they already have some
intuitive grasp of how to abstract structure underlying phenomena
and to make idealizations? The expectation of the value of knowing
what is in their repertoire and whether or not any of the procedures
are age specific is that it should be easier to train what is already
among their cognitive skills.

3. What can be achieved in the area of conceptual change in the science lab? Would computer-simulated labs do better in this area? The
predominant ideology among science educators is that hands-on
experience is at the heart of science learning. This ideology arises
from the erroneous assumption that scientific method involves primarily induction from data. It also fails to take into account the real
possibility that students will simply assimilate the new 'data' to their
pre-existing conceptualizations. Computer simulations, such as
"dyna-turtle" and "micro-worlds" (di Sessa 1982; White, in press),
might help students to think at the requisite level of abstraction for
developing a scientific representation of phenomena. A possible
avenue for exploring this question is to test the success of standard
laboratory instruction in facilitating conceptual learning as compared with computer-simulated labs.

ACKNOWLEDGMENTS

*Preparation of this paper was supported by National Science Foundation
Scholars Award DIR-8821422. I wish to thank James Greeno, Lauren Resnick,
and the editors of this volume for their helpful comments.

REFERENCES

Carey, S. (1985). *Conceptual change in childhood.* Cambridge, MA: MIT Press.

Clavelin, M. (1983). Conceptual and technical aspects of the Galilean
geometrization of the motion of heavy bodies. In W. Shea (Ed.), *Nature
Mathematized* (pp. 23-50). Dordrecht, the Netherlands: Reidel.

Clement, J. (1982). Students' preconceptions in introductory mechanics. *American Journal of Physics, 50,* 66-71.

Champagne, A. B., Klopfer, L. E., & Gunstone, R. F. (1982). Cognitive research and the design of science instruction. *Educational Psychologist, 17,* 31-53.

di Sessa, A. A. (1982). Unlearning Aristotelian physics: A study of knowledge-based learning. *Cognitive Science, 6,* 37-75.

Driver, R., & Easley, J. (1978). Pupils and paradigms: A review of literature related to concept development in adolescent science students. *Studies in Science Education, 5,* 61-84.

Feynman, R. P., Leighton, R. B., and Sands, M. (1964). *The Feyman lectures on physics.* Reading, MA: Addison-Wesley.

Galilei, G. (1974). *Two new sciences* (S. Drake, trans.). Madison: University of Wisconsin Press. (Original work published 1638)

Giere, R. (1988). *Explaining science: A cognitive approach.* Chicago: University of Chicago Press.

Halloun, I. A. & Hestenes, D. (1985). Common sense concepts about motion. *American Journal of Physics, 53,* 1056-65.

Jackson, J. D. (1962). *Classical electrodynamics.* New York: Wiley.

Keil, F. C. (1989). *Concepts, kinds, and cognitive development.* Cambridge, MA: MIT Press.

Koyré, A. (1978). *Galileo studies.* Atlantic Highlands, NJ: Humanities Press.

Kuhn, T. S. (1987). What are scientific revolutions? In L. Kruger et al. (Eds.), *The probabilistic revolution* (pp. 7-22). Cambridge, MA: MIT Press.

Larkin, J. H. & Simon, H. (1987). Why a diagram is (sometimes) worth ten thousand words. *Cognitive Science, 11,* 65-100.

McCloskey, M. (1983). Naive theories of motion. In D. Gentner & A. L. Stevens (Eds.), *Mental models* (pp. 299-324). Hillsdale, NJ: Lawrence Erlbaum.

Panofsky, W. & Phillips, M. (1962). *Classical electricity and magnetism.* Reading, MA: Addison-Wesley.

McDermott, L. (1984). An overview of research on conceptual understanding in physics. Unpublished manuscript.

Nersessian, N. J. (in press). How do scientists think? Capturing the dynamics of conceptual change in science. In R. Giere (Ed.), *Cognitive Models of Science (Minnesota Studies in the Philosophy of Science, Vol. 15.* Minneapolis: University of Minnesota Press.

Nersessian, N. J. (1989). Conceptual change in science and in science education. *Synthese, 80,* 163-83.

Nersessian, N. J. (1984). *Faraday to Einstein: Constructing meaning in scientific theories.* Dordrecht, The Netherlands: Kluwer Academic Publishers.

Nersessian, N. J., & Greeno, J. G. (1990). Multiple abstracted representations in problem solving and discovery in physics. *Proceedings of the Cognitive Science Society, 12* (pp. 77-84). Hillsdale, NJ: Lawrence Erlbaum.

Nersessian, N. J., & Resnick, L. B. (1989). Comparing historical and intuitive explanations of motion: Does 'naive' physics have a structure? *Proceedings of the Cognitive Science Society, 11* (pp. 412-20). Hillsdale, NJ: Lawrence Erlbaum.

Posner, G., Strike, K., Hewson, P., & Gertzog, W. (1982). Accommodation of a scientific conception: Toward a theory of conceptual change. *Science Education, 66*(2), 211-27.

Ranney, M. A. (1987). *Changing Naive Conceptions of Motion.* Unpublished dissertation, University of Pittsburgh.

Roschelle, J., & Greeno, J. G. (1987). *Mental Models in Expert Physics Reasoning* (Report No. GK-2). Berkeley: University of California.

Shapere, D. (1984). *Reason and the search for knowledge.* Dordrecht, The Netherlands: Reidel.

Suppe, F. (1977). *The structure of scientific theories* (2nd ed.). Urbana, IL: University of Illinois.

Toulmin, S. (1982). The construal of reality: Criticism in modern and postmodern science. *Critical Inquiry, 1,* 93-111.

Tweney, R. D. (1987). What is scientific thinking? Unpublished manuscript.

Viennot, L. (1979). Spontaneous reasoning in elementary dynamics. *European Journal of Science Education, 1,* 205-21.

White, B. Y. (in press). ThinkerTools: Causal models, conceptual change, and science education. *Cognition and Instruction.*

GREG NOWAK
PAUL THAGARD

3

Newton, Descartes, and Explanatory Coherence

OUTLINE

ABSTRACT

This paper applies a theory of explanatory coherence to model the conflict between Newtonian mechanics and the Cartesian system of the world. The theory of explanatory coherence consists of principles that establish coherence and incoherence relations among propositions. It has been implemented in ECHO, a connectionist computer program. We present a detailed simulation of Newton's comparison of his mechanics with Cartesian physics. Our simulation displays the explanatory structure of these two theories and indicates why, from Newton's perspective, his theory was greatly superior to Descartes's. Newton's theory explained more evidence than Descartes's, which also suffered from predictions that contradicted evidence. In addition, Newton's theory was simpler, in that it required fewer hypotheses in its explanations. We conclude by discussing some implications of our analysis for science education.

EXPLANATORY COHERENCE

This paper applies a computational theory of explanatory coherence to an important case in the history of physics. The theory has been implemented in a connectionist computer program called "ECHO," and ECHO has been used to model the competition between Newtonian and Cartesian physics. ECHO has also been used to model the acceptance of hypotheses in chemistry, biology, geology, and legal reasoning (Thagard 1989, in press-b, in press-c; Thagard & Nowak 1988, 1990) and in the Copernican revolution (Nowak & Thagard 1991a). Thagard (1989) provides a detailed description of the new theory of explanatory coherence and the program that implements it. Here we provide only a brief excerpt from that paper, which should be consulted for a full discussion of explanatory coherence and specification of the algorithms used in the program.

The theory of explanatory coherence, or TEC, is stated in seven principles that establish relations of explanatory coherence and make possible an assessment of the global coherence of an explanatory system S. S consists of propositions P, Q, and $P_l \ldots P_n$. Local coherence is a relation between two propositions. The term *incohere* is used to mean more than just that two propositions do not cohere: to incohere is to *resist* holding together. Here are the principles.

PRINCIPLE 1. *Symmetry.*
   (a) If P and Q cohere, then Q and P cohere.

(b) If P and Q incohere, then Q and P incohere.
PRINCIPLE 2. *Explanation.*
If $P_1 \ldots P_m$ explain Q, then:
    (a) For each P_i in $P_1 \ldots P_m$, P_i and Q cohere.
    (b) For each P_i and P_j in $P_1 \ldots P_m$, P_i and P_j cohere.
    (c) In (a) and (b) the degree of coherence is inversely
        proportional to the number of propositions $P_1 \ldots P_m$.
PRINCIPLE 3. *Analogy.*
    (a) If P_1 explains Q_1, P_2 explains Q_2, P_1 is analogous to P_2, and Q_1 is
        analogous to Q_2, then P_1 and P_2 cohere, and Q_1 and Q_2 cohere.
    (b) If P_1 explains Q_1, P_2 explains Q_2, Q_1 is analogous to Q_2, but P_1 is
        disanalogous to P_2, then P_1 and P_2 incohere.
PRINCIPLE 4. *Data Priority.*
Propositions that describe the results of observation have a degree of
acceptability on their own.
PRINCIPLE 5. *Contradiction.*
If P contradicts Q, then P and Q incohere.
PRINCIPLE 6. *Acceptability.*
    (a) The acceptability of a proposition P in a system S depends on its
        coherence with the propositions in S.
    (b) If many results of relevant experimental observations are
        unexplained, then the acceptability of a proposition P that
        explains only a few of them is reduced.
PRINCIPLE 7. *System coherence.*
The global explanatory coherence of a system S of propositions is a
function of the pairwise local coherence of those propositions.

TEC is implemented in ECHO, a computer program written in
Common LISP that is a straightforward application of connectionist
algorithms to the problem of explanatory coherence. In ECHO, propositions representing hypotheses and results of observation are represented by units. Whenever principles 1-5 state that two propositions
cohere, an excitatory link between them is established. If two propositions incohere, an inhibitory link between them is established. In ECHO,
these links are symmetric, as principle 1 suggests: the weight from unit
1 to unit 2 is the same as the weight from unit 2 to unit 1. Principle 2(c)
says that the larger the number of propositions used in an explanation,
the less the degree of coherence between each pair of propositions.
ECHO therefore counts the propositions that do the explaining and
proportionately lowers the weight of the excitatory links between units
representing coherent propositions.

Principle 4, Data Priority, is implemented by links to each data unit from a special evidence unit that always has activation 1, giving each unit some acceptability on its own. When the network is run, activation spreads from the special unit to the data units, and then to the units representing explanatory hypotheses. The extent of data priority—the presumed acceptability of data propositions—depends on the weight of the link between the special unit and the data units. The higher this weight, the more immune the data units become from deactivation by other units. Units that have inhibitory links between them because they represent contradictory hypotheses have to compete with each other for the activation spreading from the data units: the activation of one of these units will tend to suppress the activation of the other. Excitatory links have positive weights, and best performance occurs with weights around .05. Inhibitory links have negative weights, and best performance occurs with weights around -.2. The activation of units ranges between 1 and -1; positive activation can be interpreted as acceptance of the proposition represented by the unit, negative activation as rejection, and activation close to 0 as neutrality.

To summarize how ECHO implements the principles of explanatory coherence, we can list key terms from the principles with the corresponding terms from ECHO.

> *Proposition:* unit.
> *Coherence:* excitatory link, with positive weight.
> *Incoherence:* inhibitory link, with negative weight.
> *Data priority:* excitatory link from special unit.
> *Acceptability:* activation.

Recently, TEC and ECHO have been revised by the addition of a new principle concerning competition among hypotheses (Thagard in press-c). Hypotheses do not need to contradict each other to be incoherent with each other. We will see in the simulation discussed below that there are many pairs of hypotheses in opposing theories that do not directly contradict each other but are such that scientists would not want to accept both of them. TEC.2 consists of the seven principles of TEC stated above plus:

Principle of Competition
>   If P and Q both explain a proposition R, and if P and Q are not
>   explanatorily connected, then P and Q incohere. Here P and Q are
>   explanatorily connected if any of the following conditions holds:
>   (a) P is part of the explanation of Q,
>   (b) Q is part of the explanation of P,

(c) *P* and *Q* are together part of the explanation of some propositions *S*.

ECH0.2 implements this principle by finding for each piece of evidence *E* pairs of hypotheses *P* and *Q* that explain *E* but are not explanatorily related to each other. Then an inhibitory link between *P* and *Q* is constructed. In the limiting case, the inhibition is the same as that between units representing contradictory hypotheses. But if *P* and *Q* each explain *E* only with the assistance of numerous other hypotheses, then they incohere to a lesser extent; compare principle 2(c) above. Hence in ECH0.2 degree of inhibition between units representing *P* and *Q* is inversely proportional to the number of cohypotheses used by *P* and *Q* in their explanations of *E*.

After input has been used to set up the network, the network is run in cycles that synchronously update all the units. For each unit *j*, the activation a_j, ranging from -1 to 1, is a continuous function of the activation of all the units linked to it, with each unit's contribution depending on the *weight* w_{ij} of the link from unit *i* to unit *j*. The activation of a unit *J* is updated using the following equation.

$$a_j(t+1) = a_j(t)(1-\theta) + \begin{cases} net_j \, (max-a_j(t)) & \text{if } net_j > 0 \\ net_j \, (a_j(t)-min) & \text{otherwise} \end{cases}$$

Here θ is a decay parameter that decrements each unit at every cycle, min is minimum activation (-1), max is maximum activation (1), and net_j is the net input to a unit. This is defined by:

$$net_j = \Sigma_i w_{ij} a_i(t)$$

Repeated updating cycles result in some units becoming activated (getting activation > 0) while others become deactivated (activation < 0). (For full details, see Thagard in press-b).

TEC and ECHO treat theory evaluation as a process of parallel constraint satisfaction. Hypotheses should explain the evidence, be explained by other hypotheses, be analogous to other explanatory hypotheses, be part of simple explanations, cohere with other accepted hypotheses, and not incohere with rejected propositions. None of these constraints is absolute, and no simple linear method would work to satisfy them simultaneously. Many other psychological processes besides hypothesis evaluation can naturally be understood in terms of parallel satisfaction of multiple soft constraints. Much of ECHO's computational apparatus is based on the interactive activation and competition model of McClelland and Rumelhart (1981, 1989), which they applied to visual word recognition. Other visual processes can also be understood in terms of parallel competitive algorithms (Marr 1982). Kintsch (1988) has used similar techniques to model many aspects of discourse comprehension. Analogy also involves satisfaction of multiple constraints in both the construction of mappings between two analogs and the retrieval of analogs from memory (Holyoak & Thagard 1989; Thagard, Holyoak, Nelson, & Gochfeld 1990; the implications of these models for instructional use of analogy is discussed in Thagard in press-a).

TEC and ECHO are intended to model explanatory coherence, not explanation as such. They are consistent with a wide variety of views of the nature of explanation that have appeared in philosophy and cognitive science. Some researchers view explanation as a matter of constructing a deduction of what is to be explained, while others view explanation as schema application rather than deduction. A review of different perspectives on the nature of explanation is provided elsewhere (Thagard in press-c, ch. 5).

Let us now turn to a new historical application of ideas about explanatory coherence.

DESCARTES AND NEWTON

Both Descartes and Newton presented their ideas in relatively complete and carefully edited single works. Descartes's *Principles of Philosophy* was first published in Latin in 1644; an enlarged French language translation was published with Descartes's approval in 1647. An English translation of the 1644 edition by V. R. Miller and R. P. Miller was published in 1983. Newton's *Mathematical Principles of Natural Philosophy* first appeared in 1687 in Latin; it was translated into English by Andrew Motte in 1729 and updated by Florian Cajori in the 1920s. Aiton (1972) and Clarke (1982) have proved useful in elucidating the thought of Descartes.

Newton's work provided a grand synthesis that integrated Copernicus's heliocentric view, Kepler's laws of planetary motion, and Galileo's insights about terrestrial physics. The geocentric system of Ptolemy had largely dropped out of contention by the time Newton wrote his *Principia*, and he saw as the major alternative another heliocentric system, the cosmology of Descartes.

In the ECHO contest between Copernicus and Ptolemy (Nowak & Thagard 1990) both disputants agreed about the phenomena to be explained, but the simulation of the dispute between Newton and Descartes is less balanced. Whereas Newton distinguished propositions that could be formally demonstrated from hypotheses about the natural world, Descartes was intent on demonstrating the necessity of all of his ideas. This necessity rested upon two principles: Descartes's perception that matter and space were identical and his conclusion that certain features of the universe ordained by God at the creation had to remain unchanged to avoid violating the theological principle of divine immutability.

Our simulation pits the geometrical physics of Newton against the more abstract, largely qualitative physics of Descartes. While ECHO does not grant the status of necessity to propositions viewed as necessary by Descartes or Newton, it is able to capture the structure of the two explanatory systems as they appeared to the authors.

The two systems were based upon radically different metaphysics, but both aspired to explain almost all visible astronomical phenomena and a great many terrestrial phenomena as well. Because Newton's work appeared several decades after that of Descartes, he was able to respond directly to some of Descartes's hypotheses, a historical contingency which is reflected in the input we give ECHO. Although we used Descartes's own writings to construct a model of his explanatory system, our simulation is intended to be a model of Newton's view of the superior explanatory coherence of his system: it is not a model of an impartial observer. Thus, the simulation embodies both Newton's description of his own system and his critique of Descartes's. Newton's ability to rebut specific Cartesian hypotheses gave him an advantage in argumentation successfully modeled by ECHO, which judges Newtonian mechanics to be more coherent than Cartesian physics.

Most of the evidence propositions in our simulation are derived from book 3 of Newton's *Mathematical Principles*, the "System of the World". Descartes does not provide a summary description of the phenomena to be explained, but only refers to natural phenomena in passing, as if they were needed only to confirm the validity of the propositions whose necessity he had already demonstrated. In many articles in the *Principles of Philosophy*, he merely rephrases a proposition at greater length, neither demonstrating it from what had gone before nor giving any evidence it could explain. This terseness is in contrast to Newton, all of whose arguments at least aspired to the level of rigor required of mathematical proof, even if they were not complete proofs. As a result, Newtonian explanations were easier to derive from the text than Cartesian ones.

DESCARTES

Descartes's physics was a world picture incorporating religion, philosophy, and science. At the center of his metaphysics was an essentially negative principle, that there is nothing in the physical universe except matter and its motion. Descartes argued for this principle by noting that there is no feature that all matter shares except the property that it takes up space. Some matter is not hard, some matter has no color, and some matter such as fire has no weight. Since changeable properties of matter such as heat and cold could not be essential to it, Descartes concluded that there is no difference between any substance and space, and therefore any perceptible section of space must also be occupied by matter. Descartes therefore concluded that universal matter must be infinitely divisible and that the only real features of a particle of matter are its shape and motion. Hence for Descartes a scientific explanation of a phenomenon is an account of the shapes and motions of particles that can bring about the given phenomenon.

Descartes's *Principles* is divided into four parts. The first is concerned mainly with epistemological issues, such as the nature of understanding, the formation of clear concepts, the ontological proof of the existence of God, and the reasons for error in perception and philosophy. The second part introduces Descartes's theory of matter, including his concepts of place and motion and his laws of motion. It also includes a few principles of Descartes's fluid dynamics, mainly discussing the behavior of objects moving in fluids.

The appendices to this chapter state the input given to ECHO for our simulation of the competition between the Newtonian and Cartesian systems. Appendix A lists the propositions used as evidence for the competing theories, while appendices B and C contain propositions representing the theories of Newton and Descartes, respectively. Newton and Descartes agreed that motion follows certain determinate laws about the conditions under which motion changes. They differed over the content of these laws and the proper epistemological techniques to be used in science. Thus for Descartes, having a clear and simple idea of a possible property of nature was sufficient to demonstrate its truth. Newton's epistemological principles were simpler (Newton 1934, pp. 398-400): to assign similar causes to similar effects, to assume that properties omnipresent locally (e.g., inertia) are omnipresent universally, and to allow induction. Although Newton's laws were referred to as "laws of motion" and Descartes's as "laws of nature," the first laws in each set were almost identical; however, the content of the succeeding laws differed, and in fact those of Descartes end up being self-contradictory.

Descartes' first law is split into two propositions, D27 and D28, to reflect a feature of his model of motion: whereas Newton saw rest and motion as differing in degree but not in principle, Descartes saw rest and motion as opposing "states" or "modes" that a body could be in, as stated in D69. Together, D69 and D27 explain D28; for Descartes, persistence in motion is merely an application of the principle of persistence in state. The clause "as far as is in its power" in D27 is also significant; it reflects Descartes's idea that moving bodies have a "force of motion" which tends to maintain their motion in exactly the same way, and resting bodies have a similar but opposing "force of rest" which tends to maintain them in a state of rest. These forces differed from Newtonian forces; they are best understood as a kind of all-or-nothing inertial mass which is either sufficient to prevent a change in the body's motion or not sufficient.

Descartes's second law, D43, is similar to parts of Newton's first two laws, claiming that all movement is in itself along straight lines. Descartes justified the law by appealing in D46 to the immutability of God. Descartes explained that matter in motion possesses an inclination to move in a single direction, which requires that its inclination to move must be in a straight line; an inclination moving in a *curved* line would require the body to "remember" its former path, but "God maintains movement in matter it, and not as it may perhaps have been at some earlier time" (Descartes 1983, p. 60). Since Descartes believed that no motion was accomplished in an instant, he saw as one of the tasks of God a continual re-creation of the universe which transformed a succession of instants into an illusion of motion.

One of the propositions of Descartes's system which led him into the most trouble is D85, that the force of rest must be overcome by a greater force in order for the body to be moved at all. More generally he claimed in D71 that whenever two forces act in opposition to each other, only the stronger force has any effect. This principle gave support to Descartes's third law of nature, giving two principles of collision: D30, which states that a moving body could not move a resting one of greater mass, but would merely rebound off it, and D31, which states that a moving body hitting a resting one of lesser mass would merely carry along the smaller one. These laws figured in Cartesian explanations for several pieces of negative evidence that contradict actual observations. For example, NE13, concerning the motion of a loadstone and a piece of iron, contradicts E13, which is evidence presented by Newton for his third law of motion that every action has an equal and opposite reaction.

Descartes further expanded these two laws into seven rules of collision that caused him further problems, because they predict different results depending on the frame of reference used. This discrepancy in itself would not be problematic, since Descartes believed in the existence of an absolute frame of reference, but the definition of motion (D87) that he used to claim that the earth was not moving entailed changeable frames of reference. Hence, in conjunction with the two halves of the third law, D87 explains negative evidence NE9. Whereas Newton presented the evidence E9 that all motions happen on a uniformly moving ship exactly as they would on land, Descartes ended up explaining NE9 (a generalization of the explicit contradiction to E9) with his third law, thus penalizing his model of motion. A nearly identical pattern of explanation occurs with the pair E12 and NE12.

Part of Descartes's account of motion included a cosmological account of the origins of matter and motion. In addition to the immutability of God, mentioned above, Descartes believed that God was directly responsible for the conservation of motion. Descartes claimed that God bestowed upon the world its total quantity of motion at the creation (D16), and, gave God credit for actively maintaining the sum of motion in the world (D5). In order to understand Descartes, we must distinguish between his idea of the constant sum of motion and the modern idea of conservation of momentum, which is expressed as the product of mass and velocity. For Descartes, motion was defined mathematically as the product of mass and speed, which is the absolute value of velocity; it carries no directional information. This difference was part of the explanatory scheme which led to Descartes's erroneous laws of collision, since some of Descartes's rules conserved motion but not momentum. Since Descartes did not believe in forces, he held that the motion could only come from motion and thus, in order for there to be any motion in the world, God had to put it there in the first place. Thus he was able to explain E16 and E17, that matter exhibits motion and changes in motion.

Since Newton had a concept of force, he had no difficulty in explaining these pieces of evidence. Descartes, however, in addition to denying the existence of forces, had to derive a physics which was compatible with his belief that matter and space were identical. The basic proposition of Descartes' philosophy of matter was D1, that the only characteristic feature of matter was extension, or the property of taking up space. From this followed several corollaries, including D12-D14, which in turn asserted the identity of space and matter, the infinite divisibility of matter, and the impossibility of the vacuum.

One of the conceptual problems for Descartes's system was that his identification of matter with extension made clear that matter was infinitely divisible, since one could always conceive of a smaller extension. But the identification did not explain why material bodies persist, that is, what prevents them from constantly subdividing. Descartes had to explain the coherence of matter (E39) and the apparent differences of matter and "empty" space (E40). He argued that the only mechanical reason for two bodies to remain together would be relative rest, the existence of which was asserted in proposition D2, so he merely asserted that relative rest was the sufficient condition for cohesion of parts of matter in D3. These propositions allowed Descartes to explain E39 and E40, evidence which was beyond the scope of Newton's work.

The third part of Descartes's *Principles of Philosophy* is concerned with the "Visible Universe," meaning astronomical phenomena. In discussing the origins of the universe, Descartes explicitly admitted that he knows some of his views to be false, yet maintained that we can still deduce "true and certain" conclusions from them. He stated that for religious reasons he knows that the universe was created "in the beginning with all the perfection which it now possesses," but that it advances the understanding to consider how the present state might have arisen from a simpler set of initial conditions (Descartes 1983, pp. 105-7). Here Descartes reasoned from the necessity of the universe being arranged in a certain way, combined with his understanding of the current physical situation, to posit the initial conditions of the universe which would necessarily have been in effect had not God chosen to create the universe in a state of full perfection.

The third part of the *Principles* also contains Descartes's treatment of a more sensitive religious issue: the movement of the earth (Descartes 1983, p. 95). Descartes was aware of the harsh response to the politically well-connected Galileo after he advocated the movement of the earth, and as a loyal Catholic who had no wish to defy the church, Descartes felt obliged to deny explicitly the motion of the earth in proposition D42. He did this by proposing D87, an alternative definition of motion, that a body is in motion only when it ceases to touch other bodies in its neighborhood and appears in the neighborhood of others. Since by D41, the earth was surrounded by a vortex which moved with it around the sun, this was a permanent "neighborhood" in the sense of D87, and thus Descartes could conclude that the earth did not in fact move. This definition significantly added to the incoherence of Descartes's model: it entailed the two pieces of negative evidence NE9 and NE12, and explained nothing else except D42, which itself explained no evidence. Note that ECHO successfully models this component of Descartes's world system: even though the immobility of the earth explains no evidence for Descartes, it can be included in his explanatory network, since he has made clear its explanatory relations to other parts of his system such as the alternative definition of motion.

Descartes's account of the motion of the planets is much less organized than Newton's. Having abandoned his goal of demonstrating the necessity of his system, and having established to his satisfaction the necessity of the identity of matter and space and the principle of vortex motion, Descartes is content to assume that vortices behave in whatever way necessary to save the phenomena. The assumption of the existence of vortices themselves is made by Descartes less out of any sense of necessity than out of his assumption that vortices must move the planets, because he was familiar with no other form of self-sustaining physical phenomenon, and his metaphysics required him to come up with a completely kinematic (i.e., forceless, as opposed to dynamic) account of planetary motion.

One of Newton's rebuttals to Descartes was the demonstration that vortices cannot continue indefinitely unless they are maintained by some outside "active principle" (see N57). Although Descartes appealed to divine aid at many points in his physics, the maintenance of vortex motion does not appear to be one of them. In D32, he simply stated that the planets were carried around by the main vortex of the solar system, and an appeal to God in D20 merely served to start the celestial vortex off at the creation, as God was the source of the initial quantity of motion in the universe carefully conserved. D17 describes the formation of coarser particles of terrestrial matter from the celestial matter of space by the agency of relative rest; D22-D24 account for the formation of the stars and planets. In D22, Descartes described the formation of stars from the "primary particles" or finest-grained celestial matter. D23 and D24 actually contradict each other, since D23 claims that the planets used to be stars, and thus are composed of primary matter; but in D24, he claimed that the planets are made of heavy or terrestrial matter. In his discussion of the formation of matter, he claimed that terrestrial matter is composed of the coarser tertiary particles and, indeed, based his entire account of gravity on this assumption. Gravity is described in D40 as the tendency of bodies to sort themselves according to the proportion of tertiary matter they contain. Yet in his discussion of the life cycles of vortices, he maintained that when one vortex swallows another, the star in the "losing" vortex becomes a planet of the other. Descartes then gave a detailed description of how the solar system was assembled in this way, nowhere mentioning how the planets became tertiary matter.

There is a significant difference in level of detail between Descartes and Newton. Newton engaged in detailed mathematical proofs that an inverse-square centripetal force moves the planets in ellipses with the sun at one focus, which agreed well with observation, and is able to calculate disturbances in the moon's orbit caused by the sun. Descartes, not a mathematical astronomer, resolved the problem of accurate determination of the planet's orbits merely by asserting in D57 that their motions need not be circular since collisions of innumerable particles are involved and nothing beneath heaven is perfect anyway.

The most prolific source of error in Descartes's physics is his discussion of fluid dynamics. In several cases, he either explains negative evidence or derives both a piece of evidence and its contradiction. For example, Descartes presented the evidence E23 that a solid body in a fluid can be set in motion easily. He accounted for the evidence by asserting in D75 that the fluid at the back of a moving body is likely to assist it in its motion to some extent, thus creating the impression that the body is very easily moved. This contradicts Descartes's claim that resting bodies possess a force of rest which must be overcome by a greater force before they can be moved. Thus his doctrine of inertia also allowed Descartes to demonstrate the contradictory piece of negative evidence NE23. The pair E35-NE35 is provided by Newton, who claimed that Descartes violated observed astronomical fact in requiring planets to move more slowly at their closest approach to the sun instead of more quickly. Applied to the earth, this principle would affect the apparent motions of the sun.

The final part of Descartes's *Principles* concerned terrestrial phenomena, mostly what we would today call "materials science," dealing with such questions as why glass is both transparent and hard, why different substances burn differently, and so on. There is one section more relevant to astronomical questions, which concerns the reasons for the tides. We will discuss this topic in detail below, as it provides an example of the differing explanatory styles of Newton and Descartes.

One large-scale phenomenon discussed by both Newton and Descartes is that of the tides. The discussion is rendered somewhat difficult by the fact that in addition to the twice-daily cycle of the tides described in E36, there was a monthly variation apparently associated with the moon given in E37. Newton correctly observed that high tides occur about when the moon is highest on the sky, on or near the meridian (E38). The negative evidence NE38, on the other hand, is a direct consequence of Descartes' theory. Descartes attempted to explain the monthly variation of the tides, but he reversed the daily cycle, having the low tides rather than the high coincide with the appearance of the moon on the meridian or the antemeridian.

Descartes's error may have been a result of his desire to use vortices to explain the phenomenon of tides without paying sufficient attention to what was already known about the timing of the tides. Descartes had not previously discussed the possibility that the position of the planets was determined by some sort of equality of forces (D88); he used it to justify the idea that the moon restricts the celestial matter in the earth's vortex from freely circulating around the earth (D89), thus pushing the earth back (D90), and he maintained that this compression is responsible for the low tides. Without justification, Descartes also asserted (see D91) that the celestial matter on the opposite side of the earth from the moon is also constricted, providing two low tides twelve hours apart. But the tides are still not synchronized with the moon crossing the meridian. Descartes explained the monthly variation in the tides by asserting in D92, that the earth's vortex is not round, and assuming that the full moon and new moon occur when the shape of the vortex forces it closest to the earth. Therefore the celestial matter was even more constricted when the moon was full or new, and constrained the seas even more than the normal compression due to the presence of the moon.

Another problem in Descartes's system was that it did not naturally explain the motion of the moon. He had asserted in D37 that the planets found their place in the solar system by coming to equilibrium in the part of the vortex moving as fast as the planet. But the moon could not find its place in this way, since it was covering approximately the same distance as the earth but going faster since it was moving in a looping path. As the moon was sometimes inside and sometimes outside the earth's orbit, its distance could not be a factor of its speed. Hence Descartes made the distance of a planet from the sun dependent upon its density (D62) and its speed dependent upon its size (D64). Then given that the moon was smaller than (D66) but just as dense (D65) as the earth, it had to revolve around the sun at the same distance as the earth, but faster. Both of these conditions could be met only if the moon was revolving around the earth, which he concluded in D67. Descartes was able to explain the fact that only one side of the moon faced the earth by supposing, in D61, that one side of the moon was denser than the other; thus the celestial matter around the earth forced the moon to arrange itself by density, with the less dense side always facing inward. The motion of the moon serves as a good example of Descartes's strengths and failings: while he was unlikely to leave a phenomenon unexplained, he paid a heavy price for the explanation in the creation of many new hypotheses. We shall see in the discussion in "Results" section that Descartes's theory was less simple than Newton's. To provide a sense of the hierarchical structure of Descartes's system, figure 3-1 shows some of the explanatory relations of a few of the seventy Cartesian propositions.

NEWTON

Unlike Descartes's work, Newton's *Mathematical Principles* contains no detailed study of God. Whereas Descartes often cited God in explanations as a first cause, Newton began with a few simple definitions of mass, momentum, force, and centripetal force, then presenting his "Axioms, or Laws of Motion." These laws are used to derive a few corollaries about composition and resolution of forces, which in turn are used to solve various abstract physics problems. Newton's use of a tower of explanations, topped with a few very powerful, very general principles, is a hallmark of his style; of the forty-seven propositions in the model of Newton's thought, only twelve were asserted without being explained by other Propositions, while of Descartes's seventy propositions, thirty-two were asserted without explanation. The hierarchy of Newtonian explanations is shown in figure 3-2, which shows high-level hypotheses explaining lower-level hypotheses that explain pieces of evidence. Further exposition of these propositions and their explanatory relations is given below.

The organization of Newton's *Mathematical Principles* is much tighter than that of Descartes's work. The definitions of concepts and the laws of motion are given in two small sections prior to the first book of the Principia, serving to set the ground for a theoretical physics. In our ECHO analysis found in appendix C, three laws of motion are given as propositions N11, N13, and N14. We use Newton's own statements (Newton 1934, p. 13):

> *Law I:* Every body continues in its state of rest, or of uniform motion in a right line, unless it is compelled to change that state by forces impressed upon it.
> *Law II:* The change of motion is proportional to the motive force impressed, and is made in the direction of the right line in which that force is impressed.
> *Law III:* To every action there is always opposed an equal reaction: or, the mutual actions of two bodies upon each other are always equal, and directed to contrary parts.

The first law asserted that every body possesses the property of inertia. The second law embodied a principle by which every force,

Figure 3-1
Hierarchical relations in the Cartesian system.

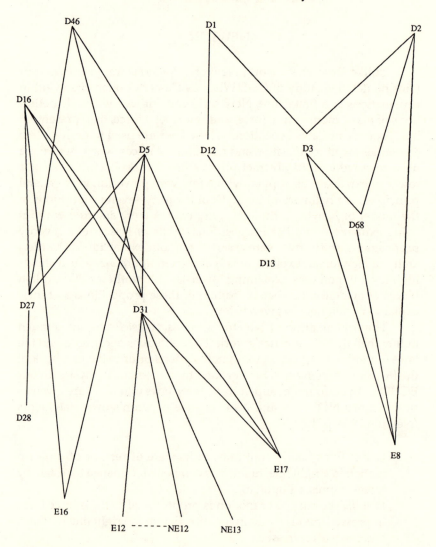

The solid lines indicate explanations, while the dotted line indicates a contradiction. E.g., D46 explains D5, which explains E17. Not shown are many other propositions and other relations, such as cohypotheses and competition.

Figure 3-2
Hierarchical relations in the Newtonian system.

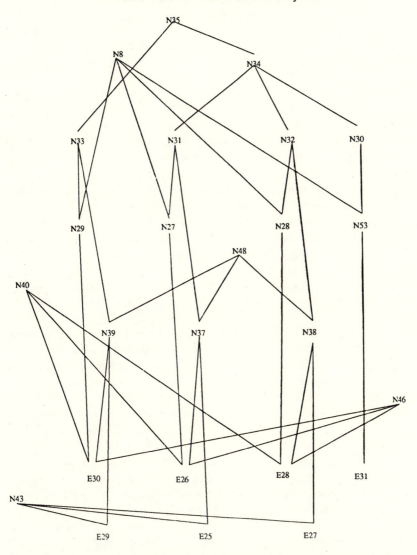

The solid lines indicate explanations. For example, N8 explains N29, which explains E30. Many other propositions and relations are not shown.

however small, has an effect, and thus contradicts D71, in which Descartes asserts that only the greater of two forces has an effect. Since D71 was an important mechanical principle for Descartes, and since it participated in the explanation of several pieces of negative evidence, this contradiction is significant in affecting ECHO's judgment in favor of Newton. The third laws of both Newton and Descartes dealt with interactions of forces and motions. Newton was able to justify his third law with the presentation of several crucial pieces of evidence. For example, he turned to magnetism, observing in E13 that a magnet and a piece of iron separated by an obstacle come to equilibrium. Newton did not discuss magnetism in detail in the *Mathematical Principles,* so his use of this example merely indicated that he thought magnetism was a force. Since two pieces of iron do not attract each other, all of the attraction between a magnet and a piece of iron must come from the magnet. Even so, the force of attraction of the magnet for the iron must be met by an equal and opposite force from the iron, since we know E13 by observation. Otherwise, the iron and the magnet could be tied together to form a single body that would experience a net force generated by the magnet and hence accelerate off to infinity. This absurd conclusion is presented as NE13; Descartes's third law of motion could entail such an event based on his doctrine that only the greater of two forces has an effect.

Several corollaries (N15-N19) to the laws of motion explain several pieces of evidence and thus contribute indirectly to the success of Newton's laws of motion. In the corollaries, there are at least three levels of hypotheses; N18 explains another hypothesis, N46, which explains several pieces of evidence. Figure 3-3 shows the structure of part of the network that ECHO creates in the Newton/Descartes simulation.

Book 1 of the *Mathematical Principles* is titled simply, "The Motion of Bodies." Although it is apparent that Newton is developing theorems for use in a terrestrial physics, at no point does he appeal to real-world examples to carry the argument. He even takes the time to derive the formal consequences of situations not found in nature; for example, the behavior of bodies subject to forces obeying an inverse-power law other than the inverse-square. In all cases the propositions are demonstrated either with reference to earlier established propositions, or with Euclidean geometry. Many of the proofs are not demonstrations of propositions but solutions of specific problems proposed by Newton.

One reason that Newton's account of motion was able to supersede Descartes's was its ability to explain numerical and geometric laws that were obtained by induction from many observations. For example, Newton observed, in E10, that the position of falling bodies was

Figure 3-3
Small fragment of the constraint network created by ECHO.

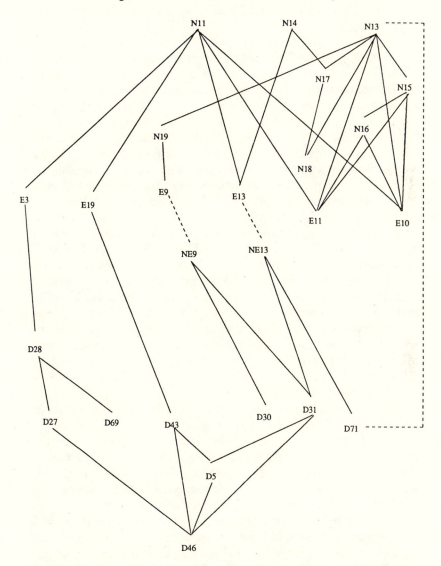

Solid lines indicate excitatory links, while dotted lines show inhibitory links. Not shown are many excitatory links between cohypotheses, and many inhibitory links due to competition.

proportional to the square of the time and, in E11, that projectiles moved in a parabola. Descartes was unable to explain such specific characterizations of the motion of bodies, but they were explicable within Newton's geometric approach.

Book 2 of the *Mathematical Principles* is much the same, discussing "The Motion of Bodies in Resisting Mediums." This book forms the foundation for Newton's response to Descartes. The propositions demonstrated are general enough to be applicable to the motion of bodies in air, water, or Descartes's "celestial matter." The style of discussion is very similar to that in the first book.

The assault by Newtonian fluid dynamics on Descartes's theory begins with the proposition that the orbital period at a certain distance from the center of a vortex is proportional to the square of the distance (N54). From this principle, Newton concludes that every vortex attempts to propagate its motion to infinity (N55) and that, therefore, motion is continuously transferred from the center to the circumference of a vortex (N56). Therefore, vortices cannot exist on their own but require some active principle to sustain them (N57). Also from N55 Newton derived N58, which stated that two spheres, both at the centers of vortices, would fly apart due to the interaction of their vortices. Descartes had supported his model of vortices carried about by other vortices with the observations that twigs in vortices of water would spin around even if they were not in the center of the vortex, and concluded that the twigs were-spinning due to the presence of secondary vortices. Newton draws the further conclusion that any "system" of spinning globes in a fluid would become unstable without the assistance of some external force.

The second key proposition of Newton's fluid dynamics was his assertion that objects maintaining an orbit within a vortex are of the same density with the vortex and thus moved with periods proportional to the square of their distances from the center of the vortex (N60). With this proposition, Newton was able to demonstrate that no object could be carried in an ellipse by a vortex (N63), thus undercutting Descartes's ability to account for the motion of the planets.

Book 3 of the *Mathematical Principles* is titled "System of the World (in Mathematical Treatment)" and is somewhat different in content but similar in style to the preceding two books. Newton referred to the first two as "mathematical" in content, as opposed to the "philosophical" discussion in book 3, which dealt with natural phenomena. Newton tells us that his original intent was to avoid the "mathematical way" of demonstration entirely in his discussion of the system of the world, but then considered that it would strengthen his argument to use a mathematical style of proof. He suggested that only the definitions, laws of motion, and the first three sections of book 1 are a necessary prerequisite for following the argument of book 3. The *Mathematical Principles* closes with a section titled simply "System of the World," which gives a less mathematical discussion of astronomical phenomena, refuting geocentric astronomy and including Newton's treatment of tides.

The success of Newton's theory of gravitation was largely measured by its ability to account in detail for the motion of the planets, partially shown in figure 3-2. (In figure 3-2, propositions aligned vertically represent statements about the same orbital system, e.g., Jupiter and its satellites; propositions aligned horizontally represent similar statements about different systems.) Almost as important as the specific, mathematical hypotheses that formed Newton's theory were the specific, mathematical observations upon which that theory was based. E25, E27, and E29 represent the observations that the planets and the moons of Jupiter and Saturn obey a 3/2-power law; E26, E28, and E30-E31 assert that the satellite systems sweep out equal areas in equal times. These observations (of 3/2-power law) first made by Kepler, were specific enough in their details to need an equally mathematical theory to explain them. Descartes's qualitatively described vortex theory simply had no way of addressing these observations, while Newton's mathematical method could explain them easily. For example, N43 claimed that bodies moved by an inverse-square force would obey a 3/2-power law. N48 asserted that gravity was an inverse-square force. So efficient was Newton's network of explanation that he was actually able to propose two distinct explanations for E26, E28, and E30. In N40, Newton proved mathematically that any centripetal force would require orbiting bodies to obey this law and then asserted that these satellites obeyed a centripetal force (N27-N29). Alternatively, he demonstrated that any inverse-square force would require orbiting bodies to obey the equal-area law (N46) and then asserted that the forces guiding each satellite system obeyed an inverse-square law (N37-N39). Newton explicitly demonstrated his ability to achieve these disjoint proofs of observational evidence. N8 asserts that gravity is a centripetal force. N27-N29 and N53 assert that centripetal forces guide the four satellite systems of Saturn, Jupiter, the earth, and the sun. Similarly, N30-33 assert that these centripetal forces are actually gravity. N34 and N35 claim the property of gravity for all planets and all bodies respectively. N37-N39 assert that the forces guiding these satellite systems obey an inverse-square law.

The propositions as originally given by Newton were more compact than the discrete propositions given in the ECHO input: Newton would just explain the proposition once with reference to the moons of

Jupiter, for example, and then mention that the statement applied equally to the moons of Saturn and the planets. It is clear from the text of the *Mathematical Principles* that Newton meant his discussion to be understood as a hierarchy of explanations. He began book 3 with several phenomena needing to be explained, then gave the hypotheses in the middle of the diagram, ending with N34 and N35, the assertions that "all bodies gravitate towards every planet" and that "there is a power of gravity pertaining to all bodies," respectively.

Newton used his work on the motion of fluids to demonstrate that it was impossible for Descartes's vortex theory to explain these pieces of evidence. Thus Newton showed that Descartes's theory was explaining negative evidence, NE25 and NE29, contradicting the observed 3/2-power law, and NE30-NE31, contradicting the observed equal-area law.

The tides illustrate the differing explanatory coherence of Newton and Descartes, since Newton needed to make no new hypotheses in order to account for the tides. The gravitational effect of all bodies for each other explained the moon's attraction for the oceans; the fact that gravity is an inverse square force means that this attraction decreases with distance, so there is a matching tide on the opposite side of the earth from the moon, since the water there is less attracted. The two monthly high tides mentioned in E38 are explained by the fact that when the moon is new or full the sun and the moon are in line with the earth, so their gravitational effects on the earth's oceans combine instead of counteracting each other. The gravitational account of the tides correctly locates the high tides at the time the moon crosses the meridian.

RESULTS

The input to ECH0.2 given in the appendices produces the following units:

Units representing Newtonian hypotheses: 47
Units representing Cartesian hypotheses: 70
Units representing evidence propositions: 39

Links between the units are created as follows:

Symmetric excitatory links created for explanations: 469
Symmetric inhibitory links created for contradictions: 20
Symmetric inhibitory links created for competition: 101

Figure 3-4 shows the connectivity of a typical unit, N13, which represents Newton's second law. Most of the inhibitory links are created by ECHO's implementation of principle C, Competition. Appendix F list the competitions between Cartesian and Newtonian hypotheses that ECHO automatically identifies.

After the network of units and links is created, ECHO0.2 adjusts the activations of the units until the network settles. This takes 109 cycles using the standard parameter values for ECHO0.2: .05 for decay, .04 for excitation, and -.06 for inhibition. More than a hundred runs with different parameter values were performed to see how sensitive the simulation is to particular values, and the results were similar to those for the Copernicus simulation: ECHO0.2 almost always settles, accepts the Newtonian units (activation > 0), and rejects the Cartesian units (activation < 0) so long as the absolute value of inhibition is greater than excitation. Figure 3-5 graphs the activation histories of selected units over the 109 cycles that it takes the network to settle using the standard parameter values.

Since we are simulating Newton's judgment that his theory is superior to Descartes's, it is fortunate that ECHO0.2 judges that Newton's theory is better. From the perspective of the theory of explanatory coherence, there are three reasons favoring Newton. First, Newton explains numerous pieces of evidence not explained by Descartes. According to the input in the appendices, there are seventeen pieces of evidence explained by Newton but not by Descartes: E1, E2, E9, E10, E11, E13, E25, E26, E27, E28, E29, E30, E31, E33, E34, E35, and E38.

In addition, two somewhat obscure observations about matter serve as evidence for Descartes but not for Newton: E39 and E40. The second advantage for Newton is that there are ten Cartesian explanations of negative evidence that bring down the activation of the Cartesian units by linking them to units that become deactivated because they are inhibited by evidence units.

The third advantage for Newton is simplicity: he explains more evidence with fewer hypotheses. Computational experiments performed by modifying the input to ECHO suggest that simplicity is more crucial in this simulation than the other two advantages. Newton's victory diminishes slightly when the evidence explained by him and not by Descartes is deleted, and the deletion of Cartesian explanations of negative evidence reduces the Cartesian disadvantage. In both cases, however, the Newtonian victory remains clear. When, however, we eliminate the simplicity factor that reduces the weights of excitatory links based on the number of cohypotheses used, the mean activation of the Cartesian hypotheses is almost equal to the Newtonian ones. From the

Figure 3-4
Connectivity of a sample unit, N13.

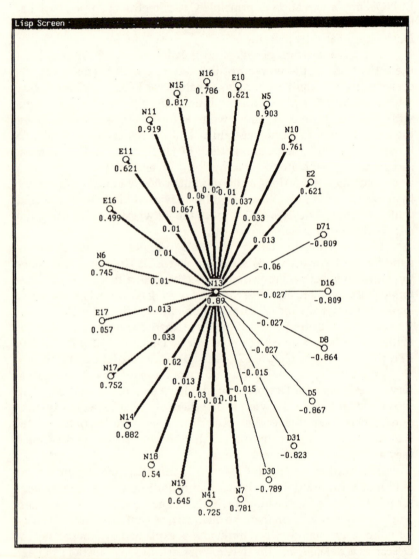

Thick lines indicate excitatory links, while thin lines indicate inhibitory links.
Numbers on lines indicate the weights of the links. Numbers under unit
names are the truncated asymptotic activations of the units.

Figure 3-5
Activation histories of selected units.

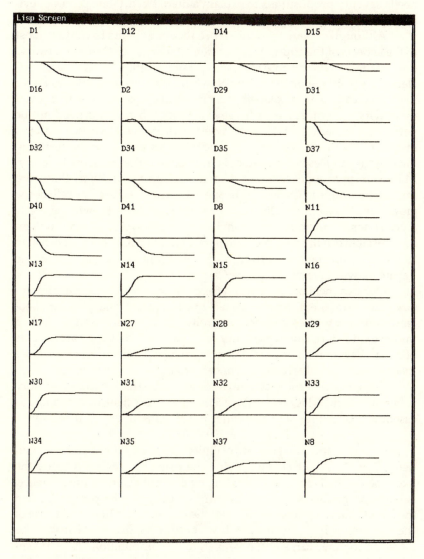

Each graph shows activation on a scale of 1 to -1, with the horizontal line
indicating the starting activation of 0.

perspective of ECHO, it is very important that Newton explains thirty-six pieces of data with only forty-seven hypotheses, while Descartes needs seventy propositions to explain a mere twenty-one pieces of evidence.

Although explanatory coherence theory appears to capture most of the aspects of the triumph of Newton's theory over Descartes, ECHO does not model the dispute completely. For example, we have not modeled the advantage perceived by Newton based on his ability to prove mathematically that the planets must move in ellipses if they are moved by gravity. The most Descartes says is that their motions need not be perfectly circular (D57). Newton's demonstration that vortices can not move objects in ellipses helps to discredit Descartes, but the resulting incoherence in Descartes system is deductive rather than explanatory. Moreover, our model does not take into account two factors that were important from the Cartesian perspective, since it does not reflect the judgments that some of Descartes principles could be known to be true a priori nor the metaphysical conviction that Newton's gravity was an inadmissible occult force. Nevertheless, using ECHO we have been able to model a substantial portion of the Newtonian perspective on the debate between Newton and the Cartesians.

Our treatment of Newton and Descartes, along with the other important cases from the history of science to which ECHO has been applied, lends support to the claim that scientific theory evaluation should be understood in terms of explanatory coherence. We challenge proponents of other views of scientific reasoning to produce models of historical cases that mirror so closely the actual concerns of the scientists involved.

Perhaps the strongest contender as an alternative to explanatory coherence and ECHO is the Bayesian view that scientific reasoning is essentially updating of probabilities in accord with Bayes' theorem:

$$P(H/E) = P(H)P(E/H)/P(E).$$

This says that the posterior probability of a hypothesis H given evidence E is the result of multiplying the prior probability of H by the likelihood of E given H, and dividing by the probability of the evidence. A Bayesian prefers Newton to Descartes if the posterior probabilities of the Newtonian hypotheses given all the evidence are high and those of the Cartesian hypotheses are low. Updating probabilities in the Bayesian manner turns out, however, to be computationally problematic. In the worst case, we would need to know the conditional probability of each propositions given all combinations of truth and falsity of all the other propositions in the system (Harman 1986, p. 26). For the Newton simulation with its 166 propositions, we would need 2^{166} conditional probabilities, which is more than 10^{43}. (For comparison, the number of milliseconds since the universe began around 20,000,000,000 years ago is only around 10^{23}.) Recently, much more efficient computational methods have been developed for updating probabilities in Bayesian fashion, making use of structural properties of networks of variables that are similar in some respects to those produced by ECHO (Pearl 1988; Neapolitain 1990). It is easy to show, however, that Pearl's algorithms still require an implausibly large number of conditional probabilities. For every proposition P explained, Pearl's algorithms require conditional probabilities of P given all the Boolean combinations of P's explainers, and the same for not-P. If E is explained only by hypotheses $H1$ and $H2$, for example, we need to know $P(E/H1\&H2)$, $P(E/H1\&\text{not-}H2)$, $P(E/\text{not-}H1\&H2)$, and $P(E/\text{not-}H1\&\text{not-}H2)$, and similar values for not-E. For proposition E17 in our Newton simulation, which has three Newtonian and five Cartesian explainers, 512 conditional probabilities will be needed, 2^8 for each of E17 and its negation. In total, a Bayesian network model of Newton versus Descartes would require 3,304 conditional probabilities if it had the same structure as our ECHO network. We find it very implausible that people either have or can generate such probabilities.

In contrast, ECHO provides a computationally efficient means of selecting the best set of explanatory hypotheses using information about explanatory relations gleanable from historical texts. We have shown how the triumph of one of the greatest theories in the history of science, Newtonian mechanics, can be understood in terms of explanatory coherence.

IMPLICATIONS FOR SCIENCE EDUCATION

In their paper in this volume, Duschl, Hamilton, and Grandy lay out an important agenda for (1) developing an integration of cognitive psychology and epistemology and (2) using the integrated view to improve science education. We are completely sympathetic to this agenda and will now briefly indicate how our explanatory coherence treatment of Newton and Descartes fits with the integrative project.

As Duschl, Hamilton, and Grandy well describe, psychologists have been looking to philosophers of science for insights into how scientific knowledge develops, while philosophers have been looking to psychology for insights into the nature of scientific knowledge. The theory of explanatory coherence (TEC) and its connectionist implementation ECHO are the direct result of such interaction. Thagard did research in the mid-1970s on the problem of theory evaluation and

started to look at interrelations between cognitive science and philosophy of science in 1978. While it may seem from the presentation in this
and other papers that TEC came first and ECHO provided a way of
implementing it, the essential insight came the other way around. In
1987, Thagard was developing with Keith Holyoak a parallel constraint
satisfaction model of analogy when it struck him that similar computational techniques could be used for theory evaluation. The connectionist approach using units connected to each other in different ways suggested a richer coherence theory than philosophers had previously
developed. The integration of philosophical, psychological, and computational ideas in TEC and ECHO is beginning to be applied to problems in science education, principally by Michael Ranney and his students (Ranney and Thagard 1988; Ranney in press).

The major difference between this path and the one outlined by
Duschl, Hamilton, and Grandy is that computational ideas provided the
theoretical glue for the joining of philosophical and psychological ones. In
addition, the methodology of writing and testing a program on diverse
examples has provided a means of evaluating theoretical ideas not available in either traditional philosophy of science or experimental psychology. Computational implementation also forces a degree of precision lacking in concepts such as *schema*, which plays a large role in the theoretical
proposals of Duschl, Hamilton, and Grandy. Thagard (1988) describes
various ways in which the concept of schema can be useful for understanding the nature of scientific knowledge, but does so in the context of a
specific computational model that pins down the nature of schemata more
than most psychological and philosophical discussions. Duschl, Hamilton,
and Grandy emphasize Rumelhart's work on schemata, but omit discussion of the dramatic impact that development of parallel distributed processing models has had on his thinking about schemata.

Thagard (1991) uses artificial intelligence ideas to provide a theory
of conceptual change that applies to all the major scientific revolutions,
including the case of Newton. Just as writing a program requires specification of data structures and algorithms, so giving a theory of conceptual change requires specification of cognitive structures and the
learning mechanisms that operate on them to develop improved structures. Thus while agreeing with Duschl, Hamilton, and Grandy that
psychology and philosophy have much to offer to each other and to
science education, we stress the advantages of developing richer computational models of learning processes that draw on philosophical and
psychological insights but develop them in much more detail.

With this methodology in mind, let us look at what might be
learned about science education from the simulation of Newton and

Descartes in this paper. At first glance, our simulation might be taken to endorse a traditional epistemological and psychological view that theories are just sets of sentences, a view that might be taken to suggest that science education should be much easier than it is, since all that would be required is that students should acquire the relevant beliefs. This interpretation is misleading for two reasons. First, as Thagard (1991) makes clear, the propositions are embedded in a complex conceptual structure. Second, as we hope our discussion in the section on Newton indicated, the Propositions themselves have considerable structure by virtue of their explanatory relations. Acquiring Newtonian theory, in our view, is not simply a matter of learning an unstructured set of propositions but requires appreciation of how they form a hierarchy of explanations leading down from theoretical principles to observed facts. Much traditional physics education consists of having students work out problems to acquire a mathematical understanding of principles such as Newton's laws. While it is important to assimilate theories as problem-solving devices, it is also important to appreciate their explanatory function. Newtonian physics is much more than just a calculating tool: it provides a deep way of understanding the world that was much superior to the previous way offered by Descartes.

We therefore suggest that research on science education can be furthered by understanding the explanatory structure of theories that students are expected to acquire. Although Ranney's work already cited is highly suggestive, it remains an open question whether explanatory coherence plays a role in students' belief revisions and rejection of old conceptual systems. Does theory competition actually occur, or do students merely incorporate old beliefs or ignore them? If students are not appreciating explanatory matters, can they be taught a greater sensitivity to explanatory coherence? Will this sensitivity then lead them to learn new scientific theories more readily? We very much hope that researchers in science education will pursue such questions and that the answers will help to improve the difficult task of science teachers.

APPENDICES: INPUT TO ECHO FOR
SIMULATION OF NEWTON AND DESCARTES

Appendix A: Evidence propositions

(E = evidence; NE = Negative evidence)

E1 Water in a spinning bucket will first be at rest, then climb the sides of the bucket as it spins.

E2 Two globes joined by a cord can be set spinning around each other such that their motions can be determined.

E3 Projectiles continue in their motions, so far as they are not retarded by the resistance of the air, or impelled downward by the force of gravity.

E5 The planets and comets, meeting with less resistance in freer spaces, preserve their motions both progressive and circular for a much longer time.

E6 If you press a stone with your finger, the finger is also pressed by the stone.

E7 If a horse draws a stone tied to a rope, the horse will be equally drawn back towards the stone; for the distended rope, by the same endeavor to relax or unbend itself, will draw the horse as much towards the stone as it does the stone towards the horse.

E8 A mallet and wedge can be used to split objects.

E9 On a ship, all motions happen in the same manner whether the ship is at rest or is carried uniformly forwards in a right line.

NE9 The behavior of two colliding bodies changes based upon the frame of reference used.

E10 The descent of bodies varies as the square of the time.

E11 The motion of projectiles is in the curve of a parabola.

E12 Colliding pendulums lose no quantity of motion after collision.

NE12 Colliding pendulums may lose some quantity of motion after collision.

E13 A loadstone and a piece of iron separated by an obstacle come to equilibrium.

NE13 If a loadstone has greater attraction for a piece of iron than vice versa, they can be separated by an obstacle and thus will not remain in equilibrium but go forwards ad infinitum with a motion continually accelerated.

E14 The planets move in the sky.

E15 Thrown objects continue to move after they have left the hand.

E16 Matter exhibits motion.

E17 Matter exhibits changes in motion.

E18 Only one side of the moon ever faces the earth.

E19 A stone released from a sling tends to move in a straight line tangent to the circle in which it was moving.

E20 All bodies about the earth gravitate towards the earth, in proportion to their mass.

E21 The moon gravitates towards the earth.

E22 The planets nearer to the sun move faster.

E23 A solid body, immersed in a fluid, can be set in motion with very little force.

NE23 A solid body, immersed in a fluid, cannot be set in motion without first overcoming the body's force of rest.

E24 Comets gravitate towards the sun.

E25 The periods of the orbits of Jupiter's moons are proportional to the 3/2 power of their distances from the center of Jupiter.

NE25 The periods of the orbits of Jupiter's moons do not follow any determinate power law.

E26 The areas swept out by Jupiter's moons to move through parts of their orbits are proportional to the times taken for the motion.

E27 The periods of the orbits of Saturn's moons are proportional to the 3/2 power of their distances from the center of Saturn.

E28 The areas swept out by Saturn's moons to move through parts of their orbits are proportional to the times taken for the motion.

E29 The periods of the orbits of the planets are proportional to the 3/2 power of their distances from the center of the sun.

NE29 The periods of the orbits of the planets do not follow any determinate power law.

E30 The areas which the planets describe in their motions with radii drawn to the sun are proportional to the times of description.

NE30 The areas which the planets describe in their motions with radii drawn to the sun are not proportional to the times of description.

E31 The moon, by a radius drawn to the earth's centre, describes an area proportional to the time of description.

NE31 The moon's motion does not describe an area proportional to the time of description.

E32 The aphelion points of the orbits of the planets are fixed against the sky.

E33 The moon's deviation from a straight path in a given time is exactly equal to the distance it would fall from its distance in that time due to earth's gravity.

E34 Jupiter and Saturn, when near their conjunction, are disturbed in their motions.

E35 The sun moves less quickly in Pisces than in Virgo.

NE35 The sun moves more quickly in Pisces than in Virgo.

E36 The oceans rise and fall in tides twice a day.

E37 The tides are greater when the moon is full or new.

E38 The two daily high tides occur almost directly under the moon and on the opposite side of the earth.

NE38 The two daily low tides occur under the moon and on the opposite side of the earth.

E39 Parts of matter cohere.

E40 Terrestrial matter appears to be different from empty space.

Appendix B: Cartesian Hypotheses in the Newton-Descartes Simulation

(D = statement by Descarte)

D1 The nature of body does not consist in weight, hardness, color, or other similar properties, but in extension alone.

D2 Bodies can be in relative rest.

D3 The parts of solid bodies are not joined by any other bond than their own rest.

D5 God maintains the total amount of motion in the world at a constant.

D6 Originally cubic parts of space were rubbed down to spheres or "globules" by collisions.

D8 Motion can only be caused by motion and can only produce motion.

D12 Space does not in fact differ from material substance.

D13 Matter is infinitely divisible.

D14 A vacuum, or space not containing matter, is a contradiction and hence impossible.

D15 At the creation, God divided space into parts of medium size.

D16 At the creation, God set parts of space in motion relative to each other.

D17 Some of the original particles have been bound by relative rest to form coarser particles of matter.

D18 The rubbings formed in globule-creation fill all the interstices between particles of the other two kinds.

D19 The rubbings formed in globule-creation move at great velocities.

D20 God caused the globules, or secondary particles, to form large vortices.

D21 The centrifugal tendency of vortices impels the rubbings, or primary particles, towards the center.

D22 Primary particles collect at the centers of vortices to form the sun and the fixed stars.

D23 The planets are formed when stars lose their vortices and are trapped by the sun's vortex.

D24 The coarser tertiary particles form the earth and planets.

D27 First law of nature: that each thing, as far as is in its power, always remains in the same state.

D28 Every body, when it is once moved, always continues to move.

D29 A moving body cannot put in motion another body which is at rest and has greater mass.

D30 Third law a: If a moving body collides with another one of greater mass, it will continue to move with the same velocity in another direction.

D31 Third law b: If a moving body collides with another one of lesser mass, it will carry the other one along, losing the same amount of momentum it imparts to the other body.

D32 The planets are carried around the sun by the heaven.

D34 Up to a certain distance from the sun, the celestial particles increase in size and decrease in angular velocity.

D35 After this distance, the size of the celestial particles remains the same, and the angular velocity increases up to the outside of the vortex.

D37 Every planet seeks the distance from the sun at which the motion of the celestial particles is equal to its own.

D40 The effects of the earth's gravity are actually caused by the tendency of bodies to attain the level of bodies of equivalent density of celestial matter due to the centrifugal force exerted by vortices of celestial matter.

D41 The earth is carried along in the diurnal axial revolution by a smaller vortex of celestial matter.

D42 The earth does not move with reference to the vortex of celestial matter, so it is at rest while revolving.

D43 Second law: All movement is, of itself, along straight lines.

D44 Every moving body, at any given moment in the course of its movement, is inclined to continue that movement in some direction in a straight line, and never in a curved one.

D45 Bodies which are moving in a circle always tend to move away from the circle which they are describing.

D46 God is immutable in His nature and actions.

D47 Centrifugal force throws the bulk of ethereal matter outward in each vortex.

D48 As a result of centrifugal force, there is a lower density of celestial matter in the center of each vortex, creating a centripetal pressure inward.

D49 A moving fluid carries along any solid body immersed in it.

D56 The heavens carry with them all the bodies which they contain.

D57 The motions of the planets are not perfectly circular.

D58 Each of the planets revolves in its own plane.

D61 One side of the moon is less dense than the other.

D62 The distances of planets from the center of the solar vortex depend upon their densities.

D63 Matter of the first element rotating in the sun augments the speed of the layers of the vortex close to it.

D64 The speed of a planet's motion around the sun depends upon its size.

D65 The moon is just as dense as the earth.

D66 The moon is smaller than the earth.

D67 The moon revolves around the earth.

D68 Relative motion of parts of matter is equivalent to division.

D69 Movement and rest are merely diverse modes of the body in which they are found.

D70 It is possible for the determination of motion in some direction to change while the quantity of motion remains intact.

D71 If two forces oppose, only the stronger one will produce its effect.

D72 The particles of fluids move with equal force in all directions.

D73 Rest is contrary to movement.

D74 The determination of movement in one direction is contrary to its determination in another direction.

D75 A solid body which has been driven by another does not receive all its movement from that other, but also acquires some motion from the surrounding fluid.

D76 The solid body cannot, however, acquire a greater speed from this fluid than it has acquired from the solid body which drives it.

D77 A solid body carried along by a fluid is not moving.

D80 There is a secondary celestial vortex which is centered at Jupiter and moves its moons.

D81 The moon is carried about the earth in its vortex of celestial matter.

D82 Several spheres joined together do not form a completely solid and continuous body.

D83 A fluid offers no resistance to a body immersed in it.

D85 Bodies at rest possess a force of rest which must be overcome before they are moved.

D87 Motion is the transport of a part of matter or of a body from the neighborhood of those which touch it immediately, and which we may consider as at rest, into the neighborhood of others.

D88 The location of heavenly bodies in a vortex is determined only by the equality of the forces of the heavenly matter flowing around it.

D89 The presence of the moon impedes the heavenly matter from being able to flow as freely between it and the earth as on the other side .

D90 The earth will always recede slightly from the moon.

D91 Not only is the space through which the heavenly matter flows between the earth and the moon made narrower by the moon, but so is the space through which the heavenly matter flows on the other side of the earth.

D92 The vortex around the earth carrying the moon is not exactly round; the diameter on which the full or new moon is situated is shorter than the one perpendicular to it.

D93 Comets are stars whose vortices have been lost, and now move through other vortices.

Appendix C: Newtonian Hypotheses in the Newton-Descartes Simulation

(N = statements by Newton)

N5 There are impressed forces, which are any actions which change an object's state of rest or uniform motion in a straight line.

N6 Any force consists only of action and does not remain in the object after the action is over.

N7 Definition 5: There are centripetal forces, by which bodies are drawn or impelled towards a point as to a center.

N8 Gravity is a centripetal force.

N10 There are absolute and relative motions, which can be detected against absolute and relative spaces.

N11 Law I: Every body continues in its state of rest, or of uniform motion in a right line, unless it is compelled to change that state by forces impressed upon it.

N13 Law II: The change of motion is proportional to the motive force impressed, and is made in the direction of the right line in which that force is impressed.

N14 Law III: To every action there is always opposed an equal reaction: or, the mutual actions of two bodies upon each other are always equal and directed to contrary parts.

N15 Corollary I: A body acted on by two forces simultaneously, will describe the diagonal of a parallelogram in the same time as it would describe the sides by those forces separately.

N16 Corollary II: And hence is explained the composition of any one direct force *AD*, out of any two oblique forces *AC* and *CD*; and, on the contrary, the resolution of any one direct force *AD* into two oblique forces *AC* and *CD*: which composition and resolution are abundantly confirmed from mechanics.

N17 Corollary III: The quantity of motion (of a collection of objects), which is obtained by taking the sum of the motions directed towards the same parts, and the difference of those that are directed to contrary parts, suffers no change from the action of bodies among themselves.

N18 Corollary IV: The common centre of gravity of two or more bodies does not alter its state of motion or rest by the actions of the bodies among themselves; and therefore the common center of gravity of all bodies acting upon each other (excluding external actions and impediments) is either at rest, or moves uniformly in a right line.

N19 Corollary V: The motions of bodies included in a given space are the same among themselves, whether that space is at rest or moves uniformly forwards in a right line without any circular motion.

N27 Theorem Ia: The forces by which Jupiter's moons are continually drawn off from rectilinear motions, and retained in their proper orbits, tend to Jupiter's centre.

N28 Theorem Ib: The forces by which Saturn's moons are continually drawn off from rectilinear motions, and retained in their proper orbits, tend to Saturn's centre.

N29 Theorem II: The forces by which the planets are continually drawn off from rectilinear motions and retained in their proper orbits, tend to the sun.

N30 The moon gravitates towards the earth and by the force of gravity is continually drawn off from a rectilinear motion and retained in its orbit.

N31 Theorem Va: The Jovian moons gravitate towards Jupiter, and by the forces of their gravity are drawn off from rectilinear motions, and retained in curvilinear orbits.

N32 Theorem Vb: Saturn's moons gravitate towards Saturn, and by the forces of their gravity are drawn off from rectilinear motions, and retained in curvilinear orbits.

N33 Theorem Vc: The planets gravitate towards the sun, and by the forces of their gravity are drawn off from rectilinear motions, and retained in curvilinear orbits.

N34 All bodies gravitate towards every planet, and the weights of bodies towards any one planet, at equal distances from the centre of the planet, are proportional to their masses.

N35 Theorem VII: There is a power of gravity pertaining to all bodies, proportional to the several quantities of matter which they contain.

N37 Theorem Ia:The forces by which Jupiter's moons are continually drawn off from rectilinear motions, and retained in their proper orbits are inversely as the squares of the distances of the places of the moons from that center.

N38 Theorem Ib: The forces by which Saturn's moons are continually drawn off from rectilinear motions, and retained in their proper orbits, are inversely as the squares of the distances of the places of the moons from that center.

N39 Theorem II: The forces by which the planets are continually drawn off from rectilinear motions and retained in their proper orbits are inversely as the squares of the distances of the places of those planets from the sun's centre.

N40 The areas which revolving bodies describe by radii drawn to an immovable centre of force are proportional to the times in which they are described.

N41 Every body that moves in any curved line described in a plane, and by a radius drawn to a point either immovable, or moving forwards with an uniform rectilinear motion, describes about that point areas proportional to the times, is urged by a centripetal force directed to that point.

N42 The centripetal forces of bodies, which by equable motions describe different circles, tend to the centers of the same circles; and are to each other as the squares of the arcs described in equal times divided respectively by the radii of the circles.

N43 If bodies are orbiting a point of centripetal force varying as the inverse of the square of the distance from that point, then their periodic times vary as the 3/2 power of the distance from the point.

N45 If a body-acted upon by any centripetal force-is moved in any manner, and another body ascends or descends in a right line, and their velocities be equal in any one case of equal altitudes, their velocities will also be equal at all equal altitudes.

N46 Bodies, whose forces decrease as the square of their distances from their centers, may move among themselves in ellipses; and by radii drawn to the foci may describe areas very nearly proportional to the times.

N47 If the periodic times of bodies orbiting a point due to a centripetal force are as the 3/2 powers of the radii from that point, then the force varies inversely as the square of the radii from that point.

N48 The force of gravity which tends to any one planet is inversely as the square of the distance of places from that planet's center.

N52 The planets move in ellipses which have their common focus in the center of the sun; and by radii drawn to that center, they describe areas proportional to the times of description.

N53 The force by which the moon is retained in its orbit tends to the earth; and is inversely as the square of the distance of its place from the earth's center.

N54 A revolving sphere immersed in a fluid of uniform density will cause the fluid to circulate around the sphere with the period of a particle of fluid being proportional to the square of its distance from the sphere.

N55 A revolving sphere immersed in a fluid of uniform density will propagate its motion *ad infinitum* throughout the fluid.

N56 Motion is continually transferred from the center to the circumference of a vortex.

N57 Therefore, in order to continue a vortex in the same state of motion, some active principle is required from which the globe may receive continually the same quantity of motion which it is always communicating to the matter of the vortex.

N58 Two spinning globes in a fluid will both create vortices and thus fly apart unless some force restrains them.

N59 In any system of several spinning globes in a fluid, as many vortices [as there are spinning globes] will be created in the fluid, and by the actions of the vortices on each other, the globes will continually be moved from their places; neither can they keep any certain position among themselves, unless some force restrains them.

N60 Bodies carried about in a vortex and returning in the same orbit are of the same density with the vortex and are moved according to the same law with the parts of the vortex, as to the velocity and direction of motion.

N61 Therefore a solid revolving in a vortex and continually going round in the same orbit is relatively quiescent in the fluid that carries it.

N62 If a vortex be of a uniform density, the same body may revolve at any distance from the centre of the vortex.

N63 The parts of a vortex can never revolve with an elliptical motion.

N64 An object denser than the fluid of a vortex will attempt to recede from the center of a vortex, while an object less dense than the matter of a vortex will attempt to move toward the center of a vortex.

N65 The moon revolves once on its axis in a sidereal month.

APPENDIX D: EXPLANATIONS IN THE
NEWTON-DESCARTES SIMULATION

Newtonian Explanations

(explain '(N10 N5) 'E1)
(explain '(NS N10 N13) 'E2)
(explain '(N11 N5) 'E3)
(explain '(N11) 'E5)
(explain '(N14 N5) 'E6)
(explain '(N14 N5) 'E7)
(explain '(N14 N16) 'E8)
(explain '(N 19) 'E9)
(explain '(N11 N13 N15 N16) 'E10)
(explain '(N11 N13 N15 N16) 'E11)
(explain '(N14 N17) 'E12)
(explain '(N11 N14) 'E13)
(explain '(N33 N41 N52) 'E14)
(explain '(N5 N10 N 11) 'E 15)
(explain '(N5 N6 N11 N13) 'E16)
(explain '(N5 N11 N13) 'E17)
(explain '(N30 N65) 'E18)
(explain '(N7 N11 N15) 'E19)
(explain '(N34) 'E20)
(explain '(N30) 'E21)
(explain '(N39 N43) 'E22)
(explain '(N6 N11) 'E23)
(explain '(N33) 'E24)
(explain '(N37 N43) 'E25)
(explain '(N37 N46) 'E26)
(explain '(N27 N40) 'E26)
(explain '(N38 N43) 'E27)
(explain '(N38 N46) 'E28)
(explain '(N28 N40) 'E28)
(explain '(N39 N43) 'E29)
(explain '(N39 N46) 'E30)
(explain '(N29 N40) 'E30)
(explain '(N46 N53) 'E31)
(explain '(N39) 'E32)
(explain '(N8 N30) 'E33)
(explain ' (N34) 'E34)

108   *Newton, Descartes, and Explanatory Coherence*

(explain '(N29 N39 N40 N52) 'E35)
(explain '(N30 N34) 'E36)
(explain '(N30 N33 N34) 'E37)
(explain '(N30 N34) 'E38)
(explain '(N13) 'N15)
(explain '(N15) 'N16)
(explain '(N13 N14) 'N17)
(explain '(N11 N13 N17) 'N18)
(explain '(N10 N13) 'N19)
(explain '(N8 N31) 'N27)
(explain '(N8 N32) 'N28)
(explain '(N8 N33) 'N29)
(explain '(N8 N30) 'N53)
(explain '(N48 N31) 'N37)
(explain '(N48 N32) 'N38)
(explain '(N48 N33) 'N39)
(explain ' (N34) 'N30)
(explain '(N34) 'N31)
(explain '(N34) 'N32)
(explain '(N35) 'N33)
(explain ' (N35) 'N34)
(explain '(N7 N11 N15) 'N40)
(explain '(N7 N11 N13 N19) 'N41)
(explain '(N7 N40 N41) 'N42)
(explain '(N42) 'N43)
(explain '(N16) 'N45)
(explain '(N7 N18) 'N46)
(explain '(N42) 'N47)
(explain '(N29 N39 N40) 'N52)
(explain '(N54) 'N55)
(explain '(N54 N55) 'N56)
(explain '(N54 N56) 'N57)
(explain '(N55 N56 N60) 'N58)
(explain '(N54 N58) 'N59)
(explain '(N54) 'N60)
(explain '(N60 N64) 'N61)
(explain '(N60 N64) 'N62)
(explain '(N58 N61 N62) 'N63)
(explain '(N60) 'N64)

Cartesian Explanations

(explain '(D28 D40) 'E3)
(explain '(D22 D20 D32) 'E5)

(explain '(D5 D69 D71) 'E6)
(explain '(D5 D69 D71) 'E7)
(explain '(D2 D3 D68) 'E8)
(explain '(D30 D31 D87) 'NE9)
(explain '(D6 D8 D30 D31) 'E12)
(explain '(D30 D31 D87) 'NE12)
(explain '(D31 D71) 'NE13)
(explain '(D22 D20 D32) 'E14)
(explain '(D8 D28) 'E15)
(explain '(D5 D8 D16) 'E16)
(explain '(D5 D8 D16 D30 D31) 'E17)
(explain '(D41 D49 D61 D62) 'E18)
(explain '(D28 D43 D45) 'E19)
(explain '(D24 D40 D41) 'E20)
(explain '(D41 D67) 'E21)
(explain '(D32 D34 D63) 'E22)
(explain '(D28 D75 D83) 'E23)
(explain '(D27 D85) 'NE23)
(explain '(D22 D32 D93) 'E24)
(explain '(D20 D80) 'NE25)
(explain '(D32 D34 D35 D37) 'NE29)
(explain '(D32 D57) 'NE30)
(explain '(D81 D92) 'NE31)
(explain '(D32 D58) 'E32)
(explain '(D32 D57) 'NE35)
(explain '(D89 D90 D91) 'E36)
(explain '(D89 D90 D91 D92) 'E37)
(explain '(D89 D90 D91) 'NE38)
(explain '(D2 D3 D27) 'E39)
(explain ' (D 17) 'E40)
(explain '(D1 D2) 'D3)
(explain ' (D46) 'D5)
(explain '(D13 D68) 'D6)
(explain '(D16 D69 D27) 'D8)
(explain '(D1) 'D12)
(explain '(D12) 'D13)
(explain '(D12) 'D14)
(explain '(D2 D3 D15 D27) 'D17)
(explain '(D13 D14 D68 D82) 'D18)
(explain '(D31) 'D19)
(explain '(D48) 'D21)
(explain '(D21) 'D22)
(explain ' (D20) 'D23)

(explain '(D5 D16 D46) 'D27)
(explain '(D27 D69) 'D28)
(explain '(D5 D8 D85) 'D29)
(explain '(D8 D29 D70) 'D30)
(explain '(D5 D16 D46) 'D31)
(explain '(D40 D47) 'D37)
(explain '(D20 D23) 'D41)
(explain '(D41 D87) 'D42)
(explain '(D5 D44 D46) 'D43)
(explain '(D28 D43) 'D45)
(explain '(D47) 'D48)
(explain ' (D49) 'D56)
(explain '(D32 D34 D37 D48) 'D62)
(explain '(D32 D62 D64 D65 D66) 'D67)
(explain '(D2 D3) 'D68)
(explain '(D43 D73 D74) 'D72)
(explain ' (D76) 'D77)
(explain '(D20 D24) 'D80)
(explain '(D20 D23) 'D81)
(explain '(D72 D74) 'D83)
(explain '(D69 D71 D73) 'D85)
(explain '(D88 D89) 'D90)
(explain ' (D57) 'D92)

Appendix E: Contradictions in the Newton-Descartes Simulation

(contradict 'NE9 'E9)
(contradict 'NE 12 'E 12)
(contradict 'NE 13 'E 13)
(contradict 'NE23 'E23)
(contradict 'NE25 'E25)
(contradict 'NE29 'E29)
(contradict 'NE30 'E30)
(contradict 'NE31 'E31)
(contradict 'NE35 'E35)
(contradict 'NE38 'E38)
(contradict 'D37 'D64)
(contradict 'D23 'D24)
(contradict 'D8 'N5)
(contradict 'D71 'N13)
(contradict 'D32 'N33)
(contradict 'D40 'N34)

(contradict 'D57 'N63)
(contradict 'D87 'N52)
(contradict 'D90 'N30)
(contradict 'D1 'N35)

Appendix F: Competitors Noted by ECHO in Newton-Descartes Simulation

N10 competes with D28 because of (E15).
N10 competes with D8 because of (E15).
N11 competes With D22 because of (E5).
N11 competes with D20 because of (E5).
N11 competes with D32 because of (E5).
N11 competes with D8 because of (E15 E16 E17).
N11 competes with D31 because of (E17).
N11 competes with D30 because of (E17).
N11 competes with D45 because of (E19).
N11 competes with D43 because of (E19).
N11 competes with D83 because of (E23).
N11 competes with D75 because of (E23).
N11 competes with D16 because of (E16 E17).
N11 competes with D5 because of (E16 E17).
N11 competes with D40 because of (E3).
N11 competes with D28 because of (E3 E15 E19 E23).
N13 competes with D30 because of (E17).
N13 competes with D31 because of (E17).
N13 competes with D5 because of (E16 E17).
N13 competes with D8 because of (E16 E17).
N13 competes with D16 because of (E16 E17).
N14 competes with D6 because of (E12).
N14 competes with D8 because of (E12).
N14 competes with D30 because of (E12).
N14 competes with D31 because of (E12).
N14 competes with D68 because of (E8).
N14 competes with D3 because of (E8).
N14 competes with D2 because of (E8).
N14 competes with D71 because of (E6 E7).
N14 competes with D69 because of (E6 E7).
N14 competes with D5 because of (E6 E7).
N15 competes with D28 because of (E19).
N15 competes with D43 because of (E19).
N15 competes with D45 because of (E19).
N16 competes with D2 because of (E8).

N16 competes with D3 because of (E8).
N16 competes with D68 because of (E8).
N17 competes with D31 because of (E12).
N17 competes with D30 because of (E12).
N17 competes with D8 because of (E12).
N17 competes with D6 because of (E12).
N30 competes with D67 because of (E21).
N30 competes with D89 because of (E36 E37).
N30 competes with D90 because of (E36 E37).
N30 competes with D91 because of (E36 E37).
N30 competes with D92 because of (E37).
N30 competes with D62 because of (E18).
N30 competes with D61 because of (E18).
N30 competes with D49 because of (E18).
N30 competes with D41 because of (E18 E21).
N33 competes with D89 because of (E37).
N33 competes with D90 because of (E37).
N33 competes with D91 because of (E37).
N33 competes with D92 because of (E37).
N33 competes with D93 because of (E24).
N33 competes with D32 because of (E14 E24).
N33 competes with D20 because of (E14).
N33 competes with D22 because of (E14 E24).
N34 competes with D91 because of (E36 E37).
N34 competes with D90 because of (E36 E37).
N34 competes with D89 because of (E36 E37).
N34 competes with D92 because of (E37).
N34 competes with D41 because of (E20).
N34 competes with D40 because of (E20).
N34 competes with D24 because of (E20).
N37 competes with N40 because of (E26).
N38 competes with N40 because of (E28).
N39 competes with D58 because of (E32).
N39 competes with D63 because of (E22).
N39 competes with D34 because of (E22).
N39 competes with D32 because of (E22 E32).
N41 competes with D22 because of (E14).
N41 competes with D20 because of (E14).
N41 competes with D32 because of (E14).
N43 competes with D32 because of (E22).
N43 competes with D34 because of (E22).
N43 competes with D63 because of (E22).

N46 competes with N27 because of (E26).
N46 competes with N29 because of (E30).
N46 competes with N28 because of (E28).
N5 competes with D8 because of (E15 E16 E17).
N5 competes with D30 because of (E17).
N5 competes with D31 because of (E17).
N5 competes with D16 because of (E16 E17).
N5 competes with D5 because of (E6 E7 E16 E17).
N5 competes with D69 because of (E6 E7).
N5 competes with D71 because of (E6 E7).
N5 competes with D28 because of (E3 E15).
N5 competes with D40 because of (E3).
N52 competes with D32 because of (E14).
N52 competes with D20 because of (E14).
N52 competes with D22 because of (E14).
N6 competes with D28 because of (E23).
N6 competes with D75 because of (E23).
N6 competes with D83 because of (E23).
N6 competes with D5 because of (E16).
N6 competes with D8 because of (E16).
N6 competes with D16 because of (E16).
N65 competes with D41 because of (E18).
N65 competes with D49 because of (E18).
N65 competes with D61 because of (E18).
N65 competes with D62 because of (E18).
N7 competes with D28 because of (E19).
N7 competes with D43 because of (E19).
N7 competes with D45 because of (E19).
Symmetric inhibitory links created for competition: 101.

REFERENCES

Aiton, E. J. (1972). *The vortex theory of planetary motions.* New York: American Elsevier.

Clarke, D. (Ed.). (1982). *Descartes's philosophy of science.* Manchester University Press.

Descartes, R. (1983). *Principles of philosophy* (V. Miller & R. Miller, Trans.). Dordrecht, The Netherlands: Reidel. (Original work published 1644)

Harman, G. (1986). *Change in view: Principles of reasoning.* Cambridge, MA: MIT Press.

Holyoak, K., & Thagard, P. (1989). Analogical mapping by constraint satisfaction. *Cognitive Science, 13*, 295-355.

Kintsch, W. (1988). The role of knowledge in discourse comprehension: A construction-integration model. *Psychological Review, 95*, 163-82.

Marr, D. (1982). *Vision*. San Francisco: Freeman.

McClelland, J., & Rumelhart, D. (1989). *Explorations in parallel distributed processing*. Cambridge, MA: MIT Press.

McClelland, J., & Rumelhart, D. (1981). An interactive activation model of context effects in letter perception: Part 1. An account of basic findings. *Psychological Review, 88*, 375-407.

Neapolitain, R. (1990). *Probabilistic reasoning in expert systems*. New York: Wiley.

Newton, I. (1934). *Mathematical principles of natural philosophy* (A. Motte & F. Cojou, Trans.). Berkeley and Los Angeles: University of California Press. (Original work published 1726)

Nowak, G., & Thagard, P., (in press). Copernicus, Ptolemy, and explanatory coherence. In R. Giere (Ed.), *Cognitive Models of Science (Minnesota Studies in the Philosophy of Science* Vol. 15). Minneapolis: University of Minnesota Press.

Pearl, J. (1988). *Probabilistic reasoning in intelligent systems*. San Mateo: Morgan Kaufman.

Ranney, M. (in press). Explorations in explanatory coherence. In E. Bar-On, B. Eylon, & Z. Schertz (Eds.), *Designing intelligent learning environments: From cognitive analysis to computer implementation*. Norwood, NJ: Ablex.

Ranney, M., & Thagard, P. (1988). Explanatory coherence and belief revision in naive physics. *Proceedings of the Tenth Annual Conference of the Cognitive Science Society*. Hillsdale, NJ: Lawrence Erlbaum. 426-32.

Thagard, P. (in press-a). Analogy, explanation, and education. *Journal of Research in Science Teaching*.

Thagard, P. (in press-b). The dinosaur debate: Explanatory coherence and the problem of competing hypotheses. In J. Pollock & R. Cummins (Eds.), *Philosophy and AI: Essays at the interface*. Cambridge, MA: MIT Press.

Thagard, P. (in press-c). *Conceptual revolutions*. Princeton, NJ: Princeton University Press.

Thagard, P. (1989). Explanatory coherence. *Behavioral and Brain Sciences, 12*, 435-67.

Thagard, P. (1988). *Computational philosophy of science*. Cambridge, MA: MIT Press.

Thagard, P., Holyoak, K., Nelson, G., & Gochfeld, D. (1990). Analog retrieval by constraint satisfaction. *Artificial Intelligence, 46,* 259-310.

Thagard, P., & Nowak, G. (1990). The conceptual structure of the geological revolution. In J. Shrager & P. Langley (Eds.), *Computational models of discovery and theory formation* (27-72). San Mateo, CA: Morgan Kaufman.

Thagard, P., & Nowak, G. (1988). The explanatory coherence of continental drift. In A. Fine & J. Leplin (Eds.), *Philosophy of Science Association 1988, Vol. 1.* East Lansing, MI: Philosophy of Science Association, 118-26.

RICHARD KITCHENER

4

Piaget's Genetic Epistemology: Epistemological Implications for Science Education

OUTLINE

I. Introduction
II. Epistemology versus Psychology
    A. Naturalistic Epistemology
    B. Epistemic Competence
    C. Epistemic Subject
III. The Epistemological Nature of Genetic Epistemology
    A. Nature of Knowledge
    B. Development of Knowledge
IV. Summary and Implications for Science Education
    A. Epistemic Competence and the Epistemic Subject
    B. Cognitive Conflict and Motivation for Change
    C. Stage Theory

ABSTRACT

Jean Piaget's theory of cognitive development had a strong influence on science education in the 1960s. But this psychological theory was just part of a larger program of genetic epistemology. As an epistemology, it has distinctively epistemological (not merely psychological) properties. I sketch the main epistemological tenets of genetic epistemology. I then point out some epistemological implications this genetic epistemology has for science education.

INTRODUCTION

Jean Piaget's theory of cognitive development had a profound impact upon science education during the 1960s and wrought changes in science curricula, conceptions of how students learn and how science should be taught. The major thrust of this impact centered on the cognitive development of students and how this development influences the learning of scientific concepts and methodology.

Although many individuals (Brainerd, 1978a; Brown & Desforges 1977; Carey 1986; Novak 1977a, 1977b, 1977c) have been critical of the educational implications of Piaget's theory, they have been critical of it fundamentally on psychological grounds, to wit, the empirical evidence does not seem to support what they take to be Piaget's psychological claims about the development of individuals. Although I believe these psychological criticisms of Piaget are wide of the mark and that the empirical evidence is basically supportive of the main tenets of Piaget's theory, I will not argue for that point. Instead, I will argue that most individuals continue to misunderstand the fundamental thrust of Piaget's theory. Although many individuals pay lip service to the claim that Piaget is a genetic epistemologist, they misunderstand the significance of this notion by equating genetic epistemology with developmental psychology. They then proceed to evaluate his epistemological theory on psychological grounds and to form (often mistaken) judgments about the validity of his genetic epistemology.

The Problem

Part of the reason for this mistaken identification of genetic epistemology with genetic psychology is the failure to recognize the fundamental difference between epistemology and psychology. Traditionally, psychology was conceived to be an empirical science, concerned with investigating empirical facts. By contrast, traditional philosophical disciplines, such as epistemology, were thought to be a priori, overly speculative, and nontestable. Hence, philosophical disciplines were thought to be basically irrelevant,to science of psychology. (The same applies, *mutatis mutandis*-allowing for the appropriate changes, to the philosophical discipline of ethics.) Since epistemology was thought to be a branch of philosophy, therefore, it was irrelevant to psychology. (Insofar as science education aims at being a purely empirical science, it too conceives epistemology as irrelevant.)

Psychologists and science educators have had difficulty in understanding the very possibility of a nonfactual realm. Consequently, anything normative (like epistemology) has been beyond their ken. Hence, when Americans first discovered Piaget in the thirties and then again in the fifties, they "assimilated" his theory to their own cognitive interpretation and consequently read his theory to be an ordinary psychological theory. Furthermore, in these early works, Piaget was not terribly explicit about the epistemological aim of his program; consequently, he indirectly encouraged a psychological interpretation of his views. In addition, the only works that were translated into English—five of his works were translated into English in the thirties and five more in the fifties—were Piaget's empirical (observational) studies of children: none of his major theoretical works and, *a fortiori*, none of his major epistemological works were translated into English during this period. (This situation has not improved much, since his major and definitive epistemological works—for example, *Introduction to Genetic Epistemology* (1950), *Logic and Scientific Knowledge* (1967), and Sociological Studies (1976)—have never appeared in English.) Consequently, the almost overwhelming temptation would have been to read Piaget as a child psychologist, engaged in the empirical observation of children's cognitive development.

Piaget—the Genetic Epistemologist

This interpretation is certainly wrong, however (R. Kitchener 1986): as Piaget has always insisted, his theory is first and foremost a theory about knowledge—the development of knowledge—and only secondarily a theory about psychological development (a point that many textbook discussions of Piaget now make). But if so, then we should take this claim seriously and attempt to understand and evaluate his theory as a *theory of knowledge*. Such a theory of knowledge has, of course, a psychological component, since according to Piaget a theory of knowledge makes empirical claims that must be evaluated empirically. However, one should not mistake this psychological component for his larger theory, nor evaluate his epistemology exclusively on psychological grounds. One must, in short, distinguish the psychological and the epistemological aspects of his theory. This involves, *inter alia*-among other things, understanding the difference between epistemic norms and psychological facts. If there is a basic difference between epistemology and psychology, as several science educators (Duschl, Hamilton & Grandy 1992; Novak 1983; Rogers 1982; Shuell 1987; Strike 1983; Summers 1982) recognize, then there may be pedagogical implications that follow from his epistemology as distinct from his psychology. These pedagogical implications may be epistemological in nature and not psychological, for if it is correct that science educators are concerned with the development of *knowledge* in their students, then any science pedagogy would seem to presuppose a view about the nature of knowledge, the acquisition and development of knowledge, and so forth. This clearly is an epistemological issue and a not psychological one. Science educators should have the best and most relevant epistemology; it may be that Piaget's theory of knowledge can provide such an epistemology.

In the following pages I will, first, set out the basic contrast between epistemology and psychology. Then I will briefly characterize Piaget's genetic epistemology. Next, I will indicate what epistemological implications follow from this epistemology and what value these may be for science educators.

EPISTEMOLOGY VERSUS PSYCHOLOGY

Piaget's theory of cognitive development is an epistemology, not an ordinary psychological theory (R. Kitchener, 1986). To understand the importance of this distinction, it is necessary to briefly discuss the traditional conception of epistemology (vs. psychology) and Piaget's particular interpretation of this distinction.

The Normative Versus the Factual

According to most epistemologists, epistemology is different from psychology in that epistemology is *normative* whereas psychology is *empirical*. Psychology (on the standard interpretation) is concerned with describing and explaining the purely factual realm of the mind and behavior, for example, the particular set of beliefs (or cognitive structures) held by an individual and why the individual holds such beliefs. By contrast, epistemology is concerned with *evaluating* the *adequacy* of these beliefs, with determining whether these beliefs are *correct, objective, rational, warranted* by the evidence, *coherent, plausible, truth-conducive,* and so forth. These latter terms have traditionally been taken to be normative concepts since they are concerned with describing how *good* or *right* (epistemically speaking) one's beliefs are, not simply with describing *what* they are or explaining *why* (causally speaking) one holds them. Thus, the distinction between epistemology and psychology is supposed to be an instance of the traditional distinction between norms and facts. Whether an individual actually holds a belief or not is a factual question, but whether she ought (epistemically speaking) to hold such beliefs, whether they are epistemically good or right, are normative questions. Epistemology is fundamentally concerned with this normative dimension of belief.

As a result of the alleged distinction between epistemology and psychology, epistemology has traditionally been viewed as a branch of philosophy. But suppose one makes the contrary assumption (as Piaget and several other contemporary epistemologists do) that *epistemology is a branch of science* or, better put (R. Kitchener, 1986), that *an essential part of epistemology is empirical science,* in particular, biology and psychology.[1] One can, consequently, be an epistemologist and be doing epistemology (in some sense) by doing science—not just any science, of course, but only that kind of empirical science relevant to epistemology, for example, empirical research designed to test the hypothesis that all ideas are acquired after birth, that only individuals possessing language can have the notion of "necessary" truth, that individuals cannot reason about science unless they possess formal deductive reasoning skills, or that concepts are acquired by abstraction from particular experience. What I am claiming, therefore, is that Piaget's general program is an example of "naturalistic epistemology" and not merely a theory of psychological development.

Naturalistic Epistemology

On the standard view (e.g., Chisholm 1977; Siegel 1980), epistemology is a completely normative endeavor, with empirical evidence from psychology having no contribution to make. In the last few decades, this view has been challenged by "naturalistic epistemologists" (Kornblith 1985).

There are several varieties of naturalistic epistemology (Maffie in press). The most famous is the reductionistic approach of Quine (1969), which argues that psychology must *replace* epistemology and hence become completely empirical. (This is also the view of Skinner 1945 [R. Kitchener 1979].) According to a second view (e.g., Goldman 1986; Corlett in press; R. Kitchener 1980), there is no sharp separation between the normative and the empirical. Epistemology has both a normative dimension and an empirical dimension and is best pursued in an interdisciplinary fashion. Piaget's epistemology can best be seen as an example of this latter version of naturalistic epistemology. Hence, there is a role for psychology to play in matters epistemological just as there is a crucial role for epistemology to play in psychology.

Epistemic Competence

In what sense is Piaget's theory of cognitive development not an ordinary theory of psychological development? As is well known, Piaget is a structuralist (Piaget 1971a; Gardner 1981) who is strongly committed to a biological or evolutionary model of knowledge (Piaget 1971b). As such, he is concerned with limning the cognitive structure(s) underlying (and explaining) one's epistemic adaptation to the environment. A central epistemological problem concerns how to explain the possibility of this epistemic behavior—a *how-possibly* type of explanation (Kitchener, 1983b). An answer to this how-possibly question involves the postulation of what we can call, borrowing from Chomsky's (1965) notion of competence, one's underlying *epistemic competence*. One's epistemic competence will consist of one's epistemic (not merely psychological) powers and abilities coupled together in a particular kind of abstract structure. These epistemic powers and abilities are powers and abilities *to know,* for example, to know how to count, to know how solve problems, to know how to adapt to one's environment. Furthermore, since these epistemic powers are related to each other—related in a logical or epistemic way— they have an underlying structure to them. Such an epistemic competence must be distinguished, of course, from one's epistemic performance, for example, an individual solving a syllogistic reasoning task at a particular time. Such epistemic behavior is not the same as one's epistemic competence, which is more abstract and general but exemplified in instances of actual epistemic performance. Public displays of epistemic performance are fallible evidence for one's underlying epistemic competence but not the same as the underlying construct.

In the epistemological tradition of Western philosophy, epistemology is concerned not merely with the existence and nature of one's *beliefs* about a particular domain of inquiry, for beliefs (along with correlative notions like schemata, mental models, categories, etc.) are taken to be *psychological* notions resident inside the individual mind and ascertained on ordinary empirical grounds. Epistemologists are interested, of course, in what beliefs one has, since beliefs are the internal carriers of knowledge, just as scientific theories are the external carriers of scientific knowledge. But knowledge is not reducible to mere belief (or cognitive schemata), since a belief can not only be *false* but can also fail to be well *justified*; according to the traditional view of knowledge, in order to know something (that p) a subject S must have not only a belief about p, but *adequate evidence* that p, and p must be *true*.[2] It is these notions of 'truth' and 'justification' that seem to require something more than merely empirical psychological concepts.[3]

If we focus on the epistemic carrier, mere beliefs are brute empirical, devoid of all normative properties, and hence (on the standard interpretation) a part of empirical psychology.[4] If one speaks of one's "competence" to do something, one is speaking not merely of psychological traits; one is saying something about the epistemic status of these traits, for if one is competent to do something, one knows-how to do something and this entails successfully satisfying certain normative standards and criteria, for example, *really* being able to do something under appropriate conditions.

Suppose one is concerned with one's epistemic competence to adapt successfully to one's environment, to know the world adequately, to solve problems, and so on. It was Kant ([1787] 1964) who attempted to describe what such competence must be by arguing that the necessary parts of this epistemic competence were "a priori forms of intuition" (space and time), a particular set of categories (e.g., causality and substance), schemata, and so on, and that this epistemic structure explained *how* it was *possible* for us to have (scientific) knowledge. In this sense he was inferring what every knower's epistemic competence must be. For Kant, such epistemic competence, lodged in our underlying cognitive structures, was *formal* epistemic competence as opposed to empirical *content* or *matter*, which came from our senses. Epistemic form was provided by the mind; epistemic content by the world. By 'formal' Kant meant (roughly) purely logical and structural relations embedded in a kind of abstract scaffolding. It had little to do with purely formal propositional logic, which was one instance of 'formal', just as Kohlberg's (1981) moral developmental theory is 'formal' without being equivalent to formal-propositional (deductive) logic. Hence, one can call 'concrete-operational' thinking an example of formal thinking without meaning the formal propositional thinking codified in Piaget's INRC group. The same ambiguity plagues Piaget's (Inhelder & Piaget 1958) construct of formal-operational thought, since it is formal but not formal-propositional (deductive) (Kitchener & Kitchener 1981).

In short, Piaget's genetic epistemology should be seen as a kind of (biological) neo-Kantianism. If this is correct, then Piaget is not interested in the merely cognitive psychological structures underlying our interactions in the world, but only with those cognitive structures that are epistemic in nature.[5]

Where is the Psychological?

One of the things absent in Piaget's account of our evolving epistemic competence is a typical or ideal *psychological explanation* of how this occurs, an explanation involving certain psychological constructs so precisely specified, measured, and quantified that one can *predict* precisely when the next stage will occur in a particular individual, explain why a particular individual solved a particular problem, and so on.

When this actually happens, Piaget tells us it occurred because of, say, equilibration, and we also know it involved biological, social, and experiential factors. But in any particular case we do not know how these factors interacted to produce actual epistemic development (hence allowing us to predict this beforehand). Piaget is virtually silent on this psychological question. Epistemic development is somehow *up to the individual* (or perhaps varies from individual to individual), but at the very least Piaget has very little to say concerning precisely how epistemic transitions occur.[6] The most he says is that equilibration is a process of *auto-* or *self-regulation*, which is "spontaneous." He certainly is not offering an explanation involving a set of variables by means of which one can *predict* behavior, any more than Chomsky is offering his theory of linguistic universals as a theory of linguistic performance. Chomsky's theory has been criticized for lacking psychological reality and for not containing a theory of performance, and similar criticisms (not surprisingly) have been made of Piaget. These criticisms have a point, of course, especially if one is offering a psychological theory—a performance level explanation. But if one is not, if one is offering explanations of epistemic competence, then other criteria of evaluation will be invoked—epistemic ones.

The Epistemic Subject

Piaget is not offering ordinary psychological explanations of behavioral performance and changes in behavior over time. Furthermore, he is not concerned with the epistemic competence of *particular* individuals. As a structuralist he is interested in a set of abstract, universal epistemic structures underlying all epistemic behavior and development. Neither Chomsky nor Piaget is interested in the underlying competence of a single individual person, since neither is concerned with particular competence but rather with *universal competence*. Piaget ([1981] 1987, p. 153) thus distinguishes *the epistemic subject* (which is nontemporal and noncausal), *the psychological subject* (which is temporal and causal), and the *individual*. (Virtually all of Piaget's work was on the epistemic subject whereas the work of his lifelong collaborator Barbel Inhelder has been on the psychological subject.)[7]

The epistemic subject, like Chomsky's ideal speaker, is not the average behavior of a group of individuals—the psychological subject—for (presumably) such an average will contain, besides the typical sources of error variance, numerous accidental features, common errors, and so forth. Instead, the epistemic subject is 'normative' in the sense of "ideal" (R. Kitchener 1990; Niaz 1990), that is to say, the epistemic subject is that set of abstract, universal epistemic structures, procedures, and so on, constituting an "ideal" knower, a knower not limited by performance errors, human frailties, unconscious motives, social class pressures, and so on, which typically operate to interfere with ideal epistemic performance.

In short, it is the epistemic competence of an ideal knower that concerns Piaget, for he is interested in *describing* our *evolving* epistemic competence and *explaining* how such epistemic development is possible.

THE EPISTEMOLOGICAL NATURE OF GENETIC EPISTEMOLOGY

Piaget's genetic epistemology should not be confused with psychology ordinarily conceived, any more than it should be mistaken for traditional epistemology. Clearly, a major concern of this program is with *knowledge*, but an even more fundamental concern is with the *development* of knowledge.

Knowledge

What is Piaget's general conception of the nature of knowledge? We can list at least five characteristics: (1) it is cognitive, (2) it is constructivist, (3) it involves the epistemic subject, (4) it is interactivist, and (5) it is rooted in operatory praxis.

Cognitivism. Like classical rationalists, Kant, and contemporary cognitive scientists (and unlike classical empiricists and recent behaviorists), Piaget believes knowledge requires antecedent categories, concepts, ideas, and so on, which make this knowledge possible. Contrary to empiricism, knowledge is not the simple, unaided recording of brute experience as such but presupposes a prior cognitive scaffolding into which incoming data can be subsumed. Kant and the rationalists were correct in arguing that cognitive categories are presupposed from the very beginning and prior to incoming sensory information. Thus the epistemic object is always "intensional" not "extensional", that is, the interpretation and description of the object-as-known depends upon the internal representation of the individual. Furthermore, as a cognitivist, Piaget believes that any "meaning" to be found in the representation will be due to the individual and is be found inherent in the stimulus material itself.

Constructivism. Like rationalists, Kant, and contemporary cognitive scientists, Piaget is also a constructivist: what is known is constructed or generated, since incoming data are processed and transformed through a series of cognitive structures, with the end result being knowledge. Knowledge is thus not a copy of sensations but the result of a long sequence of information processing. But, according to Piaget, the cognitive scaffolding necessary for knowledge is not fixed and innate but develops over time. It develops because it is constructed by the epistemic subject as a result of interactions with the environment according to certain laws of epistemic development.

The Epistemic Subject. Knowledge is constructed by the knower— the epistemic subject—whose activities result in the construction of categories of knowledge and the consequent generation of knowledge. Although one can say that individuals construct knowledge, this is potentially misleading since (1) the construction of knowledge is not idiographic but nomothetic and hence involves the psychological subject (not the individual) and (2) not all constructive activities of the psychological subject are relevant, only those constructions that are epistemic (i.e., rational constructions). Hence the epistemic subject is a double abstraction from particular individuals and a single abstraction from the psychological subject.

Although it is the epistemic subject that constructs knowledge, does this mean the knower is a solitary knower, cut off from other knowers and forced to construct knowledge by him/herself? Not at all, since Piaget (1976) claims that knowledge is also socially constructed (R. Kitchener 1989, in press-a). However, as one might surmise, it is not a group of individuals who constructs knowledge but a group of epistemic individuals, each of whom is an instance of the epistemic subject. Hence, knowledge is inescapably social for Piaget, but it is social in an epistemological, not a psychological, sense.

Interactivism. The epistemic subject constructs or generates knowledge by means of its interactions with the environment. Incoming data are assimilated to existing cognitive structures, and cognitive structures are accommodated to the incoming data. But all of this occurs in the context of an external world to which one must adapt. Adaptation, of course, is an *active* process not a passive one, but it is Piaget's biological orientation that leads him to view the basic epistemic unit as the organism-in-its-environment in which there is a series of *transactions*. Piaget's biological epistemology, with its adaptationist constraints, lands him squarely on the side of the ecological epistemologists (Carello et al. 1984; Neisser 1976) against the computer model of intelligence and its methological solipsism. If assimilation occurred without accommodation, one would have idealism; if accommodation occurred without assimilation, one would have a naive realism. Neither position is tenable for Piaget.

Praxis. These interactions or transactions occur by means of *actions* of the subject in the natural world. Piaget is thus committed to a *praxis* conception of knowledge, championed by Hegel, Marx, Bergson, and the pragmatists, as opposed to a "spectator" theory of knowledge: knowing-how (success) is primary (ontogenetically and epistemically), upon which is built knowing-that (understanding) (Piaget [1974] 1978). Hence, procedural knowledge is basic and declarative knowledge is lodged upon it. The root of all knowledge, therefore, is to be found in the primitive actions of the organism in its ecological environment. Piaget often remarks that to know an object is to act upon it, to subject it to a set of operations, transformations, and so forth. Hence we know an object by acting on it, or as Freyd (1987) puts it: "the perception of all objects depends upon knowledge of their possible transformations" (p. 436). *Praxis* (skill, knowing-how) is thus the epistemic basis of all our knowledge, upon which is constructed other levels of knowledge—first knowing-that and later meta-cognition.

The Development of Knowledge

Although these properties characterize Piaget's conception of knowledge in general, what is surely distinctive about his epistemology centers on his claims about the *development* of knowledge. The history of epistemology has largely been committed to some version of *logicism*, the thesis that a complete description of the nature of knowledge consists of certain kinds of logical relations between a belief (or theory) and a set of evidential statements. Although such a view is the basis of the traditional analysis of "*S* knows that *p*," it was Carnap's (1962) theory of scientific confirmation and Hempel's (Hempel & Oppenheim [1948] 1965) theory of explanation that most clearly exemplify this thesis. To this logicist conception of knowledge, which is a static, "frozen time-slice" view of knowledge, one can oppose a dynamic or historicist view of knowledge. (But although Piaget's genetic epistemology is a version of historicist epistemology, it is not a version of relativism as some varieties of historicism are.)

Just as there are two subfields of physics—kinematics and dynamics—so there are two subfields to a genetic (or developmental) epistemology: belief kinematics and belief dynamics. A complete developmental epistemology, therefore, should include both fields.

Epistemic Kinematics. Any historically oriented epistemology is concerned with how knowledge (beliefs, theories) change over time. Epistemic kinematics is concerned with *describing* the succession of these beliefs: B_1 at time t_1, B_2 at time t_2, and so on. Several contemporary epistemologists (Forrest 1986; Gardensfors 1988; Harman 1986; Levi 1980; Shoham 1988) are concerned with the underlying *logic* of such belief kinematics, for example, with which logical model (e.g., Bayes' Theorem) can best accommodate belief revision, belief addition, and so forth. But one can also be concerned with the logical structure of the entire (and completed) sequence of belief change from start to finish— a kind of epistemic morphology. Like those philosophers of science (T. Kuhn 1970; Lakatos 1980; Laudan 1978; Popper 1972) who are concerned with the logical structure of theory change, Piaget is concerned with the logical structure of that particular kind of cognitive change found in ontogenesis and, to a somewhat lesser extent, in the history of science (Piaget & Garcia 1989). This logical structure takes the form of a (dialectical) stage law of development that is purely kinematic in nature.

Such stage laws are of two main types: (1) *domain-specific* conceptual stage laws, for example, in physics the 'impetus' stage law of Aristotle's dual force, the single force of Philoponus, the impetus theory of Buridan and Oresme, and the stage law of acceleration (Piaget 1978), and (2) Piaget's *domain-general* or operatory stage law—preoperational, intuitive, concrete operational, and formal operational. Although critics (Carey 1985; Nersessian 1989; Novak 1977b; Viennot 1979; Vosniadou & Brewer 1987) focus on the latter type of stage law, they seem to have forgotten that from the very beginning of his career (Piaget [1923] 1955) up until his death (Piaget & Garcia [1983] 1989), Piaget has always been interested in domain-specific stage laws. Most science educators have simply overlooked this type of stage law in Piaget's work and its implications for science education.

Although this matter is far too complicated to go into here, it is a fundamental assumption of Piaget's epistemic kinematics that, since beliefs and cognitive structures do not change without reason (*la raison n'en peut changer qu'avec raison*), there are rational (morphological) constraints operating to constrain the very *form* of the trajectory of such a stage law, for example, any conceptual stage S_j subsequent to S_i must incorporate the epistemic competence of the preceding stage. The similarity to morphological constraints in biological evolution should be apparent (see Gould & Lewontin 1979).

Epistemic Dynamics. In addition to changing belief structures, the evidential basis for these beliefs also change over time, for example, the set of scientific observations is increasing steadily, epistemic criteria are changing, social conditions (to which theories must adapt) are changing, and so forth. Consequently, in a developmental epistemology, what is crucial is the set of changing theory-evidence relationships. One's beliefs (theories) must obviously change to meet this changing evidential basis. When theories change to meet these evidential constraints, questions of epistemic dynamics obviously arise, for it is here that we are interested in *explaining* the course of development (just as in physics Newtonian dynamics explains Galilean kinematics).

When it comes to explanation, however, we must distinguish what I will call *purely psychological* (brute empirical) *explanation* from *epistemic explanation*. In a purely psychological explanation, one explains a belief transition (why individuals made the transition) by reference to some psychological cause, for example, Skinnerian reinforcement, Hullian need-reduction, personality characteristic, social pressure, toilet training, and so forth. Such causes are brute empirical facts, empirical facts with no normative (epistemic) dimension.

In an epistemic explanation, however, one explains why belief B_1 led to B_2 by showing it was the rational thing to do, by citing the evidential justification for the transition. In the typical case, for example, theory T_1 was replaced by T_2 because there was better evidence for T_2, T_1 had encountered negative evidence, T_2 could solve more problems than T_1 could, T_2 was more promising, and so on. In Piaget's genetic epistemology, one epistemic structure is replaced by a subsequent one because the latter is more *equilibrated,* a complex (and rather vague) notion that includes the key property of "greater problem-solving power." As such equilibration is epistemic and not merely psychological.

Equilibration is clearly the key explanatory construct in Piaget's genetic epistemology. Because of its epistemic nature, this concept allows us to speak of a developmental sequence as being a case of *rational* change and as demonstrating *progress*. In offering an equilibrium-type explanation of epistemic change, therefore, Piaget is offering us not an efficient psychological cause of the transition but rather an explanation in terms of reasons.[8] As such, genetic epistemology is providing an "internalist" explanation, not an "externalist" one (R. Kitchener 1987), even though it may be a social explanation (R. Kitchener 1989, in press-a).

SCIENCE EDUCATION

I have suggested that most individuals have misunderstood Piaget's program of genetic epistemology by mistaking it for an ordinary psychological theory. By assuming that psychology investigates the purely empirical—a holdover from the era of logical positivism— they have either reduced the epistemological component to a merely psychological one or denied it has any relevance at all.

Having taken Piaget's theory to be an ordinary psychological theory, many individuals have proceeded to evaluate it as a psychological theory. Often this has meant employing some outmoded logical positivist criterion of empirical testability, the necessity of defining all psychological concepts in terms of operational definitions, restricting all constructs to the category of intervening variables, and so forth. (R. Kitchener 1983a). These strictures about theory construction were characteristic of an earlier era of logical positivism, one which soon gave way (around 1935) to a quite different philosophy of science—"logical empiricism," the characteristic feature of which was a weakening or abandonment of virtually all the constraints adumbrated earlier. But this earlier, more radical positivism continued to be dominant in mainstream psychology (e.g., Kimble 1989), including developmental psychology (Baltes, Reese & Nesselroade 1977; Brainerd 1978b). Consequently, much of Piaget's theory has been analyzed and criticized in terms of criteria that are (at best) applicable to ordinary psychological theory (not an epistemology), criteria that are, in fact, logically inadequate from a philosophy of science perspective.

Most science educators have been influenced by what they took to be Piaget's psychological theory. What I now want to suggest, however, is that this genetic epistemology has epistemological implications for science education. I want to discuss three areas in which one can find such implications: (1) competence explanations and the epistemic subject, (2) the issue of "cognitive conflict" and motivation for change, and (3) the question of stages of development.

Epistemic Competence and the Epistemic Subject

If Piaget is fundamentally concerned with the epistemic subject and not with particular individuals and if he is doing epistemology and not ordinary psychology, what is the role of the actual behavioral performance of individuals in evaluating this model of epistemic competence? As several individuals have argued (e.g., R. Kitchener 1990; Niaz 1990), empirical psychological data from particular individual performance will play less than a conclusive role in assessing the conceptual and empirical status of Piaget's theory.

Assuming this structuralist notion of competence is conceptually tenable, actual performance will be tenuously related to underlying competence in several senses. First, it will not be possible to operationally *define* competence in terms of performance (as Brainerd 1978b and several others require). We must treat "competence" not as an intervening variable but as a hypothetical construct (MacCorquodale & Meehl 1948) anchored to performance in multiple ways such that these behavioral indices function as "converging operations" (Garner, Hake & Eriksen 1956). It will not be possible, therefore, to make a direct, unambiguous, and certain inference from performance to competence since the appropriate scientific methodology here is that of a "multiple indicator" model in which various behavioral indices provide (at best) probabilistic evidence for this underlying intellectual capacity (Campbell & Fiske 1959).

Furthermore, even the employment of a multiple indicator model will be more problematic in determining and validating the construct of "competence" than in determining other constructs (such as need achievement or dreaming) because performance, even multiple performances, will "underdetermine" one's theoretical conclusion in a more radical way than in ordinary construct validation (Cronbach & Meehl 1955). This is because competence, like learning, is an ideal state, only tenuously related to real behavior because of performance debilitation, motivation, and so on. As an ideal epistemic state, it must be accompanied by a psychological theory of how structural competence is transformed into behavior manifestations, and this psychological theory has yet to be provided by Piaget (Pascual-Leone 1976). Consequently, it will not do (contrary to Novak 1977b) simply to consult the various training studies, which often involve only *single* performances, to identify and evaluate competence. But even in employing several tasks to evaluate underlying competence (D. Kuhn 1974), one always runs the risk of underestimating competence. This is an inherent problem with all competence explanations and applies to Chomskian linguistics and artificial intelligence models of cognition. What this means, therefore, is that most of the empirical studies in science teaching designed to test Piaget's theory will not be successful. This is not because the theory is empirically false but rather because of the inherent difficulties in empirically testing a theory of epistemic competence. (See R. Kitchener [1990] for a positive discussion of how one can empirically test Piaget's theory.)

Cognitive Conflict and Motivation for Change

A key issue for science educators concerns the "motor" of change: when students change from one conceptual structure to another, what motivates this change? Suppose we can epistemically explain the change (and hence "rationally reconstruct" it) by means of something like the principle of equilibration. What was the underlying *motive* for such a change? Once we can discover this underlying motivation, we can provide such motivation to other students and hence produce a change in their conceptual structures.

Issues of motivation typically have been thought to fall under the purview of ordinary empirical psychology which invokes causal explanations in terms of drive-reduction, incentive motivation, reward, and so forth. But if I am correct about the nature of Piaget's theory, it involves *epistemic explanations* (not ordinary psychological ones) as a motivational basis for change. Such explanations will involve *reasons*, not ordinary *causes*. Indeed, in genetic epistemology (Mischel 1971; Piaget 1954), there is no need for a *separate* theory of motivation: cognitive change can be explained on cognitive grounds alone without the need for a separate theory of affective motivation.

Simply put, the reason individuals make such conceptual change, and hence the underlying motive operating in such cases, is epistemic in nature: the earlier cognitive structure was disequilibrated, inadequate as a problem-solving device, cognitively inconsistent, and so forth. Because such epistemic structures are inadequate, this is a sufficient condition for rational change; hence it is sufficient as a motivating condition for making the change in question. The only motive needed to explain conceptual transitions, therefore, is a logical and rational one.

One consequence of this view is the following: if one wants to facilitate the epistemic transition from one conceptual scheme to another, the best way to do so is to produce a disequilibrated situation, a situation of cognitive dissonance, cognitive conflict, and so on. Although there are various ways of producing such a situation, two in particular stand out as important for science education. First, as is evident in Piaget's *methode clinique*, one can engage the student in "Socratic" discussion in which he is forced to give reasons for what he believes, says, does, and so forth. Presumably, if the student cannot provide adequate logical justification for what she says, this will produce disequilibrium and cognitive conflict.[9]

Secondly, one can provide cognitive conflict in the student by means of other students who are at a higher epistemic stage and who engage in discussions, cooperative problem-solving ventures, and so on, with the first student. As several empirical studies have shown (e.g., Doise, Mugny & Perres-Clermont 1975) what seems important is the experience of encountering a higher stage of epistemic development (although one not too much higher). Presumably, the effect is similar to that of the first method in that the student not only becomes aware (on some nonconscious level) of what a higher stage of epistemic functioning is and the superiority of such a stage, this "awareness" must result in some kind of epistemic conflict. A similar notion has been defended by Bower (1989); Nussbaum & Novick (1982); Posner (1983); Posner et al. (1982);[10] Rowell (1984) and others. Nothing I have said about inducing cognitive change is of course new; what is new is the explanation (or rationale) for this change—such cognitive conflict explanations are epistemic ones, not ordinary psychological ones.

If I am correct, how should science education be changed? Science education must be viewed as cognitive change, and this means epistemic change. It will not do, therefore, merely to get students to change their beliefs or cognitive structures, for after all this could be done, as a Skinnerian would suggest, by changing the reinforcement contingencies. What is important is not mere belief-revision, but rather belief-revision based upon epistemic grounds, motivating the student to change his/her beliefs for good epistemic reasons. They must (on some level) come to see the epistemic inadequacy of their belief structures and, if I am correct, the motivation for such change must be epistemic in nature, not merely psychological (Posner et al. 1982). Even if science educators speak of cognitive conflict as the motivation for change, it is important to understand the conceptual nature of this cognitive conflict.

Stage Theory

If what I have said about the concept of knowledge acquisition is correct, then a *cognitive theory of knowledge acquisition must be an epistemic stage theory*. Something like epistemic stages are necessary both for individual development and for a historical philosophy of science, for if (scientific) knowledge is progressing and if the carrier of knowledge is a theory (or scheme), then such theories (schemata) must be progressing. Consequently, there must be a series of (scientific) theories research programmes, research traditions, schemata, programs, and so forth, which are constrained by developmental-epistemological criteria. If there is progress with respect to this sequence C_1-C_2-C_3, then there must be a progressive increase in its overall epistemic power (however epistemic progress is to be conceptualized and measured). This need not be a simple linear accumulation model, since the latter epistemic entity can "integrate" and "reorganize" the earlier one, nor need there be a radical discontinuity between successive ones. But some kind of linear ordering seems necessary. If all of this is correct, then we seem to have the beginnings of an *epistemic stage sequence*. Such stages are, however, *weak* stages and need not be the *strong* stages characterized by domain-independent, content-independent Piagetian *structures d'ensemble*. One can choose to reject Piaget's strong stages, of course, but the alternative of weak stages should be endorsed, I suggest, for epistemological reasons. Moreover, as I suggested earlier, Piaget has always been concerned with these domain-specific stages in a wide variety of areas. If so, then the demise of stage theory (Hodson 1988; Linn 1986; Novak 1977b) seems greatly exaggerated and premature.

I have suggested there are several epistemological implications which follow from Piaget's genetic epistemology and that these implications are important for science education. Their importance is epistemological in nature, not just psychological, since they concern the nature of knowledge, knowledge acquisition, and epistemological change. These implications are not new, of course, since they are already accepted by many science educators, but their nature and rationale are different since science educators have thought they were psychological in nature.

To this, the science educator might well respond: So what? Why should science educators care about epistemological issues at all? And even assuming they do (or should) care, practical implications concerning the teaching of science that follow from these epistemological matters?

Why Epistemology is Important to Science Education

To the question, Why is epistemology important to science education?, the appropriate answer is the following.

Science educators have largely become convinced that philosophy of science is relevant to science education. If one is going to teach science, then it is obviously important to have an adequate conception of what science and scientific knowledge are. Consequently, it has been important for science educators to give up outmoded philosophies of science and adopt more epistemologically adequate ones. But philosophy of science is primarily concerned with the nature of scientific knowledge, that is, with epistemology.

A similar point can also be made with regard to general epistemology: if science educators are to teach students certain systems of knowledge, that is, scientific theories, they should have an adequate conception of the nature of knowledge. Epistemology, therefore, will be relevant to science education (just as philosophy of science is to science education), and science educators should thus come to appreciate what is distinctive about knowledge as opposed to mere belief (epistemology vs. psychology), namely, the normative dimension of epistemology as opposed to the merely factual dimension of ordinary psychology.

Practical Epistemological Implications for Science Education

The above point is a purely logical point about the conceptual nature of the subject matter of science education. But more than this, there are practical implications which follow from this point, analogous way practical implications follow from having an adequate philosophy of science underlying one's science education, namely, how one teaches science. It concerns the importance, first, of making sure that science students actually have good reasons, evidence, and so on, for their beliefs. When science educators discuss science with their students, the answers of the students must be *evaluated*, evaluated according to criteria or standards of correctness. Here it is important for science educators to distinguish the mere beliefs of students from beliefs backed by good evidence. In short, science educators must see the importance of normative standards of knowledge in relation to how they teach science.

But more than this, students must come to see not only the need to justify their answers by reference to standards of correctness, they must also come to see what these (good) standards of correctness are. For example, they must come to see that one need not have *absolute certainty* in order to have knowledge, that this normative criterion is too stringent and a mere will-o'-the-wisp. They must come to see that scepticism is an untenable epistemic position and correlatively that epistemological relativism is inadequate as a basis of knowledge. They must come to see that a standard of correctness or norm suitable for knowledge must be something in between skepticism and absolute certainty, a fallibilistic criterion of "adequate evidence."

How do science educators actually get their students to see this? How can they get their students to abandon an inadequate epistemological "scheme" and accept a more adequate one? Here we are talking about *epistemological change*, a change in their theory of knowledge, and how to produce it. Furthermore, how does all of this relate to Piaget's genetic epistemology, with its stress on the growth of knowledge through stages via epistemic construction as a result of epistemic conflict?

Although there are several theoretical models that address some of these questions (see Commons, Richards & Armon 1984; Mines & Kitchener 1986 for useful collections), none of them are as explicitly epistemological and, at the same time, as empirically based as the reflective judgment model of K. Kitchener and King (1981; K. Kitchener 1983). They have collected longitudinal data on the epistemic development of adolescents for over ten years (King, et al. 1983).

Their model is an epistemological stage model in which students pass through seven epistemological stages, the most important of which are absolute certainty (absolutism), skepticism, relativism, and finally probabilistic knowledge (fallibilism), which is attained only in the mid-twenties (or later), that is, in the post-graduate years! There are, therefore, definite developmental constraints on when a *fully* developed epistemological stage of "probabilism" can be reached. But Kitchener and King have also found that science students at lower stages (for example, high school) can make progress towards attaining this higher stage.

Improvement among high school science students' ability to think in epistemically probabilistic terms (and presumably change their underlying epistemological structures) comes, first of all, from the science teacher teaching them that scientists have disagreed, that theoretical pluralism is not an anomaly in science but the norm. Such a realization is basic to the transition from "absolute certainty" to a more relativistic conception of science. This can perhaps most easily be done through a historical approach to science (for example, the change from the Ptolemaic theory to the Copernican theory or the change from spontaneous generation theory to germ theory) in which students learn that there were different (and competing) scientific theories, that these theories were backed by good (although not absolutely certain) scientific reasons, that scientists nevertheless disagreed about which theory was most adequate, and that one theory was finally abandoned in favor of another theory. What is especially important is teaching science students what epistemic considerations led the scientific community to abandon one theory and adopt a different one, for example, the discovery of new evidence, the (superior) simplicity of one theory over another, changing theoretical support from other sciences, technological applications, new mathematical techniques, and so forth. Thus they should learn that although theory choice is not incorribly certain or algorithmic, nevertheless there were good (probabilistic) reasons for such a choice. Finally, students can also be taught (although this is more controversial in contemporary philosophy of science) that the epistemic norms governing theory choice in science have changed over the years, for example, scientists have abandoned the criterion that a scientific theory must be consistent with and derivable from one's theology. These norms or criteria for evaluating and choosing a theory have changed over the course of history, but (more importantly) this change has been a rational affair; there has been an improvement or development in such epistemic norms as scientists have not only learned about nature but have learned how to learn (Laudan 1984: Shapere 1984). Learning how to learn means learning which epistemic norms should be retained and which ones abandoned. Correlatively, students should not only learn the cumulative facts of science; they too should "learn how to learn." This involves not only the development of logic and scientific reasoning skills (D. Kuhn, Amsel & O'Loughlin 1988; Moshman, 1990), but also the development of epistemic skills.

In the development of these epistemic skills—skills involving reasoning about epistemic questions—what seems crucial is the teaching of *ill-structured problems* (Newell 1969; Simon 1973; Wood 1983) and how various kinds of evidence and rational considerations are relevant to addressing such problems. Ill-structured problems are those that have poorly defined goals or solutions, an absence of-a predetermined decision path from the initial state to the goal, lack of well-defined criteria for what an acceptable solution is, etc. For example, how to solve the world's overpopulation problem is one such ill-structured problem, as is the question of whether it is possible to have a fully complete and comprehensive theory of the cosmos (R. Kitchener & Freeman, in press).

Science students need to be taught that it is possible to make progress on solving such ill-structured problems by showing them how various scientific data are relevant to the problems, how such data lend credibility to one proposed solution over against another proposed solution, what new data, experimental techniques or mathematical tools might be relevant to answering such questions more fully, how one could go about conducting an experiment to obtain new data, and so forth. In short, students can learn there are numerous ill-structured problems in science, that conclusive answers to such problems are difficult if not impossible to obtain, but that nevertheless some answers are epistemically better—in a probabilistic, fallibilistic sense—than others. Hence, relativism and skepticism are no more tenable than is the quest for absolute certainty.

Of course all of this will take valuable classroom time and science teachers may well reply: "but we have so little time and we need to teach students the facts." Such responses not only are wrong (since teaching them the facts does not work) but also betoken an earlier and outmoded epistemology, one that is wrong on epistemological grounds. Such a belief will inhibit the epistemological development of science students, and if we have such development as our goal in science education, we must develop pedagogical techniques that are efficacious in producing such epistemic development.

In conclusion, what science educators should teach thus depends on the psychological evidence about epistemic development, for example, the important empirical research of K. Kitchener and King. But it also depends upon what prior epistemology science educators bring to bear on the teaching of science. Once again, the science educator must realize the importance of having both an adequate epistemology and adequate empirical (psychological) evidence. As Jean Piaget has always insisted, both epistemology and psychology are relevant to "the growth of knowledge."

NOTES

1. Which interpretation should be ascribed to Piaget clear, since sometimes he seems to advocate one interpretation and sometimes a different view. The point is important, however, since it divides contemporary "naturalistic epistemologists" (Kornblith 1985) into those who believe the strong thesis that epistemology can be *reduced* to science and those that believe the weaker thesis that science is *evidentially relevant* to traditional epistemology.

2. Of course, this simplified version of the traditional view of propositional (declarative) knowledge is widely taken to be inadequate due to the seminal paper of Gettier (1963). It still provides the backdrop, however, against which other theories of knowledge are developed.

3. This is because most philosophers have been suspicious of any version of *psychologism*, the view (roughly) that attempts to reduce normative notions (e.g., "validity") to empirical ones (e.g., "felt conviction" or "social reinforcement.")

4. 'Cognition' is ambiguous on this point since "to be aware of" something seems to imply something more than just believing something, for example, one can believe in the Holy Grail but not be cognizant of it. It is because of this intermediate conceptual nature of 'cognition' that cognitive psychology and cognitive science are widely taken to be equivalent to epistemology. Few cognitivists have worried about this point.

5. It is not easy to provide examples of cognitive states that are nonepistemic. It depends, of course, on what one takes the domain of knowledge to be: if it is scientific knowledge of the natural world, then cognitive states involving, say, self-concept, sexual image, or emotional feeling, such cognitions would be nonepistemic. If, however, one extends the domain of knowledge to include psychological knowledge and social knowledge, then virtually everything cognitive would be epistemic. I believe Piaget was never clear on this point but leaned toward the former, since his main concern was with scientific knowledge.

6. This is the standard psychological criticism of Piaget (e.g., Meadows 1988) and from a psychological point of view, it is well taken. Several psychol-

ogists (e.g., Pascual-Leone 1976) have attempted to supplement Piaget's epistemology by providing the "missing" psychological counterpart. The move
towards "Genevan functionalism" (Inhelder 1978) can be interpreted in the
same way. Even Piaget (Inhelder & Piaget [1979] 1980) seemed to realize the
necessity for such a psychology. Currently, Genevan functionalism provides
the swiss bridge between Piaget's genetic epistemology and information processing psychology (Leiser & Gillieron 1990).

7. The competence-performance distinction is not to be identified with
the epistemic subject-psychological subject distinction, since one can give a
competence-type explanation of nonepistemic behavior involving, for example, the persuasion of others by means of one's social power and prestige.
Although an explanation of actual epistemic behavior would have to involve a
theory of the psychological subject, since such a theory would tell us how individuals actually function in real time to solve a problem, the functioning of the
psychological subject is not restricted to epistemic behavior; indeed, it incorporates everything psychological, including distortions due to unconscious processes and personality disturbances and so forth. Indeed, according to Piaget
([1970] 1974; Beth & Piaget [1961] 1966), the psychological subject is not "decen-
tered" at all but rather fundamentally irrational, whereas the epistemic subject
is rational and objective.

8. Although I employ the terminology of "causes versus reasons," I do
not believe this distinction is a sharp one. In fact, on a sufficiently broad reading
of "cause," reasons are causes of a particular kind.

9. It should be pointed out that it is not enough simply to have an open-
ended discussion with students in which they merely express their views; the
student must be forced to rationally defend such views in reaction to the inter-
viewer/teacher's probing questions (Kitchener, in press-b).

10. Posner et al. (1982), however, employ a model of conflict that relies
too much, in my opinion, on *conscious* reasoning and *conscious* factors. Such
reasoning certainly occurs in daily life and in science, but much problem solving
and reasoning involve *unconscious* processes (Piaget 1974; Rozin 1976). One of
the problems with the "child as scientist" metaphor (Carey 1985) is the notion
that a two-year-old child could engage in processes like considering the plausibility of a new conceptual scheme; certainly this doesn't occur consciously
and seems to be much too rational an affair for a young child. This is one consequence of failing to take "'rationality' to be a developmental entity."

REFERENCES

Baltes, P., Reese, H. W., & Nesselroade, J. R. (1977) . *Lifespan developmental psychology: Introduction to research methods*. Monterey, CA: Brooks/Cole.

Beth, E. W., & Piaget, J. (1966). *Mathematical epistemology and psychology.* (W. Mays, Trans.) Dordrecht, The Netherlands: Reidel. (Original work published 1961)

Bower, T. G. R. (1989). *The rational infant: Learning in infancy.* New York: Freeman.

Brainerd, C. J. (1978a). Cognitive development and instructional theory. *Contemporary Educational Psychology, 3,* 37-50.

Brainerd, C. J. (1978b). The stage question in cognitive-developmental theory. *The Behavioral and Brain Sciences, 2,* 173-213.

Brown, G., & DesForges, C. (1979). *Piaget's theory: A psychological critique.* London: Routledge & Kegan Paul.

Brown, G., & DesForges, C. (1977) . Piagetian psychology and education: Time for revision. *British Journal of Educational Psychology, 47,* 1-17.

Campbell, D. T., & Fiske, D. W. (1959). Convergent and discriminate validation by the multitrait-multimethod matrix. *Psychological Bulletin, 56,* 81-105.

Carello, C., Turvey, M. T., Kugler, P. N. & Shaw, R. E. (1984). Inadequacies of the computer metaphor . In M. S. Gazzaniga (Ed.), *Handbook of cognitive neuroscience* (pp. 229-48) . New York: Plenum.

Carey, S. (1986). Cognitive science and science education. *American Psychologist, 41,* 1123-30.

Carey, S. (1985). *Conceptual change in childhood.* Cambridge, MA: MIT Press.

Carnap, R. (1972). *The logical foundations of probability* (2nd ed.). Chicago: University of Chicago Press.

Chisholm, R. (1977). *Theory of knowledge* (2nd ed.). Englewood Cliffs, NJ: Prentice-Hall.

Chomsky, N. (1965). *Aspects of the theory of syntax.* Cambridge, MA: MIT Press.

Commons, M. L., Richards, F. A., & Armon, C. (1984). *Beyond formal operations: Late adolescent and adult cognitive development.* New York: Praeger.

Corlett, J. A. (in press). On some relations between epistemology and psychology. *New Ideas in Psychology.*

Cronbach, L. & Meehl, P. (1955). Construct validity in psychological tests. *Psychological Bulletin, 52,* 281-302.

Doise, W., Mugny, G., & Perres-Clermont, A. N. (1975). Social interaction and the development of cognitive operations. *European Journal of Social Psychology, 5,* 367-93.

Duschl, R. A., Hamilton, R., & Grandy, R. E. (1992). Psychology and epistemology: Match or mismatch when applied to science education. In R. Duschl & R. Hamilton (Eds.), *Philosophy of Science, Cognitive Psychology, and Educational Theory and Practice*. Albany, NY: SUNY Press.

Forrest, P. (1986). *The dynamics of belief: A normative logic*. Oxford: Blackwells.

Freyd, J. J. (1987). Dynamic mental representations. *American Psychologist, 94,* 427-438.

Gardenfors, P. (1988). *Knowledge in flux: Modeling the dynamics of epistemic states*. Cambridge, MA: MIT. Press.

Gardner, H. (1981). *The quest for mind: Piaget, Levi-Strauss and the structuralist movement* (2nd ed.). Chicago: University of Chicago Press.

Garner, W. E., Hake, H. S., & Eriksen, C. W. (1956). Operationaism and the concept of perception. *Psychological Review, 63,* 149-59.

Gettier, E. L. (1963). Is justified true belief knowledge? *Analysis, 23,* 121-23.

Goldman, A. I. (1986). *Epistemology and cognition*. Cambridge, MA: Harvard University Press.

Gould, S. J. & Lewontin, R. C. (1979). The spandrels of San Marco and the panglossian paradigm: A critique of the adaptationist programme. *Proceedings of the Royal Society of London, B205,* 581-98.

Harman, G. (1986). *Change in view: Principles of Reasoning*. Cambridge, MA: MIT Press.

Hempel, C., & Oppenheim, P. (1965). Studies in the logic of confirmation. In C. G. Hempel (ed.), *Aspects of scientific explanation and other essays in the philosophy of science* (pp. 3-46). New York: Free Press. (Original work published 1948)

Hodson, D. (1988). Toward a philosophically more valid science curriculum. *Science Education, 72*(1), 19-40.

Inhelder, B. (1978). De l'approache structurale a l'approache procedurale: Introduction a l'etude des strategies [From the structural approach to the procedural approach: Introduction to the study of strategies]. In *Actes du XXIe Congres international de Psychology* (pp. 99-118). Paris: Presses Universitaires de France.

Inhelder, B., & Piaget, J. (1980). Procedures and structures. In D. R. Olson (Ed.), *The social foundations of language and thought* (pp. 19-27). New York: Norton. (Original work published 1979)

Inhelder, B., & Piaget, J. (1958). *The growth of logical thinking from childhood to adolescence*. (A Parsons & S. Milgran, Trans.). London: Routledge &

Kegan Paul. (Original work published 1955)

Kant, I. (1964). *Critique of pure reason* (2nd ed.). (N. Kemp Smith, Trans.). New York: St. Martin's. (Original work published 1787)

Kimble, G. A. (1989). Psychology from the standpoint of a generalist. *American Psychologist, 44,* 491-99.

King, P. M., Kitchener, K. S., Davison, M. L., & Parker, C. A. (1983). The justification of beliefs in young adults: A longitudinal study. *Human Development, 26,* 106-16.

Kitchener, K. S. (1983). Cognition, metacognition and epistemic cognition: A three-level model of cognitive processing. *Human Development, 26,* 227-232.

Kitchener, K. S., & King, P. M. (1981). Reflective judgment: Concepts of justification and their relationship to age and education. *Journal of Applied Developmental Psychology, 2,* 89-116.

Kitchener, K. S., & Kitchener, R. F. (1981) . The development of natural rationality: Can formal operations account for it? In J. Meacham & M. R. Santilli (Eds.), *Social development in youth: Structure and content* (pp. 231-62). New York: Karger.

Kitchener, R. F. (in press-a). Jean Piaget—the unknown sociologist. *British Journal of Sociology.*

Kitchener, R. F. (in press-b). Do children think philosophically? Thoughts after Piaget. *Metaphilosophy.*

Kitchener, R. F. (1990, April). *Piaget's epistemic subject and science education: Epistemological vs. psychological issues.* Paper presented at the 63rd meeting of the National Association for Research in Science Teaching, Atlanta, GA.

Kitchener, R. F. (1989). Genetic epistemology and the prospects for a cognitive sociology of science. *Social Epistemology, 3,* 153-69.

Kitchener, R. F. (1987). Genetic epistemology, equilibration and the rationality of scientific change. *Studies in the History and Philosophy of Science, 18,* 339-66.

Kitchener, R. F. (1986). *Piaget's theory of knowledge: Genetic epistemology and scientific reason.* New Haven: Yale University Press.

Kitchener, R. F. (1983a). Changing conceptions of the philosophy of science and the foundations of developmental psychology. In D. Kuhn & J. Meacham (Eds.), *On the development of developmental psychology* (pp. 1-30). Basel: Karger.

Kitchener, R. F. (1983b). Developmental explanations. *Review of Metaphysics, 36,* 791-818.

Kitchener, R. F. (1980). Genetic epistemology, normative epistemology and psychologism. *Synthese, 45,* 257-80.

Kitchener, R. F. (1979). Radical naturalism and radical behaviorism. *Scientia, 114,* 141-60.

Kitchener, R. F., & Freeman, K. P. (in press). *The origin of the universe: Scientific and philosophical perspectives.* Albany, NY: State University of New York Press.

Kohlberg, L. (1981). *Essays on moral development: Vol. 1. The philosophy of moral development.* New York: Harper & Row.

Kornblith, H. (1985). *Naturalizing epistemology.* Cambridge, MA: MIT Press.

Kuhn, D. (1974). Inducing development experimentally: Comments on a research paradigm. Developmental Psycholoav, 10, 590N600.

Kuhn, D., Amsel, E., & O'Loughlin, M. (1988). *The development of scientific reasoning skills.* New York: Academic Press.

Kuhn, T. (1970). *The structure of scientific revolutions.* (2nd ed.). Chicago: University of Chicago Press.

Lakatos, I. (1980). History of science and its rational reconstruction. In J. Worrall & G. Currie (Eds.), *Imre Lakatos: Philosophical papers, Vol. 1.* (pp. 102-38). Cambridge: Cambridge University Press.

Laudan, L. (1984) . *Science and values: The aims of science and their role in scientific debate.* Berkeley and Los Angeles: University of California Press.

Laudan, L. (1978). *Progress and its problems.* Berkeley and Los Angeles: University of California Press.

Leiser, D., & Gillieron, C. (1990). *Cognitive science and genetic epistemology.* New York: Plenum.

Levi, I. (1980). *The enterprise of knowledge.* Cambridge, MA: MIT Press.

Linn, M. C. (1986). Science. In R. F. Dillon & R. J. Sterberg (Eds.), *Cognition and instruction* (pp. 155-204) . New York: Academic Press.

MacCorquodale, K., & Meehl, P . (1948) . On a distinction between hypothetical constructs and intervening variables. *Psychological Review, 55,* 95-107.

Maffie, J. (in press). Recent work on naturalized epistemology. *American Philosophical Quarterly.*

Meadows, S. (1988). Piaget's contribution to understanding cognitive development: An assessment from the late 1980's. In K. Richardson (Ed.), *Cognitive development in adolescence* (pp. 19-32). East Sussex: Open University.

Mines, R. A., & Kitchener, K. 5. (1986). *Adult cognitive development: Methods and models*. New York: Praeger.

Mischel, T. (1971). Piaget: Cognitive conflict and the motivation of thought. In T. Mischel (Ed.), *Cognitive development and epistemology* (pp. 311-56). New York: Academic Press.

Moshman, D. (1990). The development of metalogical understanding. In W. Overton (Ed.), *Reasoning, necessity and logic: Developmental perspectives*. Hillsdale, NJ: Lawrence Erlbaum.

Neisser, U. (1976). General, academic, and artificial intelligence. In L. B. Resnick (Ed.), *The nature of intelligence* (pp. 135-44). Hillsdale, NJ: Lawrence Erlbaum.

Nersessian, N. J. (1989). Conceptual change in science and in science education. *Synthese, 80*, 163-83.

Newell, A. (1969). Heuristic programming: Ill-structured problems. In J. Aronofsky (Ed.), *Progress in operations research* (pp. 360-414). New York: Wiley.

Niaz, N. (1990). Role of the epistemic subject in Piaget's genetic epistemology and its importance for science education. Paper presented at the 63rd meeting of the National Association for Research in Science Teaching, Atlanta, GA.

Novak, J. D. (1983). Can metalearning and metaknowledge strategies to help students learn how to learn serve as basis for overcoming misconceptions? In H. Helm & J. D. Novak (Eds.), *Proceedings of the international seminar on misconceptions in science and mathematics* (pp. 118-30). Ithaca, NY: Cornell University Press.

Novak, J. D. (1977a). Epicycles and the homocentric earth: Or what is wrong with *stages* of cognitive development? *Science Education, 61*, 393-95.

Novak, J. D. (1977b). An alternative to piagetian psychology for science and mathematics education. *Science Education, 61*, 453-77.

Novak, J. D. (1977). *A theory of education*. Ithaca, NY: Cornell University Press.

Nussbaum, J. & Novick, S. (1982). Alternative frameworks, conceptual conflict and accommodation: Toward a principled teaching strategy. *Instructional Science, 11*, 183-200.

Pascual-Leone, J. (1976). Metasubjective problems of constructive cognition: Forms of knowing and their psychological mechanism. *Canadian psychological Review, 17*, 109-25.

Piaget, J. (1987). *Possibility and necessity. Vol. 1: The role of possibility in cognitive development* (H. Feider, Trans.). Minneapolis: University of Minnesota Press. (Original work published 1981).

Piaget, J. (1978). Die historische Entwicklung und die Psychogenese des Impetus-begriffs [The historical development and psychogenesis of the concept of impetus]. In G. Steiner (Ed.), *Psychologie in die 20. Jahrhunderts. Vol. 7: Piaget und die Folge* (pp. 64-73). Zurich: Kindler.

Piaget, J. (1978). *Success and understanding* (A. J. Pomerans, Trans.). Cambridge, MA: Harvard University Press. (Original work published 1974)

Piaget, J. (1976). *Etudes sociologiques* [Sociological studies] (2nd ed.). Geneva: Droz.

Piaget, J. (1974). Affective unconscious and cognitive unconscious. In *The child and reality: Problems of genetic epistemology* (pp. 31-48). New York: Viking.

Piaget, J. (1974). *The place of the sciences of man in the system of sciences.* New York: Harper. (Original work published 1970).

Piaget, J. (1971a). *Structuralism* (C. Maschler, Trans.). New York: Harper.

Piaget, J. (1971b). *Biology and knowledge: An essay on the relations between organic regulations and cognitive processes* (B. Walsh, Trans.). Chicago: University of Chicago Press. (Original work published 1967)

Piaget, J. (Ed.). (1967). *Logique et connaissance scientifique* [Logic and scientific knowledge]. Paris: Gallimard.

Piaget, J. (1955). *The language and thought of the child* (M. Gabain, Trans.). Cleveland: World. (Original work published 1923)

Piaget, J. (1954). *Les relations entre l'affectivite et l'intelligence dans le developpement mental de l'enfance* [The relations between affect and intelligence in the mental development of the infant]. Paris: Centre de Documentation Universitaires.

Piaget, J. (1950). *Introduction a l'epistemologie genetique* [Introduction to genetic epistemology] (Vols. 1-3). Paris: Presses Universitaires de France.

Piaget, J., & Garcia, R. (1989). *Psychogenesis and the history of science* (H. Feider, Trans.). New York: Columbia University Press. (Original work published 1983)

Popper, K. (1972). *Objective knowledge.* Oxford: Oxford University Press.

Posner, G. (1983). A model of conceptual change: Present status and prospect. In H. Helm & J. D. Novak (Eds.), *Proceedings of the international seminar on misconceptions in science and mathematics* (pp. 71-75). Ithaca, NY: Cornell University Press.

Posner, G. J., Strike, K. A., Hewson, P. W., & Gertzog, W. A. (1982). Accommodation of a scientific conception: Toward a theory of conceptual change. *Science Education, 66*(2), 211-27.

Quine, W. V. O. (1969). Epistemology naturalized. In his *Ontological relativity and other essays* (pp. 69-90). New York: Columbia University Press.

Rogers, P. J. (1982). Epistemology and history in the teaching of school science. *European Journal of Science Education, 4,* 1-10.

Rowell, J. A. (1984). Many paths to knowledge: Piaget and science education. *Studies in Science Education, 11,* 1-25 .

Rozin, P. (1976). The evolution of intelligence and access to the cognitive unconscious. In J. M. Sprague & A. A. Epstein (Eds.), *Progress in psychobiology and physiological psychology, Vol. 6* (pp. 245-80). New York: Academic Press.

Shapere, D. (1984). *Reason and the search for knowledge.* Dordrecht, The Netherlands: Reidel.

Shoham, Y. (1988). *Reasoning about change: Time and causation from the standpoint of artificial intelligence.* Cambridge, MA: MIT Press.

Shuell, T . (1987) . Cognitive psychology and conceptual change: Implications for science teaching. *Science Education, 71,* 239-50.

Siegel, H. (1980). Justification, discovery and the naturalizing of epistemology. *Philosophy of Science, 47,* 297-321.

Simon, H. A. (1973). The structure of ill-structured problems. *Artificial Intelligence, 4,* 181-201.

Skinner, B. F. (1945). The operational analysis of psychological terms. *Psychological Review, 52,* 270-77.

Stich, S. (1985). Could man be an irrational animal? Some notes on the epistemology of rationality. *Synthese, 64,* 115-35.

Strike, K. A. (1983). Misconceptions and conceptual change: Philosophical reflections on the research paradigm. In H. Helm & J. D. Novak (Eds.), *Proceedings of the international seminar on misconceptions in science and mathematics* (pp. 83-97). Ithaca, NY: Cornell University Press.

Summers, M. K. (1982) . Philosophy of science in the science teacher education curriculum. *European Journal of Science Education, 4,* 19-27.

Viennot, L. (1979). Spontaneous reasoning in elementary dynamics. *European Journal of Science Education, 1,* 205-21.

Vosniadou, S., & Brewer, W. F. (1987). Theories of knowledge restructuring in development. *Review of Educational Research, 57*(1), 51-67.

Waterson, M. A. (1983). Alternative conceptions of the tentative nature of scientific knowledge. In H. Helm & J. D. Novak (Eds.), *Proceedings of the international seminar on misconceptions in science and mathematics* (pp. 300-9). Ithaca, NY: Cornell University Press.

Wood, P. K. (1983). Inquiring systems and problem structure: Implications for cognitive development. *Human Development, 5,* 249-65.

KENNETH A. STRIKE
GEORGE J. POSNER

5

A Revisionist Theory of Conceptual Change

OUTLINE

ABSTRACT

The authors of this paper have previously published a theory of conceptual change. This paper begins by restating the theory and exploring some of the motivation for it. It then examines several lines of criticism. It restates some aspects of the theory more clearly, and it makes several revisions in the theory. There are principle modifications required of the theory:

1. A wider range of factors needs to be taken into account in attempting to describe a learners' conceptual ecology. Motives and goals and the institutional and social sources of them need to be considered.
2. Current scientific conceptions and misconceptions are parts of the learner's conceptual ecology. Thus they must be seen in interaction with other components.
3. Conceptions and misconceptions can exist in different modes of representation and different degrees of articulateness.
4. A developmental view of conceptual ecologies is required.
5. An interactionist view of conceptual ecologies is required.

The paper concludes with a discussion of empirical support of an interactionist interpretation of conceptual change. It concludes that there is a mutually reinforcing interaction between the tendency to see science as a rational enterprise and the learning of physics.

THE INITIAL THEORY

The question to which our initial theory of conceptual change was an answer is: "How do learners make a transition from one conception, C_1, to a successor conception, C_2." We used the word *conception* to mark the plurality and internal complexity of these objects of change, and to distinguish it from the term *concept* as used in normal discourse. The theory was meant to apply to concepts that play a generative or organizing role in thought. Thus we were interested in a phenomenon that is analogous to Kuhn's notion of a paradigm shift (Kuhn 1970) or Piaget's notion of an accommodation (Piaget 1950, 1952, 1971). A learner who is able to replace a Newtonian or Aristotelian view of motion with Einstein's has undergone the kind of conceptual change with which we were concerned. Someone who learns that it is raining outside or who learns that hot air rises, has not. This distinction holds even if the latter cases of learning involve the replacement of one belief or concept with another. Our theory of conceptual change concerns the alteration of conceptions that are in some way central and organizing in thought and learning. Most cases of altered belief do not count.

Thus it is important to note that we did not claim that all learning involves this form of conceptual change. Our model of conceptual change assumed that there are also cases of learning in which central concepts are not at issue. (See, for example, Peter Hewson's [1981] notion of "conceptual capture.") Moreover, any theory of learning that assumes that current conceptions are important in learning must, to be fully adequate, also provide an account of the sources of the learner's initial concepts. Since an infinite regress of prior conceptions seems unlikely, it must be the case either that there are some innate ideas or that some concepts can be acquired apart from there being prior conceptions. (See Garrison & Bentley 1989.) Our theory does not address this issue.

The answer we gave to our question about conceptual change (Strike & Posner 1982) was that much literature in philosophy of science suggests the following conditions for a successful conceptual change to take place:

1. *There must be dissatisfaction with current conceptions.* People do not alter concepts that play a central role in their thinking unless and until they see them as having become dysfunctional. Moreover, even when their current concepts are not performing well, they are likely to attempt to solve such problems as arise with more modest changes in their conceptual schemata unless it has become apparent that only a major overhaul of their concepts will repair the dysfunction. People do not accommodate while assimilation is still reasonable. Their concepts must be, in Kuhn's words, "awash in a sea of anomalies."

2. *A new conception must be intelligible.* Learners can begin to explore a new concept only if it makes minimal sense to them. One of the difficulties to overcome in bringing off a dramatic conceptual change is that a new conception is often not only counterintuitive, but incomprehensible (see Strike & Posner 1985) to those committed to the old conception. Learners do not understand what they mean and what the world would be like if they were true. Thus a new conception cannot become a candidate to replace some dysfunctional conception until learners are able to make some sense of it.

3. *A new conception must appear initially plausible.* To be a candidate for adoption, a new conception need not be seen as true, but it must at least appear as a candidate for the truth. Crucial factors in initial plausibility are a potential to solve or dissolve outstanding problems with current conceptions and consistency with other well-established beliefs.

4. *A new conception should suggest the possibility of a fruitful research program.* The new conception should do more than seem to have the potential to solve current problems. It must also suggest ways of approaching the world and open new avenues of inquiry. It must appear to have the potential to be a productive tool of thought.

These conditions assume that learning takes place in a conceptual context. Old conceptions and candidates for their replacement are understood and appraised by learners in terms of concepts they already possess. Following Toulmin (1972), we used an environmental concept to label this conceptual context, calling it a "conceptual ecology."

The conditions of conceptual change not only assume that there is a conceptual ecology but also provide some clues as to its composition. We suggested that a conceptual ecology consists of such cognitive artifacts as anomalies, analogies, metaphors, epistemological beliefs, metaphysical beliefs, knowledge from other areas of inquiry, and knowledge of competing conceptions. These aspects of a conceptual ecology are pedagogically interesting in two respects. First, they provide an inventory of the kinds of cognitive artifacts that learners are likely to possess and that must be taken into account by teachers. Such cognitive artifacts may be either assets or liabilities in instruction, depending on their capacity to promote or frustrate progressive conceptual change. Second, they suggest the kinds of things that teachers may provide in instruction in order to facilitate conceptual change.

In describing this view of conceptual change, we did not suppose that we were describing a detailed account of learning that could be immediately applied to the classroom. Instead we saw ourselves as describing the "hard core" of a research program (Lakatos 1970, 1976) that could be extended in profitable directions by further work. The various concepts in our description should be seen as variables that require concrete specification in particular instances of learning.

BACKGROUND COMMITMENTS

What are the intellectual motives for this theory? The first thing to notice is that this theory is largely an epistemological theory, not a psychological theory. It follows that it is also a normative theory. It is rooted in a conception of the kinds of things that count as *good* reasons. We believe that these features explain both some of the theory's strengths and some of its blind spots.

Several decades ago the boundaries between an epistemological theory and a psychological theory could have been easily stated. Epistemology sought to specify the logical parameters of rational belief. Its chief task was to specify criteria that enable us to distinguish true or reasonable beliefs from false or unreasonable ones. Its method was analytic and a priori. Formal logic was the basic tool. Psychology was concerned to discover the laws of learning. Its method was empirical and experimental. These enterprises at best seemed unrelated and often appeared antagonistic. (See Strike 1974.)

But much has changed. Philosophy has become more descriptive in its approach to rationality. It has been especially interested in the history of science. Cognitive psychology no longer seeks "laws of learning," at least not in the sense that this phrase would have been meant by a behaviorist. It, too, is interested in describing rationality, and it does not understand this task in a way that is radically different from how it would be understood by many philosophers. While differences in aspirations and approach remain, and while psychology retains a concern for the operation of "cognitive hardware" that is not a part of philosophy, epistemology and cognitive psychology now seem more complementary than competitive. (See Goldman 1986; Strike & Posner 1976.) Thus our task is not to stake out an approach that is competitive with cognitive psychology.

Currently to say that our theory has its roots in epistemology instead of psychology is largely to make a point about the kinds of literature and the aspirations that inform it. It also says something about what we perceive the dominant opposition theory to be. We have been substantially influenced by those theories of rationality that have been developed by authors such as Kuhn, Toulmin, and Lakatos. What these authors have in common, despite some notable differences, is a regard for the history of science and the practice of science as sources of information about the nature of rationality. They also exhibit a basic opposition to the empiricist tradition in epistemology as well as its manifestations in psychology.

Empiricists of various stripes have historically been committed to an account of rational belief that sees knowledge as grounded in uninterpreted experience to which it is attached by formal logic. Empiricists thus sought to characterize experience and to specify, using the tools of formal logic, how knowledge systems were derived from it or grounded in it (Brown 1977). More recent work in philosophy of science has emphasized the role of substantive belief in scientific reasoning and method. Scientific method cannot be characterized solely by formal logic. Instead, the approach to scientific problems is generated by substantive belief systems such as Kuhn's paradigms or Lakatos's research programs. These substantive conceptions suggest what are to count as problems and what is to count as relevant evidence. Indeed, they provide the perceptual categories by which the world is perceived.

It follows that an argument for a given scientific conception is never merely stated as a logical relationship between a set of theoretical claims and a set of unconceptualized observations. Instead, scientific arguments must be framed against the background of current conceptions. Thus, arguments are historically conditioned. What counts as evidence at a given period depends on what is currently believed. Descriptions of scientific method are similarly historically conditioned and must be formulated by historical and logical investigations.

Such accounts of rationality can be easily turned into accounts of rational learning suitable for pedagogical purposes. The major modifications required are to take into account the immaturity and novice standing of the learner and to deemphasize those aspects of the sociology of scientific communities that have figured in the philosophical theories of conceptual change. Novice learners have not been initiated into a scientific community with its current conceptions and commitments. Nor do the politics or social behavior of such communities figure in learning. Notwithstanding, novice learners do not approach learning as blank slates. They approach new ideas with prior conceptions that govern their interactions with them.

The epistemological theories that grounded our view of conceptual change are concerned to describe rational belief. Thus, our theory is normative at least to the extent that it is not equally interested in all sorts of belief acquisition. The philosophical tradition from which are viewpoint derives leads to a preferred standing given to the formation of rational belief. This concern for rational belief is thus a characteristic of our pedagogical application of the theory of conceptual change. However, for pedagogical purposes, a preoccupation with rational belief may generate blind spots. A preoccupation with rational belief, perhaps, may be taken for granted in scientific communities. There an account of what counts as a rational approach to learning something may go a long way toward explaining what scientists do. One should not uncritically assume that novices are likely to be rational in quite the same way.

A second influence on our views of conceptual change has been the voluminous literature on misconception that has emerged in the last fifteen years (Novak 1987; Helm & Novak 1983; Perkins & Simmons 1988). This literature suggests that learners do not approach the learning of science as blank slates. Instead, they come to school with already formed views on many scientific matters. These prior conceptions seem resistant to modification by instruction. Thus, effective pedagogy must take them into account.

This literature is easily assimilated to the theory of conceptual change. One must relate misconceptions to the kinds of conceptions dealt with by the theory of conceptual change. Thus, a misconception is not merely a mistake or a false belief. Either it must also play the kind of organizing role in cognition that paradigms play, or it must be dependent on such organizing concepts (Strike 1983). A misconception, thus, may become a candidate for change. The theory of conceptual change provides an account of how such change may be brought about.

The initial formulations of our work were significantly influenced by the misconceptions literature and our epistemological assumptions. One of the most important finding of the misconceptions literature (in addition to the fact that there are such things) is that misconceptions are highly resistant to change. (See, for example, Clement 1982, 1983.) The philosophical literature on conceptual change in science, especially Kuhn's work (1970), provides the rudiments of both an epistemological and a sociological account of why this might be so. The sociological account emphasizes the importance of a paradigm to individual careers and its connection to the authority structure of intellectual communities. For obvious reasons, this part of the account is of limited value in explaining the cognitive growth (or lack thereof) of students.

The epistemological account, however, provides a view of how paradigms are maintained that is readily applied to misconceptions. This account turns on how some concepts are connected to others, how they function in thought, and how they structure perception. Concepts are not isolated cognitive artifacts. They exist in semantic and syntactical relations with one another so that they are interdependent for their meaning and are not readily appraised in isolation. Thus, even if Kuhn is wrong concerning the extent to which those concepts that constitute a paradigm must stand or fall as a whole (Toulmin 1972), he provides good reasons to suppose that the reappraisal of one concept will require the reappraisal and modification of others. Likewise, he provides good reasons to suppose that some conceptions will be quite resistant to change, if they are embedded in a web of other concepts that lend them plausibility or intelligibility.

Concepts are also seen not only as objects of thought but as the tools of thought. Scientific method is not specified solely by formal logic. Instead, the approach to the investigation of scientific phenomena is generated by paradigms. They determine what questions are appropriate to ask and what is to count as evidence.

Finally, concepts function as perceptual categories. According to Kuhn, they structure perception in such a way that people who have different concepts live in different perceptual worlds (Kuhn 1970). Most significantly, people with different paradigms will not agree as to what constitutes relevant evidence for resolving their disagreement, nor will they perceive the evidence in the same way.

If one assumes that misconceptions are similar to paradigms, these views provide obvious reasons why misconceptions will be resistant to change, even given contrary instruction. When a misconception is firmly embedded in a conceptual context, the cost required for its revision is high. Students will have to alter other concepts as well. Moreover, unless these other concepts are altered, they will continue to maintain the misconception. Also, students are being asked to abandon a concept that has seemed to them to be successful in explaining a range of experience. Finally, misconceptions may have some built in "defense mechanisms." They may lead students to perceive the world in ways that are inconsistent with alternative concepts and that support the misconception. In effect, conceptions often come with their own *cognitive support group*. They will resist modification so long as this support group continues to play its role.

The link between our epistemological views and the misconceptions literature also suggests the type of explanation that is most appropriate in accounting for the origins of misconceptions. Some authors (e.g., McCloskey 1983) have argued that misconceptions are generated by misperceiving the world. It is as though explanations of events (even false ones) are on the surface of things in the sense that a given perception or misperception strongly points to a certain account of a phenomenon.

Our epistemological assumptions point to a different approach. Since we assume that explanations are not on the surface of things, we are more likely to seek explanations for misconceptions by looking for ways that misconceptions are generated and maintained by other concepts in a student's conceptual ecology. Moreover, the fact that students misperceive the world is seen as a phenomenon in need of an account. We do not deny that misperceptions may be implicated in the etiology of misconceptions. Indeed, the examples that follow suggest how this might be the case. However, we are suspicious of the assumption that there are perceptions that, in and of themselves, without conceptual mediation, suggest one kind of explanation over others. Instead, misperceptions are most plausibly viewed as a tendency to see the world in one way or another that results from something in the individual's conceptual ecology. An epistemology that emphasizes the central role that concepts play in mediating perception seems simply inconsistent, if it uncritically assumes that some conceptions are accounted for by unmediated perceptions.

These comments, of course, are consistent with a rather diverse range of accounts of the genesis of specific concepts. And they require a deeper explanation of the source of the various components of a student's conceptual ecology than we have given. Nevertheless, they suggest that accounts of misconception that emphasize misperception apart from some form of conceptual mediation are overly empiricist in their formulation.

Misconceptions thus play two crucial roles in the application of our general views of epistemology to pedagogy. First, they function to confirm the reasonableness of these views. It is far easier to explain the relevance of misconceptions given our epistemological views than it is on empiricist assumptions. On empiricist assumptions, it is not obvious why misconceptions are resistant to instruction and cannot be easily replaced merely by supplying students with a modest piece of empirical evidence.

Second, misconceptions provide a point of applicability for our theory. They are initial conceptions, the things that change in conceptual change. The existence of misconceptions guarantees the applicability of the theory to real problems of learning. Indeed, to put the point more forcefully, misconceptions provide a paradigm case of what the problem to be solved by a theory of conceptual change is. To some extent, the elaboration of our views that follows is a result of recognizing the ways in which this problem focus has limited our understanding and development of our theory.

We have dwelt on the connection between our epistemological assumptions and the misconceptions literature, because that connection is crucial for understanding the problem that our theory of conceptual change is intended to solve and the kind of solution preferred. The initial formulation of our theory is not a general theory of cognitive development. It is an attempt to suggest how concepts that have proven resistant to instruction might be altered. It assumes that these concepts have a certain character, that they are paradigm-like. Our theory is not grounded in any experimental evidence. Instead it points out those kinds of evidence that research in the philosophy and history of science has suggested are relevant to major conceptual revisions. This foundation, it should be noted again, gives the theory something of a normative character. Our theory of conceptual change is first and foremost an attempt to describe the kinds of evidence that are relevant to generating a major conceptual revision. Insofar as learning is or should be a rational activity, these kinds of evidence should have pedagogical relevance. They do not, however, describe the typical workings of student minds or any laws of learning. Nor do they predict any very specific learning outcomes. Mapping then onto actual cognitive processes is a further task.

At the same time, this theory of conceptual change is embedded in a set of epistemological assumptions that are far more generalizable than our application to misconceptions has exploited. These epistemological assumptions suggest that the basic problem of understanding cognitive development is to understand how the components of an individual's conceptual ecology interact and develop and how the conceptual ecology interacts with experience.

The generality of these background epistemological assumptions suggests the possibility of expanding the range of application of our views on conceptual change and, at the same time, of deepening our understanding of its details. What follows traces some of our thought along these lines. Thus, what follows is not merely an attempt to accommodate criticism. It is also an attempt to achieve and express a deeper understanding of our views and to state them in a more general way.

CRITIQUE

What problems does this view have? Let us emphasize at the outset that we see no reason to reject the basic epistemological commitments that we have articulated above. Nevertheless, their elaboration in our initial formulation of the theory of conceptual change contains several implicit assumptions that now seem to us to be questionable. We will discuss three.

1. In our original formulation we often talked as though misconceptions or prior conceptions are clearly articulated and expressly and symbolically formulated. Our theory is expressed as a view about how some conception, C_1, is transformed into a second conception, C_2. It is easy to assume that a theory of conceptual change applies only in cases where there is some clear case of a prior conception. What would count as a prior conception is a symbolically formulated view that functions as an alternative account of the phenomena that are thought to be best explained by C_2. This assumption no longer seems obvious to us. It is doubtful in two different respects.

    First, it seems entirely possible that misconceptions, especially those of younger or novice learners, exist in either iconic or enactive forms of representation (Bruner 1966). That is, people may not have beliefs about how something works so much as they have images of how it works or "body language" about how it works. These representations may function as a source of initial and incorrect "intuitions."

    Second, it may be that misconceptions do not exist in any form of representation as alternative formulations to preferred conceptions. Instead, misconceptions may exist as various factors in a conceptual ecology that function to select for or prefer some representation of a misconception when the opportunity to do so exists. This second point is complex. Let us elaborate.

Imagine some hypothetical learner, Fred, who is asked by a teacher or researcher to choose between two views of motion. Fred is asked about what happens when a force is applied to an object. He is given a choice between the view that the force is transferred to the object and erodes, resulting in the object gradually slowing and coming to rest, and the view that the application of the force to the object imparts some motion to the object that continues indefinitely until some other force is applies. Fred does not know, but he does have a store of recollections about moving objects. He is a baseball fan. So he inspects his images of moving baseballs. It seems to Fred that there are many cases where forces are applied to baseballs. The subsequent motion of the balls suggests that these forces are transferred to the balls, at which point the forces gradually begin to erode. This hypothesis seems compelling because Fred can detect no other forces being applies to the balls. Yet batted balls always come down eventually. Moreover, this initial intuitive understanding of forces may have been suggested to Fred by the "language games" that are often played with the concept of force in ordinary language. Fred may have learned to talk about force in a way that requires force to have an agent. Hitting balls with bats thus counts as applying force. Also, force-talk may be associated with fatigue. One's ability to apply force is limited by stamina. Or sometimes in ordinary speech force is associated with coercion. Normally, when people are coerced, they cease doing what they are coerced to do as soon as the coercion is withdrawn. Fred thus has ways of talking about force that lead to and reinforce a way of seeing. Fred thus decides that forces are transferred to objects and erode during motion.

Or consider Fred's sister Freddie. She is asked to choose between two views of heat (Hewson & Hamlyn, 1983). In one case, heat is viewed as a kind of fluid. In the second case, it is treated as a form of molecular motion. Freddie does not have any images of heat that seem decisive here. But she does have a way of talking about heat. She has some metaphors about heat that associate heat with human emotions and with devices that "move" heat (like "heat pumps"). These ways of talking about heat all seem to treat heat as something that flows. Freddie thus concludes that it is most reasonable to view heat as a fluid.

In neither of these cases does the individual involved have a prior misconception, if what one means by that is a symbolically formulated conception, C_1, that functions as a competitor for C_2. What Fred has are some ways of talking and some images of motion that provide a context for his judgments about motion. What Freddie has might be described as a verbal template, or schema, that prescribes some of the syntactical features that a properly formulated theory of heat must have. These aspects of a conceptual ecology are not physical conceptions or misconceptions, but, under proper conditions, they select for them or generate them. They may do so powerfully, so that misconceptions may seem highly plausible or compelling to learners, and scientific conceptions may seem implausible or counterintuitive.

In instructional or research situations the kinds of situations described above may easily lead teachers or researchers to believe that learners enter instruction with articulated misconceptions. In fact, the actual misconception may be generated on the spot as a consequence of instruction. The learner is given a problem to solve or some alternatives among which to choose. A misconception is produced to solve the problem at hand. This immediate generation of the misconception may cloud the fact that misconceptions are generated by other factors in the conceptual ecology.

It follows that what may be most important in instruction is understanding the factors in learners' conceptual ecologies that generate and maintain misconceptions. It is these factors that may account for both the durability of misconceptions and their commonalities across learners and even sometimes cultures. (See Eylon & Linn 1988.)

Two conclusions should be drawn. First, it is very likely wrong to assume that misconceptions are always there in developed or articulated form during science instruction. This conclusion may be wrong even in those cases where widespread misconceptions have been documented. Misconceptions may be weakly formed, need not be symbolically represented, and may not even be formed prior to instruction. Second, misconceptions have developmental histories. They are generated by something else in the conceptual ecology. It may be more important for instruction to understand what it is that produces them than it is to understand the character of the misconception itself.

This discussion suggests a further way that student's misconceptions may differ from the paradigms of scientists. While scientists' paradigms are supported by various things in their conceptual ecology, one may suppose that they have achieved a reasonably sophisticated degree of symbolic expression. This assumption need not be valid for students. This difference may turn out to be pedagogically important. Our initial formulation of a theory of conceptual change emphasized the importance of creating dissatisfaction with current conceptions. This emphasis may seem appropriate if one assumes that misconceptions are like paradigms, in that they exist in high articulated form and are supported by much current evidence and a history of successful use. Under such conditions they may need to be beaten into submission by contrary evidence.

However, if a misconception is weakly conceptualized and tends to be preferred by the learner because of something in the student's conceptual ecology, such as a misleading metaphor or way of talking, strategies that focus on rooting out those pieces of a conceptual ecology that generate the misconception and replacing them with more felicitous concepts may be more appropriate. Perhaps we need to replace a misleading metaphor with a better one or to suggest different ways of seeing familiar events. What needs to happen will depend on how the learner's misconception is embedded in the conceptual ecology. Trying to drown a students misconception into a "sea of anomalies" may not be the best strategy when the misconception is weakly conceptualized.

This leads to a way of viewing our theory of conceptual change. We had never viewed teaching for conceptual change as something for which effective teaching routines could be developed. The steps of a conceptual change that we outline were seen by us as an inventory of the kinds of evidence that are appropriate when a major conceptual revision seems required. This inquiry reinforces this interpretation. The point is not to execute the steps as though they were some form of magic ritual that would lead to success if correctly executed. Instead, one needs to discover the features of a student's conceptual ecology, find the trouble point, and introduce into the student's experience something that is appropriate. For the novice or the immature student, a strategy that is attentive to the student's collections of metaphors or that addresses how ordinary language analogues of scientific terms structure perception may be more important than a frontal assault on the misconception.

To put this point a different way, our theory can be stated in a more general form by emphasizing that what it centrally requires is a focus on the learner's conceptual ecology and how that ecology structures learning. Our views on accommodation are a special case of this, and even here our views are best understood as a statement of the kinds of features of a conceptual ecology that are likely to prove relevant to the problem, rather than as a set of steps to be uncritically executed whenever an accommodation is required.

2. A second assumption that seems implicit in the way in which we have talked about conceptual change is that conceptions or misconceptions are acted on by the conceptual ecology, but are not themselves part of it. While we do recognize that conceptions or misconceptions play a generative role in learners' thought (like that played

by paradigms or the hard core of a research program), our initial theory of conceptual change generally sees conceptions or misconceptions as cognitive objects that are affected by a learner's conceptual ecology, but does not much attend to the ways in which conceptions or misconceptions interact with that ecology.

This assumption may be unfortunate in at least two respects. First, it may lead to being inattentive to the ways in which current conceptions or misconceptions function to influence new perceptions or new ideas. Our conceptions provide perceptual categories. We are inclined to perceive the world in ways that are consistent with our current conceptions. Misconception may, therefore, mask, or lead to the misinterpretation of, counter examples (Perkins & Simmons 1988). Or counter examples may simply not be attended to.

Moreover, misconceptions may interact with current features of a conceptual ecology. Let us imagine a teacher who is trying to get a learner who is convinced of scientific creationism to at least consider the theory of evolution. The teacher proceeds to attempt to generate some anomalies by pointing out to the learner that if the universe were only 6,000 or so years old, the light from all but the nearest stars would not yet be visible. Here the teacher assumes that the learner already believes that the universe is quite large and that the speed of light is finite. If the learner in fact has all these beliefs and can perform the required inferences, the learner will be trapped in a contradiction. But the nature of the response is still open. The learner may come to take the current scientific view of the age of the universe more seriously. Other options are possible. The learner may reject the facts that contradict the belief in a recent creation. Or the learner may become metaphysically or epistemologically inventive. Perhaps the learner will believe that God created the light from distant stars already in transit. Or perhaps he or she will believe that religion and science deal with different spheres of knowledge and that the apparent conflict between religious convictions and current science is not real. The possibilities are numerous.

What this example suggests is that scientific conceptions and misconceptions are also part of a conceptual ecology and that all the parts of a conceptual ecology must be seen as dynamic and in constant interaction and development. While it may be useful from time to time to look at the effects of one part of the conceptual ecology on another and thus differentiate between what acts and what is acted upon, such strategies must be seen as simplifications. They are ultimately misleading if their status as simplifications is not recognized.

3. A third difficulty with our initial formulation of the theory of conceptual change is our tendency to see it as overly rational. This tendency leads to an understatement of the range of factors that might function as part of a conceptual ecology. Our list of factors of a conceptual ecology that were held to function in facilitating a transfer from C_1 ro C_2 were those that seemed to us to be logically relevant to appraising the worth of two competing scientific conceptions. We do not represent ourselves as providing an exhaustive list of such factors, but we do assume that what is going on in the classroom is that learners and teachers are conducting a rational appraisal of competing scientific conceptions. (This, perhaps, is a significant weakness on relying heavily on philosophy of science as a source of models of rationality.) Clearly, for learners, what we assume about classroom events is not all that is going on. For some learners, it may not be what is going on at all. The problem to be solved in the classroom for some learners is that of discovering how to get a good grade. For others the problem may be discovering how to maintain a sense of self-worth in the face of a subject matter that is unintelligible. Or students may conceptualize the task as a piece of academic work instead of a scientific inquiry (Doyle 1983). There are many possibilities.

Students may very well approach these classroom problems rationally, but they will not, as a consequence, be engaging in a rational appraisal of a scientific conception. Thus, learners for whom the paramount concern in the class is not the solution of the scientific problem being posed by the teacher may very well elect responses that are rational from the point of view of the learner's problem, but that are irrational from the perspective of solving the scientific problem. Consider again two hypothetical possibilities.

John is taking physics. He is not doing well. He generally does not understand what is said in class, and he is very concerned about his grade. He responds to this situation by becoming a rote learner. He spends much time memorizing formulas. As a consequence, he is able to do better on tests, but he understands very little of what he is learning.

Jean is also doing poorly in physics. For her the real problem, however, is not so much her grade as it is her self-esteem. She has always thought of herself as a good learner. She is very frustrated by the fact that she finds it difficult to understand what she is learning and that additional effort is not rewarded. Her response is to begin to devalue the subject matter, and her way of doing this is to lapse into relativism. Physics, she tells herself, is only one way among many of looking at the world. Its views have no special truth that make them worth knowing. Perhaps they help some people to make better widgets, but for someone who is not interested in a technical career, there is little reason to be concerned about it. After all, one interpretation of reality is as good as another.

These stories suggest three things. First, the problem the learner is solving in a classroom may often not be the scientific problem. Second, it is necessary to include motivational variables and views as to the nature and value of a subject matter in an account of a conceptual ecology. And third, such variables can affect the approach taken to a subject, the manner in which it is represented, and the conception of the subject matter developed. These effects, in turn, may be expected to further influence learning. John, for example, is solving a problem about grades. He is motivated not so much by a desire to understand physics as he is by a desire to do well in it. This leads him to a learning strategy that emphasizes rote learning. It is reasonable to suppose that this strategy and the kind of representations of physical knowledge that result will affect further learning and the perception of physics. That John does not understand what he learns will preclude using what he learns to judge other ideas, because that use of physics concepts requires their comprehension. John may be led to a perception of physics as merely an aggregation of apparently arbitrary facts. These disabilities may, in turn, reinforce his dependence on rote learning.

These various criticisms of our initial formulation of the theory of conceptual change suggest five specific conclusions about modifications required. These are as follows:

1. A wider range of factors needs to be taken into account in attempting to describe a learner's conceptual ecology. Motives and goals and the institutional and social sources of them need to be considered. The idea of a conceptual ecology thus needs to be larger than the epistemological factors suggested by the history and philosophy of science.
2. Current scientific conceptions and misconceptions are not only objects on which a learner's conceptual ecology acts, they are themselves parts of the learner's conceptual ecology. Thus they must be seen in interaction with other components.
3. Conceptions and misconceptions can exist in different modes of representation and different degrees of articulateness. They may not exist at all but may easily appear to do so, because under instruction or in research they are generated by other elements of a conceptual ecology.

4. A developmental view of conceptual ecologies is required.
5. An interactionist view of conceptual ecologies is required.

It is these last two points that seem to us to be most important. In the study of conceptual change, we need to note that all the elements have developmental histories and that these histories cannot be understood apart from their interaction with other elements in the learner's conceptual ecology. Our view of conceptual change must therefore be more dynamic and developmental, emphasizing the shifting patterns of mutual influence between the various components of an evolving conceptual ecology. We must say with Heraclitus that all is in flux. In conceptual change theory, it is difficult to step into the same conceptual ecology twice.

EMPIRICAL SUPPORT

These philosophical assertions about conceptual change receive at least indirect support from some of our recent empirical work. Only those results that are relevant to an interactionist view of conceptual change will be presented. Moreover, what follows is not intended as a detailed account of our empirical work. It is, rather, a sketch that should give the reader the feel of our thinking.

Our empirical work on conceptual change was motivated by a desire to understand in more detail the way in which a learner's epistemological views interact with physics learning. We began by developing a questionnaire that allowed students to express their views on a variety of epistemological questions. Our subjects for most of the developmental phase of this questionnaire were college students, most of whom had taken at least two semesters of college physics. Our questionnaire also included a few qualitative physics questions. Early on, we observed that responses to a few of the epistemological questions seemed to be associated with getting the answers to the physics questions right. Our development of the instrument after this was designed to exploit this lead. We developed more epistemological questions of the sort that seemed associated with success in physics and more qualitative physics items. At a later stage in the development of our thinking, as we began to see the need to look at other aspects of a conceptual ecology, we began to add items that dealt with views of the subject matter, motivation, or learning style. These we have called "learning-attitude" items. Figure 5-1 gives a few examples of each type of item.

Our work with college students continued to support the view

Figure 5-1
Sample Items from "Ideas of Science" Questionnaire

PART I. EPISTEMOLOGICAL ITEMS

Please indicate how much you agree or disagree with each of the following statements.

1. Every culture has its own kind of science. Just because some other culture's science is different from ours does not mean that the science of that culture is less valid.

2. Since scientific theories are creations of the human mind, they do not necessarily describe things the way they really are.

3. Recent debates among science historians have produced two views on how science has changed. Which of these views is closest to your own? (Circle one.)

    (a) <u>View A</u> holds that science changes as a result of the failure of current theory to solve important scientific problems. Old theories are rejected and replaced by new ones, which often have different assumptions.

    (b) <u>View B</u> holds that science changes as a result of the accumulation of new facts and observations and the refinement of generalizations based on them. New theories tend to be expansions or refinements of old theories.

PART II. PHYSICS ITEMS

<u>Rocket Problem</u>: A rocket is moving sideways in deep space, with its engine off, from point A to point B. It is not near any planets or other outside forces. Its engine is fired at point B and left on for two seconds while the rocket travels from point B to some point C. In other words, the engine is turned on at B and off at C. The illustration below shows the rocket path until the engine is turned off at C.

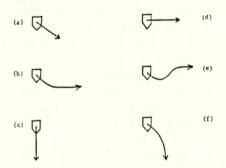

<u>Rocket Problem</u> Which drawing below represents your best guess of the rocket path <u>after</u> point C (when the rocket engine is turned off)? (Circle one.)

<u>Skylab Problem</u>: Two astronauts are working in Skylab while orbiting the Earth. In orbiting satellites such as Skylab, objects and people float around, and we say they are "weightless."

A. In this situation, what is the force of gravity on the astronauts? (Circle one.)

    (a) Close to zero.
    (b) Close to what it is on Earth.

Figure 5-1 (continued)

B. Which of the following explanations best represents your reason for choosing the answer you did? (Circle one.)

    (a)   There is little or no gravity at this distance from the earth.
    (b)   There is no gravity beyond the earth's atmosphere.
    (c)   A weightless state means there is no gravity.
    (d)   An orbiting satellite is still within the earth's gravitational field.
    (e)   Other (Please specify.)_____

PART III. LEARNING-ATTITUDE ITEMS

Please indicate how often the following statements have been true for you in science classes.

1. I try to relate what I learn in science class to what I learn in other classes.
2. I can remember facts and details, but I don't know how to fit them together into an overall picture.
3. I can usually remember formulas, but without class notes or the textbook, I am not sure which formula to use in a particular problem.

For the next few items, we would like you to indicate how much you agree or disagree with each item.

4. I tend to do my science homework very carefully and thoroughly.
5. I want to learn physics mainly because it helps me to understand the world in which I live.

that there was a relationship between epistemological conceptions and physics learning. We began to develop a more refined view of the kinds of responses that seemed associated with success on our physics items. The kinds of items that were predictive of physics performance seemed generally linked to the view that physics gave us reliable and objective knowledge of the real world. Students who did well in physics were more inclined to be realists about physics, to demand consistency in their beliefs, to be empiricists in their views of scientific method, and to reject cultural relativism about physics. While correlations between the various items we developed to measure these attitudes and scores on physics items were generally significant, they were, for the most part, low. However, in aggregate, they were both significant and large enough to be interesting.

Given the above patterns, we hypothesized three possible relationships between these variables. One possibility is that a student's epistemological views and attitudes affect the learning of physics. The second is that a student's competence in physics affects epistemological conceptions and attitudes. Finally, all three variables might be a product of some third thing such as general intelligence.

Our next step was to try to distinguish between these possibilities by using the questionnaire as both a pre- and a post-test. We also decided to use high school physics students as our sample in order to investigate these variables at an earlier point in their development. We administered the questionnaire twice to 236 high school students enrolled in physics classes of six different teachers in Ithaca, New York, and Madison, Wisconsin, and their surrounding areas. The first testing took place in September, 1986, and the second occurred in May, 1987.

The initial analyses of results were disappointing. Correlations among various epistemological items and between epistemological items and physics items were generally low and not statistically significant. Aggregating them in various ways helped little. Certainly there were no ascertainable patterns of much interest. (The initial analysis of the learning-attitude items produced larger numbers, but hardly led to profound conclusions.) It seemed that the conclusions that were best warranted by these initial results were that students had hardly begun to formulate epistemological views on the topics we were asking about and that such views as they had had little connection with their physics competence.

These rather gloomy results changed somewhat when we began to look at directions of change among items. Our procedure here was as follows. The epistemological scale was constructed by factor analyzing the data on the epistemological items. One unambiguous factor (EFac) was identified. EFac represents a view of science as logical, concrete, and about the real world. We interpret this factor as representing an assumption that the universe is a rational place and that one can figure it out empirically; that is, this factor represents a realist and empiricist set of beliefs. A student's EFac score was compiled by adding the scores that student earned on each of the eight items that loaded most heavily on EFac.

An analogous procedure was followed for the learning-attitude items. This procedure also yielded one unambiguous factor (LFac). We interpreted this factor to represent students' confidence in their ability to learn science meaningfully. Specifically, students scoring high on items loading heavily on LFac felt capable of getting a sense of the overall picture of the content, knowing which formulas to use in particular problems, and remembering the course material after the test was over. Interestingly, items signifying diligence, compliance, and a lack of intrinsic motivation also loaded heavily on this factor. For example, students who scored high on items associated with LFac claimed that they avoid trying to solve problems in novel ways and refrain from extra reading on a topic so as not to be confused. Interestingly, one item signifying a desire to avoid extra reading in order to avoid confusion also loaded heavily on LFac. As with the epistemological scale, students' scores on the learning-attitude scale was computed by adding their scores on each of the eight items loading most heavily on LFac. Following this we computed gain scores for each of the three scales by subtracting scores on the pre-test from those on the post-test. Finally, we looked at the relationships between gain scores on the three scales. Table 5-1 presents our results.

Here there are results that are both statistically significant and, if not huge, are at least large enough to be of interest. Our measure of gain on the epistemological factor correlates with the measure of gain on the physics items at a level of .220. The gain scores for the learning-attitude items correlate with the physics gain scores at .215.

A further analysis enhanced these results. We constructed additional scales based on each of our three gain scales by using those items that had changed the most from pre- to post-test. (About half of the items from each scale were used.) This procedure allowed us to look more closely at the characteristics of the changes that seemed to be taking place. The procedure resulted in a modest increase in each correlation. The correlation between the epistemological and physics items became .304 (from .220) and that between the learning-attitude items and the physics items became .236 (from .215).

We interpret these results as consistent with an interactive model of conceptual change. None of the three possibilities that we originally identified as potential accounts of the connection between the epistemological and the physics items in college students receive much support from our analysis. We believe that the reason for this is that the epistemological beliefs of high school students are only beginning to form. High school students are unlikely to have given a great deal of thought to epistemological issue such as the relativity of truth, the ways in which scientific knowledge grows and changes, and the relation between scientific theory and everyday experience. Thus the character of students' epistemological beliefs explains and is explained by little. On the other hand, there is a modest, but noteworthy, tendency for there to be a relationship between the direction of change in the epistemological items and increases in physics competence. What this suggests is an interaction between the development of physical conceptions and epistemological ones. Indeed, what is suggested is that the growth of physical knowledge both facilitates and is facilitated by the changes in epistemological beliefs.

We would draw the same conclusion for the relationship between the learning-attitude items and the physics items. While, unlike our epistemological items, there is a significant relationship between scores on certain learning-attitude items and performance on the physics

Table 5-1
Intercorrelations of Factors and Gains

	LFac	LPFac	LFacGain	EFac	EPFac	EFacGain	PScale	PPScale	PGain
LFac	1.0								
LPFac	.563	1.0							
LFacGain	-.393*	.539	1.0						
EFac	.018	-.042	-.065	1.0					
EPFac	-.096	-.067	.023	.449*	1.0				
EFacGain	-.075	-.023	.162*	-.408*	.313	1.0			
PScale	.330*	.258*	-.049	.180*	.081	-.174*	1.0		
PPScale	.327*	.457*	.175*	-.084	-.029	.087	.394*	1.0	
PGain	.084	.271*	.215*	-.221*	.031	.220	-.352*	.722*	1.0

Key:
LFac: Learning-attitude scale pre-test scores
LPFac: Learning-attitude scale post-test scores
LFacGain: Learning-attitude scale gain scores
EFac: Epistemological scale pre-test scores
EPFac: Epistemological scale post-test scores
EFacGain: Epistemological scale gain scores
PScale: Physics scale pre-test scores
PPScale: Physics scale post-test scores
PGain: Physics scale gain scores
*Significant at the .05 level

items, we believe for both empirical and theoretical reasons that an interactionist account is still the best one.[1] Perhaps the difference is that students are farther along in forming those attitudes measured by our learning-attitude items than they are in forming epistemological beliefs. For our learning-attitude items, we have entered in the middle of a story. For the epistemological beliefs, we are closer to the beginning.

What is the character of these interactions? Our results suggest the following. On the epistemological side they show that a belief that the physical world is rational and a rejection of epistemological relativism both support and are supported by a growth in physics competence. On the side of our learning-attitude items, they suggest that having confidence in one's ability to understand physics, approaching learning as a matter of understanding the material instead of learning it by rote, and valuing learning science for its own sake tend to facilitate and are facilitated by growth in physics competence.

Two final comments on the import of these conclusions: In an article in *The Review of Educational Research*, Perkins and Simmons (1988) discuss the theory of conceptual change generally and touch on our work at several points. Some of their conclusions are quite consonant with ours. Their discussion of different views about the status of formal systems of rules such as algebra (p. 307) supports our view that seeing the world as rational and intelligible facilitates learning and is inconsistent with rote learning. Moreover, they argue persuasively (against our initial formulation) for a more interactionist view of conceptual change and for a view of a conceptual ecology that has more aspects than those we list. (They list four "frame factors" that are part of a conceptual ecology that they call the "content frame," the "epistemic frame," the "inquiry frame," and the "problem-solving frame.")

We agree with most of what they have to say, including their criticisms of our initial formulation. Moreover, their comments have helped us formulate our own views and have suggested to us the label "interactionist" as preferable to the label "dialectical," to which we had first inclined. However, one of their final observations requires comment. They write, "Conceptual change theory does not appear to include a position on the importance of explicit instruction involving the epistemic and inquiry frames" (Perkins & Simmons 1988, p. 322). In one respect this is correct. Our theory, in both of its incarnations, sheds little light on the argument between advocates of direct instruction and the advocates of discovery learning.

We are not, however, inclined to see this as a defect of our theory. As we have noted repeatedly, our theory is fundamentally a theory about the kinds of evidence that function in a rational appraisal of various ideas. Obviously it is reasonable to conclude that we believe that processes such as reasoning, persuasion, and inquiry are central to instruction. We should again emphasize that we believe this for reasons that are as much normative as they are empirical. Rational belief is preferable. Such claims, however, become arguments for discovery learning (where discovery learning is seen as the opposite of direct instruction) only if one assumes that evidence for or against various ideas cannot be communicated verbally. We see no reason to make any such general assumption. Indeed, it seems obvious to the point of requiring no argument, that a great deal of inquiry involves much talk. Explaining, arguing, constructing metaphors, giving counter examples, and the like express the social character of rationality. Views that assume that people are being rational only when they discover things for themselves (where discovering is somehow juxtaposed to being told about) strike us as so wrongheaded as to require some inquiry into why people should believe them. Perhaps they result from "constructivist" epistemologies that have forgotten the social character of knowledge and that assume that people do not understand any conceptions that they have not constructed for themselves. (See Strike 1987.) Or perhaps they result from an unfortunate tendency to identify verbal instruction or direct instruction with indoctrination.

Of course it may be that discovery learning has an important role to play in effective instruction. We do not seek to prejudge this issue. Our point is that our view is grounded in an inquiry about what counts as relevant evidence for conceptual change. It is quite neutral as to the way in which this evidence is represented or presented to students. Almost every modern epistemology is likely to see scientific inquiry as involving a mix of observation and discourse. It would be hard to take an epistemology seriously if it excluded either component. A pedagogy that is dominated by epistemological considerations is likely to involve a similar mix. At the same time, it is important to be clear that our view is not neutral about the social character of knowledge. While scientific concepts may be human constructions, they are predominately social constructions into which the young are initiated. No account of learning or of conceptual innovation that misses the fact that conceptions (and misconceptions) are parts of "forms of life" (Wittgenstein 1953) into which human beings are initiated is likely to be reasonable.

While our theory is neutral between direct instruction and discovery learning, it has a great deal to say about the conditions under which direct instruction (indeed, any form of instruction) can be intelligible (Strike & Posner 1985). Verbal messages that are at odds with the learner's conceptual ecology are quite likely to be ignored, disbelieved, or misconstrued. Thus, occasional epistemological sermons (or courses in philosophy of science) should not be expected to enhance a student's conception of science as a rational activity if the student's prior experience and current outlook are at odds with them.

What in our judgment seems principally required by our theory is for teachers to teach science as though the world were a rational and intelligible place. Perhaps it would be better to say that they should teach science so that students can see that it is a rational and intelligible place. There is much to be said for the place of showing in pedagogy. The Johns and Jeans among our high school population are, after all, responding not just to physics but to their physics instruction and to the emotional and social requirements of schools and classrooms. Perhaps what conceptual change theory requires is fewer teachers who emphasize calculating the right answer in their tests and instruction, and more teachers who emphasize the connections between physical conceptions, experimental evidence, and students' current conceptual ecology. If conceptual change theory suggests anything about instruction, it is that the handles to effective instruction are to be found in persistent attention to the argument and in less attention to right answers. Better to act as though the world is rational than to produce homilies on the theme. Perhaps debates about direct instruction versus discovery learning miss the central point. It may be that what is crucial is for teachers to function as models of rational inquirers and for them to exhibit the practices and values of inquiry in their teaching. Effective modeling, no doubt, will involve both direct instruction and discovery learning. Indeed, since scientific inquiry involves both observation and discourse, this borders on the self-evident.

One final caveat: One should be cautious about moving too quickly from the premise that some set of epistemological views or attitudes about learning facilitates the learning of science, to a conclusion that these views or attitudes are true and should be promoted. The reason is that an empirical connection between an epistemological view or some attitude toward learning and efficient science learning does not guarantee the truth, reasonableness, or desirability of these views or attitudes. It is entirely possible that false beliefs can have desirable consequences. Thus the claim that a belief has desirable consequences is not logically relevant to establishing the reasonableness of what is believed. Independent reasons must be given. The matter is especially complex for values and attitudes. We must be especially cautious in treating any empirical connection between attitudes or values and learning as a sufficient reason to promote these values and attitudes in schools. Here too, independent reasons for the appropriateness or desirability of these attitudes and values are required. While, in the case at hand, we believe that it is possible to provide independent reasons for many of the epistemological believes and attitudes about learning that are associated with physics competence (here, at least the world is not perverse), we also must insist that the case for promoting such beliefs and attitudes depends as much on providing such reasons as it does on any empirical associations with good learning outcomes.

IMPLEMENTATION AND RESEARCH

In order to avoid misinterpreting our work it is crucial that the reader understand that we see ourselves as attempting to describe the features of a research program into teaching and learning science. Research programs suggest directions for further inquiry, and they articulate basic assumptions to keep in mind in such enterprises as devising pedagogical strategies or creating curricula. At the same time, we have said little that can, without further elaboration, be directly applied to instruction. We have always regarded attempts to turn our four components of conceptual change into four steps of instruction as misinterpretations of our intent. Any such construction of the work of this paper is similarly misguided. Much as we would like to specify some direct implications for instruction, we do not believe that our work has such direct implications. This is not to say that it lacks implications for how one approaches problems of developing instructional strategies and resources. Some of these are sketched below.

The implications of this paper for research and development can be sketched under two topics. The first concerns the theoretical articulation of the details of the research program. The second concerns the kinds of work that are required in order to bridge the gap between the research program and the classroom setting.

Concerning the theoretical articulation of the research program, we see the need for work of two sorts.

1. *Articulation with other supportive viewpoints.* As we have noted, the approach in this paper seems consonant with other approaches to teaching and learning, especially with various cognitive approaches. At the same time, the apparent convergence between various conceptual traditions should not lead us to an uncritical view of their essential compatibility. Epistemological approaches and those of cognitive psychology and cognitive science represent different traditions. Their dominant problems are different, their vocabularies are

different, and their investigatory approaches are different. Careful investigation of the meaning of these differences is required. It will be difficult because of differences in vocabulary. In what ways, for example, are schema like paradigms? Are such differences as may exist between the concepts of different traditions merely difference of terminology where translations between these vocabularies should be easy and not risk loss of meaning, or are there subtle incommensurabilities between various "converging" traditions? Such questions require careful analysis, but might prove quite illuminating. (See Duschl, Hamilton & Grandy this volume.)

2. *A view of boundary conditions is required.* We have claimed that our theory is not properly regarded as a complete theory of cognitive learning. It has a normative character to it, and it must be supplemented by some account of initial conceptions. If so, some fuller account of how our theory of conceptual change relates with other views of learning is required. What exactly are the boundaries of the theory? What facts should it account for, and what facts are appropriately beyond its reach?

For instructional purposes the crucial line of inquiry is to describe the conceptual ecologies that interact with instruction, to understand how they interact, and to devise instructional strategies that interact in productive ways with the students current concepts. Our work has always been intended primarily to illuminate these questions. The work of this paper suggests three lines of inquiry that might not have been evident from our prior work.

1. *There is a need for investigation of the sources of misconceptions prior to classroom instruction.* We are impressed with how much work on misconceptions is based on work with students in classroom settings. Such work is no doubt revealing about how students currently think about various scientific matters. It is less clear that such work fully reveals the features of the conceptual ecology that support or generate misconceptions. If instruction is to be responsive to the features of students' conceptual ecologies, it may be important to develop fuller histories of their development. This may require research that goes beyond the classroom site and investigates how concepts are acquired in early childhood.

2. *There is need to expand the account of a conceptual ecology.* Our initial theory developed the idea of a conceptual ecology by emphasizing accounts of rationality found in philosophy of science. This account needs to be expanded to consider the attitudes that novices have

toward the nature of science and scientific inquiry and to include the learner's perceptions of the classroom task. No doubt a much expanded account of the factors that form the student's "problem space" will eventually be required.

3. *An account of how the student comes to see the world as a rational place is needed.* Our work suggests an interaction between success in learning physics and coming to see the world as a rational place. Even if this result does not hold up under further empirical investigation, there are nevertheless good reasons why seeing the world as a rational place is a desirable educational outcome. Work that tries to understand exactly what this might mean and how it occurs seems especially important to a theory of conceptual change.

NOTES

1. The correlation between certain learning-attitude items on the pre-test and the physics score on the post-test is .327. The correlation between the same learning score and the physics gain score is .084. The correlation between the post-test learning-attitude items and the post-test physics score is .457. The correlation between the post-test learning-attitude items and the physics gain score is .271. Two conclusions are suggested. First, while attitudes toward learning are notably correlated with physics performance, they explain little of the gain from pre- to post-test. Second, both the increase in correlations from pre- to post-test and the correlation between the learning-attitudes gain score and the physics gain score are suggestive of our interactionist interpretation.

REFERENCES

Brown, H. I. (1977). *Perception, theory and commitment.* Chicago: University of Chicago Press.

Bruner, J. S. (1966). *Toward a theory of instruction.* Cambridge, MA: Harvard University Press.

Carey, S. (1986). Cognitive science and science education, *American Psychologist, 41,* 1123-30.

Carey, S. (1985). *Conceptual change in childhood.* Cambridge, MA: MIT Press.

Clement, J. (1983). A conceptual model discussed by Galileo and used intuitively by physics students. In D. Gentner & A. L. Stevens (Eds.), *Mental models.* Hillsdale, NJ: Lawrence Erlbaum.

Clement, J. (1982). Students' preconceptions in introductory mechanics. *American Journal of Physics, 50,* 66-71.

Doyle, Walter. (1983). Academic work. *Review of Educational Research, 53*(2), 159-99.

Eylon, Bat-Sheva, & Linn, Marcia C. (1988). Learning and instruction: An examination of four research perspectives in science education. *Review of Educational Research, 58*(3), 251-301.

Garrison, J. W., & Bentley, M. L. (1989). Science education, conceptual change and breaking with everyday experience. *Studies in Philosophy and Education, 10*(1), 19-35.

Gilbert, J. K., & Swift, D. J. (1985). Towards a Lakotosian analysis of the Piagetian and alternative conceptions research programs. *Science Education, 69*(5), 681-96.

Goldman, A. I. (1986). *Epistemology and cognition.* Cambridge, MA: Harvard University Press.

Gunstone, R. F., White, R. T., & Fensham, P. J. (1988). Developments in style and purpose of research on the learning of Science. *Journal of Research in Science Teaching, 25*(7), 513-29.

Helm, Hugh, & Novak, Joseph D. (Eds.). (1983). *Proceedings of the International Seminar on Misconceptions in Science and Mathematics.* Ithaca, NY: Cornell University, Department of Education.

Hewson, M. G., & Hamlyn, D. (1983, April). The influence of intellectual environment on conceptions of heat. Paper presented at the Annual Meeting of the American Educational Research Association, Montreal.

Hewson, P. W. (1981). A Conceptual Change Approach to Learning Science, *European Journal of Science Education, 3*(4), 383-96.

Kuhn, T. S. (1970). *The structure of scientific revolution* (2nd ed.). Chicago: University of Chicago Press.

Lakatos, Imre. (1976). *Proofs and refutations: The logic of mathematical discovery.* New York: Cambridge University Press.

Lakatos, Imre. (1970). Falsification and the methodology of scientific research programs. In I. Lakatos and A. Musgrave (Eds.), *Criticism and the growth of knowledge* (pp. 91-196). New York: Cambridge University Press.

McCloskey, M. (1983). Naive theories of motion. In D. Gentner & A. Stevens (Eds.), *Mental models.* Hillsdale, NJ: Lawrence Erlbaum.

Novak, Joseph D. (Ed.). (1987). *Proceedings of the Second International Seminar on Misconceptions and Educational Strategies in Science and Mathematics.* Ithaca, NY: Cornell University, Department of Education.

Perkins, D. N., & Simmons, Rebecca (1988). Patterns of misunderstanding: An integrative model for science, math, and programming. *Review of Educational Research, 58*(3), 303-26.

Piaget, J. (1971). *Biology and knowledge.* (B. Walsh, Trans.). Chicago: University of Chicago Press. (Original work published in 1967).

Piaget, J. (1952). *The origins of intelligence in children.* (M. Cook, Trans.) New York: International Universities Press.

Piaget, J. (1950). *The psychology of intelligence.* (M. Piercy and D. Berlyne, Trans.). London: Routledge & Kegan Paul. (Original work published in 1947).

Pines, A. L., & West, L. H. T. (1986). Conceptual understanding and science learning: An interpretation of research within a source-of-knowledge framework. *Science Education, 70*(5), 583-604.

Posner, George J., Strike, K. A., Hewson, P. W., & Gertzog, W. A. (1982). Accommodation of a scientific conception: Toward a theory of conceptual change. *Science Education, 66*(2), 211-27.

Strike, Kenneth A. (1987). Toward a Coherent Constructivism. In J. D. Novak (Ed.), *Proceedings of the Second International Seminar on Misconceptions and Educational Strategies in Science and Mathematics, Vol. 1* (481-89). Ithaca, NY: Cornell University, Department of Education.

Strike, K. A. (1983). Misconceptions and conceptual change: Philosophical reflection on the research program. In H. Helm and J. Novak (Eds.), *Proceedings of the International Seminar on Misconceptions in Science and Mathematics* (pp. 67-78). Ithaca, NY: Cornell University, Department of Education.

Strike, K. A. (1974). On the expressive potential of behaviorist language. *American Educational Research Journal, 11*(2), 103-20.

Strike, Kenneth A., & Posner, George J. (1985). A conceptual change view of learning and understanding. In Leo West and Leon Pines (Eds.), *Cognitive structure and conceptual change* (pp. 211-31). New York: Academic Press.

Strike, Kenneth A., & Posner, George J. (1982). Conceptual change and science teaching. *European Journal of Science Education, 4*(3), 231-40.

Strike, Kenneth A., & Posner, George J. (1976). Epistemological perspectives on conceptions of curriculum organization and learning. In Lee Schulman (Ed.), *Review of Research in Education, 4,* 106-41.

Toulmin, S. (1972). *Human understanding: An inquiry into the aims of science.* Princeton, NJ: Princeton University Press.

Vosnaidou, S., & Brewer, W. F. (1987). Theories of knowledge restructuring in development. *Review of Educational Research, 37*(1), 51-67.

Wittgenstein, L. (1953). *Philosophical investigations.* Oxford: Blackwell.

JEFFREY W. BLOOM

6

Contexts of Meaning and Conceptual Integration: How Children Understand and Learn

OUTLINE

I. Introduction
II. Theoretical background
III. Contexts of meaning
    A. Background to two sets of studies
    B. Typology of contexts of meaning
    C. Summary of contexts of meaning
IV. Discussion and implications

ABSTRACT

This chapter explores the contention that meaning as defined by epistemology and cognitive psychology does not capture the variety and richness of meanings derived from experience. These two disciplines describe meaning as being propositional or semantic in nature. The tension discussed in this chapter occurs between this sense of meaning and a different notion of meaning that emerges from data drawn from several recent studies on the perspectives of children. The notion of "contexts of meaning" suggests that meaning includes not only semantic knowledge but also episodic knowledge, the products of various mental processes, interpretive frameworks, and emotions, values and aesthetics. The result is a view of meaning that is dynamic, a view that can accommodate multiple perspectives and understandings.

Duschl, Hamilton and Grandy's (this volume) focus on the tensions between epistemology and cognitive psychology is a critically important issue that should be brought to the forefront of cognitive research and curriculum planning and implementation. The point I would like to explore in the present chapter is the issue of "meaning." The tension discussed in this chapter is one between current thinking about meaning in philosophy and psychology (i.e., meaning is propositional and semantic in nature) and the notion of meaning derived from data drawn from several recent studies on children's perspectives. Initially, I will provide a brief overview of the relevant research and how it relates to my view of the tension. This section will be followed by an examination of the data from my own research: "contexts of meaning." The final section will discuss the implications of contexts of meaning and the concomitant tension for educational research and curriculum development.

THEORETICAL BACKGROUND

Traditionally, epistemological concerns have served as the basis for designing curricula and instruction in science education. Formal knowledge or the knowledge of the discipline has determined not only what was to be taught but also how such instruction was to be delivered. According to Pines and West (1986) "formal knowledge . . . is a product of planned instruction, . . . is someone else's interpretation of the world, someone else's reality . . . [and] is approved by the consensus of adults who are usually older and more highly respected than the students" (p. 586). In other words, formal knowledge is the concern of epistemology. The intended outcome of instruction based on formal knowledge has been that students will learn what is taught in a form close to that of the structure of knowledge of the discipline.

According to Duschl, Hamilton, and Grandy (this volume), philosophers are concerned with formal knowledge, while cognitive psychologists are concerned with what and how individuals know. They see this as a fundamental tension, that is, what philosophers see as beliefs, psychologists see as knowledge. However, as suggested in the above paragraph, science education is concerned with how well individuals learn formal knowledge. When teachers, students, and curriculum come together, the tension between formal knowledge and cognition becomes confounding to the educational enterprise.

However, the tension is not simply between epistemology and cognitive psychology. The intent of curricula is the acquisition of formal knowledge. Such an intent appears to have confounded the way psychologists view cognition. Since the supposition is that children will learn formal knowledge, psychologists go about the task of investigating how children learn formal knowledge. The cognitive psychologist's task becomes one of comparing formal knowledge structures to what children "know." The focus of such research is on the formal or semantic knowledge of children. With the advent of constructivism, psychologists and other researchers interested in children's learning have begun to appreciate that children construct their own versions of knowledge. However, the dominant view is still one of seeing children's learning as acquiring formal semantic knowledge. The influence of the highly organized and semantic characteristics of formal knowledge from the philosopher's view has carried over to the way children's personal knowledge is represented. Evidence of this influence can be seen in the work of numerous researchers in psychology and science education (Champagne & Klopfer 1984; Driver & Bell 1986; Finley & Stewart 1982; Gilbert, Osborne & Fensham, 1982; Hills 1989; Kiel 1989; Markman 1989; Novak 1987; Pope & Gilbert 1983; White 1988).

The conflict or tension becomes one between "meaning" according to the presuppositions arising out of epistemology and what actually constitutes meaning for children. The view of what is meaningful to children comes from the perspective of formal knowledge structures. Such a perspective is evident in Ausubel's (1963) classic work and has been reiterated more recently by Novak (1987), who suggests that human constructivism

> . . . is an effort to integrate the psychology of human learning and the epistemology of knowledge production . . . [by placing] emphasis on the idea that in both psychology and epistemology we should focus on the process of *meaning making* that involves acquisition or modification of concepts and concept relationships. (p. 356)

Both Ausubel and Novak make an explicit connection between formal knowledge structures and meaningful learning. Meaning, from such a perspective, is based on formal knowledge.

The notion of "meaning" from both a disciplinary and an information processing psychology point of view is that meaning is propositional. Meaning is semantic in nature and as Macnamara (1982) contends, in psychology, meaning and concept are rarely distinguished. If information about a certain topic is related or linked together according to logical principles and if that information is understood, then it is meaningful to the people who understand it. For example, if we were to consider an exclusive definition for *amphibian,* we would encounter the following: (a) amphibians are vertebrate animals (which would be linked to characteristics of both vertebrates and animals), (b) amphibians lay eggs underwater, (c) amphibians have a three-chambered heart, (d) amphibians have moist skin, (e) and so forth. If someone were to understand these and associated propositions, then "amphibian" would have meaning for that individual. However, is such a notion of meaning a complete representation of what actually constitutes meaningful understanding to children or adults? Is there more to personal meaning than sets of related propositions? Is personal meaning governed by the rules of formal logic?

The answers to such questions appear to lie beyond the bounds of a purely semantic view of meaningful learning. Pepper's (1970) work with world hypotheses has influenced some researchers' work with the influence of world views on learning (Anderson & Kilbourn 1983; Roberts 1982b). Other researchers (Cobern 1988, April; Gauld 1987) are exploring the role of beliefs (including a distinctively different sense of world views) in learning science. Still others have looked at belief systems as cultural phenomena that influence learning in terms of cognitive ecology or the social and environmental context of learning. Mariana Hewson's (1988) research looked at how children in developing African nations constructed scientific knowledge according to prevailing cultural beliefs. Berlin, Breedlove, and Raven (1966) considered the social and environmental context of learning in their study of folk taxonomies. Although the inclusion of beliefs and other epistemological commitments provides a broader understanding of meaningful learning, the predominant view of conceptual ecology is still primarily semantic.

Even though beliefs appear to be another aspect of semantic knowledge, the notion of beliefs as guiding frameworks for the construction of knowledge may offer a more productive way to view their function. Take for example, Gilbert, Osborne, and Fensham's (1982) discussion of children's science. Egocentric, anthropocentric, anthropomorphic, zoomorphic, and other viewpoints are treated as principles that guide children's thinking processes. The view that such guiding principles affect children's thinking about science topics is of importance in understanding how personal meaning is constructed.

Beliefs and belief frameworks are frequently shared among individuals in a particular cultural context. Such a notion leads us to the conception of meaning as imbedded in a social context. Socially embedded meaning has been of interest to anthropologists and sociologists of education but has not been given much consideration in the constructivist circles of science education. From an anthropological view, Burtonwood (1986) discusses how the Kuhnian sense of paradigm can be applied to learning or socialization within specific cultural settings. Such a paradigmatic view of learning within social contexts provides an intriguing demonstration of how contradictory or anomalous conceptual commitments can lead to stresses on the social structure or to revolutions. From a constructivist perspective, Hewson's (1988) discussion of the difficulties encountered by native African children when their culturally embedded beliefs clash with Western science beliefs is an appropriate example of the stresses confronted on a cognitive level when two socially embedded meanings come into conflict.

Although personal meaning is strongly influenced by the sociocultural context, individuals use resources other than semantic information, belief frameworks, and the sociocultural context to construct meaning. Emotions are a critical component of meaning. Both Hofstadter (1979) and Bruner (1986) consider emotions as "triggers" of meaning. Triggers function in a similar way to Bateson's (personal communication, July 21, 1975) notion of context markers. Emotions, from a contextual point of view, can trigger specific meanings.

The idea of context begins to take on somewhat different characteristics from the sense of sociocultural contexts discussed previously. According to Bateson (1979), context is "pattern through time" (p. 15) or "a little knot or complex of that species of connectedness which we call relevance" (p. 14). In addition, "'context' is linked to another undefined notion called 'meaning.' Without context, words and actions have no meaning at all" (p. 16). Context determines meaning, in terms of both sociocultural contexts and a variety of other potential contexts. In fact, multiple contexts can be operating concurrently. Both Bruner (1986) and Bateson (1972) see the effect of the multiplicity of contexts as an individual's ability to hold multiple perspectives of his or her world. Bruner explains his notion of multiple perspectives in the following way:

> We know the world in different ways, from different stances, and each of the ways in which we know it produces different structures of representations, or, indeed, 'realities.' As we grow to adulthood (at least in Western culture), we become increasingly adept at seeing the same set of events from multiple perspectives or stances and at entertaining the results as, so to speak, alternative possible worlds. The child, we would all agree, is less adept at

achieving such multiple perspectives—although it is highly dubious . . . that children are as uniformly egocentric as formerly claimed. (p. 109)

Each perspective represents a different context in which phenomena are understood or a different "context of meaning." Such contexts of meaning can overlap producing a multiplicity of meaning around any given phenomenon. The following section elaborates on such contexts of meaning in light of data from two recent studies.

CONTEXTS OF MEANING

The idea that a child's understanding takes on the characteristics of contexts of meaning first developed as I sifted through mounds of interview transcripts from a study with two classrooms of twenty-three first-, second-, and third-grade children. One part of this study using interviews with ten children is described elsewhere (Bloom, in press). In a series of more recent studies with fifth-grade students, similar semi-structured interviews with nine children as well as a variety of other tasks with twenty-four children explored the characteristics and dynamics of contexts of meaning (Bloom 1990, April; 1990, June). In two of these studies, one set of interviews centered around observations of live earthworms. Earthworms, as it turned out, had not been the object of formal study in the classroom, but were familiar to all of the children. For the sake of clarity in the following discussion, the children's pseudonyms have been arranged according to grade level. Grade 1 children's names begin with *A*, while grade 2 names begin with *B*, grade 3 names begin with *C*, and grade 5 names begin with *E*.

In order to establish a descriptive basis for discussing contexts of meaning, I have developed a typology from the data of the two studies. The typology contains four general divisions: (a) knowledge; (b) mental processes; (c) interpretive frameworks; and (d) emotions, values, and aesthetics. In addition, the divisions are subdivided into a number of components, some of which contain further subcomponents (see table 6-1). As we explore this typology in more detail, it is important to realize that children's contexts of meaning are not static. They are dynamic systems of continuously changing information.

In the original study (Bloom, in press), the typology was established to describe patterns evident in the data. The definitions of some of the category labels are relatively standard, such as semantic and episodic knowledge. However, the other categories warrant brief expla-

Table 6-1
A typology describing the components of the context
of children's thinking in biology

Division	Components
Knowledge	Semantic knowledge
	Episodic (experiential) knowledge
Mental processes	Inferring
	Perceiving
	Describing
	Explaining
	Comparative processes
	Generating metaphors and analogies
	Comparing
	Discriminating
Interpretive Frameworks	Anthropocentrism
	Anthropomorphism
	Zoomorphism
Emotions, Values, and Aesthetics	

nations. Mental processes are obvious at one level, especially considering the amount of research devoted to the description of such processes (e.g., inferring, elaborating, recalling, perceiving, etc.). However, the important notion is that such processes are constantly changing the nature of what children understand by changing knowledge and by adding new information. New information added to an individual's context of meaning may be the product of a specific process, such as metaphors. Interpretive frameworks were originally referred to as "belief frameworks," but "belief" is not an adequate descriptor. The confusion between the psychologist's and the philosopher's definitions of belief detracts from the intended operational nature of the typological category. Interpretive frameworks describe how a certain point of view, belief system, or knowledge set influences the operations of various mental processes. For example, anthropomorphism may influence the way an inference is made. The subcomponents of anthropomorphism and zoomorphism both refer to the process of transferring the characteristics of human's and other animals' (respectively) to the object or organism at hand. Anthropocentricism, on the other hand, concerns the view that focuses upon human needs, desires, concerns, and so forth. The category of emotions-values-aesthetics was formulated to describe what appeared to be the basis of various statements. These aspects have been combined because of the difficulty in separating them as they manifest in children's speech. A child may be disgusted by earthworms, think they are ugly, and not like them. All three aspects of emotions, values, and aesthetics are strongly associated. Separating them makes little sense in terms of the operationalization of contexts of meaning. Each of the typological categories will be elaborated upon in the following discussion.

The major component of the typology responsible for the dynamic quality of contexts of meaning is mental processes. Mental processes not only construct semantic knowledge but also generate new ideas from previous knowledge and new experiences. For example, Emily's observations of an earthworm show a progression of perceptions that lead to the formulation of an inference:

> now it's turning green . . . a little bit . . . it looks like they kind of change colors as they move . . . the dark pink and there's red and there's green and there's a brown and there's that purple color . . . there's even that orange . . . I think that's the vein and then there's that . . . ugh . . . yellow [ring] . . .

In another instance, Emily demonstrates how a number of ideas can be generated as explanations of a particular phenomena:

> I think that's kind of a sensor . . . something like that so they can find their way around . . . well, it looks like it because it's going around and around . . . it looks like it's kind of sniffing to see what's there . . . [Interviewer: Do they have noses?] . . . I think it's kind of like cats' whiskers . . . you know . . . they don't smell but they feel . . . they've got kind of a nerve . . . maybe . . . maybe that line in there . . . maybe that's a nerve . . . connecting to the head . . .

In this latter example, we can see how Emily notices a particular behavior and infers that a specific structure has an associated function. At first she thinks of this function as sniffing, then she compares the function to that of cats' whiskers. From this comparison she infers the existence of a nerve, which she thinks she sees as a line down the center of the body. In both examples, Emily is actively constructing knowledge from previous knowledge and her new experiences. The meaning attached to this newly constructed knowledge extends beyond the evident semantic information. The notion that earthworms have ". . . a sensor . . . so they can find their way around" suggests a zoomorphic, if not anthropomorphic, framework of intentionality. Such a connection is meaningful. In the same way, the comparison to cats' whiskers is potentially laden with meaning stemming from personal experiences with cats.

Another powerful influence on the construction of meaning is a combination of emotions, values, and aesthetics. These three aspects of contexts of meaning have been combined because of the difficulty in clearly distinguishing them. For instance, at the beginning of the interview with Elliot, he broke an earthworm in two while digging around. He was quite upset. As he continued to look for more earthworms, he proceeded with greater caution saying, ". . . don't want to [break one] this time." Near the end of the interview, he mentioned that fish eat earthworms and "for fishing they make good bait [Interviewer: Do you go fishing?] . . . yeah . . . [5] . . . I use bread though" ("5" refers to length of pause in seconds). In a similar way, Andy comments that fishing is ". . . sort of bad because he's [earthworm] sort of killable . . . eaten by fish." Cindy mentions that, "I'm afraid I'm going to kill it," then goes on to say, "I don't feel like doing this . . . I keep killing things." In all three cases, their sensitivity towards earthworms appears to based on a particular set of personal values that are closely linked with emotions. Such strong connections with emotions and values impact on the way children proceed with tasks and on how they integrate and utilize new and prior knowledge.

Aesthetics and the lack of aesthetic appreciation are frequently evident in children's conversations about earthworms. Adam talked with a lot of confidence in his own knowledge of earthworms. His excitement carried through the whole session. His aesthetic appreciation of earthworms is demonstrated in the following excepts: (a) "they are really neat . . . ," (b) ". . . the fatter ones are pretty," and (c) ". . . they also hear with their mouth . . . isn't that neat." By contrast, Curtis did not have an aesthetic appreciation for earthworms. Some examples of Curtis's comments about earthworms include, (a) "I know a lot about worms . . . but I don't like them," (b) ". . . they are slimy . . . 'cause they look funny," and (c) ". . . a snake is cute . . . [worms] are ugly." Becky, on the other hand, changed from being afraid of earthworms to liking them: ". . . used to be scared of worms . . . felt . . . they were going to slither . . . on me . . . [now] they are quite cute." In each of these cases, emotional reactions to earthworms are closely tied in with an aesthetic appreciation or lack of appreciation.

The previous examples point not only to the intermingling of emotions, values, and aesthetics, but also to the importance they play in influencing the construction of meaning. For example, in addition to Cindy's fear of killing the earthworms she remarks that ". . . they are depressingly see-through." The fact that she can see what is inside the earthworm has a certain amount of impact on her. Such an emotional link with an observation is meaningful to her. In a similar way, Andy's comment that "they're both boy and girl mixed up . . . yuck" reflects prior knowledge that obviously had considerable valuational and emotional impact. The semantic knowledge associated with emotions and values was particularly meaningful to him. Such links with emotions, values, and aesthetics create extremely rich and diverse contexts of meaning.

Frequently in combination with emotions, values, and aesthetics, interpretive frameworks add to the richness and power of children's contexts of meaning. By placing the qualities of humans or of other animals onto other objects (earthworms in the present discussion), children create personally meaningful constructs. An almost classic example of such a construct is Beth's statement that the earthworm is "wagging it's tail." Although earthworms do not have tails, their appearance is suggestive of tails. Tails are not only long, thin, and round, but are commonly known to wag. In addition, wagging tails connote an array of emotions, depending on the animal. In a similar way, Andy's comment that a particular earthworm ". . . is hunting for dirt" suggests that earthworms exhibit the intentional behavior of hunting. The behavior of the earthworm is embedded in a meaningful context of associations, like a cat hunting its prey or a squirrel hunting for a buried nut.

The meaningful connections displayed by anthropomorphic statements are even more powerful in that children can personally identify with the earthworms. Amy's comment that one earthworm is ". . . playing with all that fuzzy wuzzy . . ." suggests a behavior (playing) which is familiar to her. When Andy says that an earthworm ". . . needs to be careful of birds," his understanding that birds eat worms is enriched by attributing earthworms with cognizant abilities: "If you know you can be eaten by birds, then you had better be careful." The emotions alluded to in such anthropomorphic and zoomorphic statements are again a strong component of the contexts of meaning.

Although the effect of mental processes (perceiving, inferring, etc.) on the construction of knowledge and meaning receives considerable treatment in the literature, one aspect of mental processes is worthy of further discussion. The generation of metaphors and analogies are a significant contributor to contexts of meaning. Even among very young children, the generation of metaphors is a common occurrence. Some examples of the metaphors used by grade 1 and 2 children include, (a) "Slinkies" as a descriptor of movement (Amy, also used by Emily), (b) "jump rope" as an imagined action (Amy), (c) "scooter boards" as a descriptor of movement ("slipping on ice like . . .") (Amy), (d) "trapeze" as a descriptor of action (Amy), (e) "playing" as an anthropomorphic descriptor of action (Amy), (f) "clothes" as an anthropomorphic comparison of skin to the function of clothes transposed to skin as clothes (Amy), (g) "drill" as a descriptor of digging action (Adam), (h) "springs" as a descriptor of movement (Alex), (i) "dragon's mouth" as a descriptor of the structure of the worm's mouth (Andy), (j) "big swords" as a descriptor of shape (Becky), and (k) "Jell-o" as a descriptor of touch (Bonnie). In each of the previous examples, metaphors add to the dimensions of contexts of meaning by extending the breadth of connections.

A different type of metaphor occurred with two children who imagined themselves as an earthworm or other organism. In response to a question about what the heart does, Cindy says, "I don't know about my body [laughs] . . . well I don't know about my worm body . . . [laughs] . . . it moves the same way so it probably has the same inside." She starts off by taking the position of being the worm and then infers that humans and earthworms have similar structures. Whether or not such a metaphorical transposition aided the inferential process is uncertain. From the moment Evan sat down for the interview he concerned himself with what it would be like to be a tiny organism: "have you ever tried thinking about what it would be like to be a bug?" A few moments later after finding an earthworm, he continued, "what does it feel like . . . to be a worm under the ground all the time . . . [after a brief diversion] . . . I just think it would be dark . . . it would be a bit boring . . . I think it would be lonely." He continued with a discussion of how it ". . . feels weird to be a human being." Flipping back and forth, Evan's particular feelings were difficult to distinguish from those imagined of the earthworm. At the very least, such transpositions between oneself and another organism appear to be very powerful vehicles for developing personal meaning.

Up to this point we have examined various aspects of the notion of contexts of meaning. I suspect that other components could be added to the typology. However, the major point is that children's, indeed human beings', understanding of their world is far more complex than what most research leads us to believe. Although propositional knowledge is a major component of children's construction of meaning, other components and processes play important roles in meaning-making. The products of some mental processes and other context of meaning components are frequently not considered relevant to the development of scientific knowledge. For instance, anthropomorphism and emotional statements, such as "it *won't let* me pick it up" or "pretty *scary* for the worm," are discouraged among science teachers and scientists. However, from the point of view of children's understanding, anthropomorphism, emotions, and so forth are powerful facilitators of meaning-making .

Summary of Contexts of Meaning

Contexts of meaning are not strictly scientific in nature, nor are they necessarily logical or rational. Instead, such contexts point to a wide variety of associations with different types of information, beliefs (as a component of interpretive frameworks), emotions, values, and aesthetics. For example, contexts of meaning are often indicated by context markers. As discussed previously, the statement, "wagging it's tail," marks a context of meaning about "tails" and their structure and function. In the same way, heads, eyes, hunting, and so forth, point to or trigger further meaning. Heads and eyes orient the child to worms. The head and eyes deal with knowing the world, they are the essence of being alive from the child's point of view. If a worm is alive, it has to have a head and maybe eyes. The action of hunting provides a way to interpret the behaviour of worms. When the worm is moving its "head" around, it looks as if it is "hunting" and hunting is what "animals" do.

Contexts of meaning are dynamic and ever-changing arrays of information imbedded in a variety of emotions, values, aesthetics, and beliefs. The action of various processes (inferring, comparing, perceiving, etc.) continuously alter the content and meaning of these contexts. Such contexts of meaning are highly personal because of the influence of individual (episodic) experiences, emotions, values, interpretive frameworks, and so forth. Various context markers, such as "tails," may trigger similar meaning in different children, but in the larger context, in the present case "worms," each child's meaning is quite individualized and different.

If we consider children's contexts of meaning in the spirit of "alternative" frameworks by not judging their "correctness," we can begin to see how children construct and modify concepts along with associated meaning. For example, the children discussed in this chapter may not have developed any concepts of how earthworms move, yet as they examined the worms in front of them the children described what they saw. In their descriptions, the children used other concepts available to them, such as "pulling" as an explanation for how worms were able to make one part of their bodies move and then another part move. Some children made metaphoric associations with objects, such as Slinkies. Other children inferred that worms must have muscles, because humans have muscles. In most cases, children actively sought out associations with their own experiences and previous knowledge.

Contexts of meaning expand and change as they overlap and interact with other contexts. Individual concepts clearly occur in a complex arena of interrelated concepts, emotions, values, beliefs, and so forth. Isolating specific concepts in the study of children's knowledge and conceptual change, as is being done in much science education research, can pose some serious problems. For instance, when researchers think they have identified a concept, such as "worms have tails," they label it as a misconcept or alternative concept. Such a concept is viewed as needing to be changed to conform with the scientific concept. The problems are (a) that there is a substantial amount of meaning attached to the concept, worms have tails; (b) that by not paying attention to and appreciating the significance of that meaning, we may be missing most of what a child understands; and (c) that by not working with the child's contexts of meaning that surround concepts, we will have greater difficulty helping children to meaningfully incorporate scientific versions of concepts.

DISCUSSION AND IMPLICATIONS

The tension between epistemology and cognitive psychology is a bit more extensive than that laid out by Duschl, Hamilton and Grandy (this volume). In some ways, the tension is more triadic: epistemology, cognitive psychology, and actual cognition. The dominant paradigm governing much of cognitive psychology is epistemological, in the sense that the logical structure and semantic nature of meaning is modeled in the way meaning is represented in cognitive psychology. The logic of this connection between epistemology and cognitive psychology is typified by Finley and Stewart (1982) in their discussion of developing artificial intelligence systems for representing meaning and knowledge:

> The original purpose of these systems was to represent knowledge as it is stored in human memory. These same systems are applicable to representing the substantive structure of disciplines because both the substantive structures and an individual's knowledge are products of the same human thought processes. Expecting the substantive structures of disciplines to be greatly different from the structures of human memory would require positing different mechanisms of human thought for scientists than for other individuals. (p. 595)

The problem with Finley and Stewart's contention is that a substantial number of different mechanisms of thought are categorically ignored in developing formal knowledge structures. Although certain types of nonsemantic mechanisms may be evident in a scientist's thinking (Bloom 1988, April), evidence of such thinking would never make it into the writings of that scientist. Formal knowledge is the product of a great deal of highly rational thinking over a long period of time by many individuals. The emotions, values, interpretive frameworks, metaphors, and so forth that originally may have played a part in developing the insights and hypotheses leading up to present-day knowledge have long since been omitted from formal knowledge descriptions.

In the everyday thinking of children, the same or similar rational processes operate along with emotionally driven or interpretive framework-guided processes. One child may conceptually organize his or her ideas about a topic, while another may not (Bloom 1990, April). One child may seem to rely heavily upon her emotions for interpreting information, while another child may rely upon his personal experiences (episodic knowledge). All of the cognitive processes evident from the perspective of contexts of meaning are powerful tools for creating meaning, although they may not be valid from a traditional epistemological point of view. On the other hand, such processes and their products may be valid from an artistic, literary, or other creative point of view.

Problems arise when these various cognitive processes come together to create, what Bateson (1979) calls a "muddle." In a previous study of student teachers (Bloom 1989), the conflicts between individuals' beliefs or interpretive frameworks and their formal knowledge of science confounded the way in which the student teachers viewed evolution and the teaching of evolution. The same sort of conflict was evident in the study of evolutionary biologists (Bloom 1988, April). Even though the biologists had extensive experience and formal knowledge backgrounds, some of them were more strongly influenced by personal interpretive frameworks in terms of their inflexible approach to research and to working with alternative hypotheses.

The danger has been that as we explore children's and adults' understandings, we tend to become reductionist to the point that we miss the forest for the trees. We isolate a specific conceptual structure, while missing the greater understanding or context of meaning behind it. Conceptual change-based instruction from a perspective of knowledge that focuses on isolated and specific concepts misses a significant portion of children's constructed meaning. From a cognitivist point of view, we must consider the complexity, variety, and interrelatedness of mental events as a whole. For instance, rather than ignore the influence of anthropomorphism in making inferences, we need to acknowledge and explore the power of this particular mechanism.

Any thinking about curriculum and instruction has to be grounded, at least in part, in a broader view of children's construction of meaning. If we consider Roberts's (1982a) description of seven curriculum emphases and his suggestion for a more eclectic, yet critical, approach to science education, the approach being proffered in the present chapter is more or less aligned with his "self as explainer" emphasis. The major difference between Roberts's "self as explainer" and what I am suggesting is that we need to deal with more than children's semantic knowledge about specific objects or events and with more than the scientific understanding. As mentioned previously, we, as human beings, understand our world from many different perspectives. As science educators, not only should we help children develop a critical understanding of scientific explanations, but we should help children develop a critical understanding of other perspectives and the thinking mechanisms that contribute to their construction as well.

The earthworm wagging its tail is a useful example to consider. Rather than simply dealing with the specific concept itself, we could have young children explore what a wagging tail means. A variety of examples could be collected and analyzed, such as, the "wagging" of tails by dogs, cats, alligators, tigers, and so forth. Within this exploration the notion of how the meaning of a wagging tail varies depending upon whether you are a human being or another dog, cat, or whatever will emerge. At the same time, the idea of tail can be explored. Examples of tails could be examined. Children could try to invent their own definition of tail. In the process of testing out their definition of tail, they may realize that worms do not have tails. In that case, the new concept, "worms do not have tails," is incorporated into the contexts of meaning surrounding earthworms along with the idea that earthworms look like tails.

Maybe what we should be concerned with instead of "conceptual change" is "conceptual integration." From the scientific point of view, some concepts, such as worms wagging their tails, are erroneous, but from a poetic or other creative point of view, the same concepts may be very powerful. Trying to replace potentially powerful but scientifically erroneous ideas perpetuates a certain scientistic presumptuousness. The power of viewing learning within the notion of contexts of meaning lies in the capacity of individuals to hold a multitude of diverse and often contradictory ideas, images, and emotions. Even young children are capable of recognizing the differences between the ideas they hold. For example, Cindy related a tale of how snakes ended up without any legs. In short, after humans and other animals got their legs, the millipede asked for all the rest, leaving the snake with none. Afterwards I asked if she believed it and she said, "no, it's a folk tale . . . like geese can talk."

Curriculum development could incorporate the view of multiple perspectives and multiple meanings. What is being suggested is a new and broader view of an existing idea, the integrated curriculum. The arts, the humanities, the social sciences, mathematics, and the natural sciences are all concerned with understanding our world and expressing that meaning in some way. Schools have, for the most part, clearly separated and divorced these aspects of meaning (subject matter disciplines) from individual children's experiences. Children's thinking, as we have seen, does not operate along disciplinary lines, but incorporates the seeds, if not the richness, of varied disciplinary thinking. If we want to develop this richness of thinking, then we need to rethink how we organize school curricula, how we train teachers, and how we implement instruction.

REFERENCES

Anderson, T., & Kilbourn, B. (1983). Creation, evolution, and curriculum. *Science Education, 67,* 45-55.

Ausubel, D. P. (1963). *The psychology of meaningful verbal learning: An introduction to school learning.* New York: Grune & Stratton.

Bateson, G. (1972). *Steps to an ecology of mind.* New York: Ballantine. (Originally published in 1972)

Bateson, G. (1979). *Mind and nature: A necessary unity.* New York: Dutton.

Berlin, B., Breedlove, D. E., & Raven, P. H. (1966). Folk taxonomies and biological classification. *Science, 154,* 273-75.

Bloom, J. W. (In press). Contexts of meaning: Young children's understanding of biological phenomena. *International Journal of Science Teaching.*

Bloom, J. W. (1988, April). *A case study of evolutionary biologists: Implications for secondary biology curriculum and teacher training.* Paper presented at the annual meeting of the American Educational Research Association, New Orleans.

Bloom, J. W. (1989). Preservice elementary teachers' conceptions of science: Science, theories, and evolution. *International Journal of Science Education,* *11*(4), 401-15.

Bloom, J. W. (1990, April). *Methodological perspectives in assessing and extending the scope of children's contexts of meaning: Context maps and drawing tasks.* Paper presented at the annual meeting of the American Educational Research Association, Boston.

Bloom, J. W. (1990, June). *Contexts of meaning and children's understanding of the world.* Paper presented at the annual meeting of the Canadian Society for Studies in Education, Victoria, BC.

Bruner, J. S. (1986). *Actual minds, possible worlds.* Cambridge, MA: Harvard University Press.

Burtonwood, N. (1986). *The culture concept in educational studies.* Windsor, England: Nfer-Nelson.

Champagne, A. B., & Klopfer, L. E. (1984). The cognitive perspective in science education. In R. W. Bybee, J. Carlson, & A. J. McCormack, *Redesigning science and technology education: 1984 Yearbook of the National Science Teachers Association.* Washington, DC: National Science Teachers Association.

Cobern, W. W. (1988, April). *World view theory and misconception research.* Paper presented at the annual meeting of the National Association for Research in Science Teaching, Lake of the Ozarks, MO.

Driver, R., & Bell, B. (1986). Students' thinking and the learning of science: A constructivist view. *School Science Review, 67,* 443-56.

Finley, F. N., & Stewart, J. (1982). Representing substantive structures. *Science Education, 66*(4), 593-611.

Gauld, C. F. (1987). Student beliefs and cognitive structure. *Research in Science Education, 17,* 87-93.

Gilbert, J. K., Osborne, R. J., & Fensham, P. J. (1982). Children's science and its consequences for teaching. *Science Education, 66,* 623-33.

Hewson, M. (1988). The ecological context of knowledge: Implications for learning science in developing countries. *Journal of Curriculum Studies, 20*(4), 317-26.

Hills, G. L. C. (1989). Students' "untutored" beliefs about natural phenomena: Primitive science or commonsense? *Science Education, 73*(2), 155-86.

Hofstadter, D. R. (1979). *Gödel, Escher, Bach: An eternal golden braid.* New York: Basic Books.

Keil, F. C. (1989). *Concepts, kinds, and cognitive development.* Cambridge, MA: MIT Press.

Macnamara, J. (1982). *Names for things: A study of human learning.* Cambridge, MA: MIT Press.

Markman, E. M. (1989). *Categorization and naming in children: Problems of induction.* Cambridge, MA: MIT Press.

Novak, J. D. (1987). Human constructivism: Toward a unity of psychological and epistemological meaning making. *Proceedings of the Second International Seminar on Misconceptions and Educational Strategies in Science and Mathematics, 1,* 348-60.

Pepper, S. C. (1970). *World hypotheses: A study in evidence.* Berkeley and Los Angeles: University of California Press.

Pines, A. L., West, L. H. T. (1986). Conceptual understanding and science learning: An interpretation of research within a sources-of-knowledge framework. *Science Education, 70*(5), 583-604.

Pope, M. & Gilbert, J. (1983). Personal experience and the construction of knowledge in science. *Science Education, 67*(2), 193-204.

Roberts, D. A. (1982a). Developing the concept of "curriculum emphases" in science education. *Science Education, 66*(2), 243-60.

Roberts, D. A. (1982b). The place of qualitative research in science education. *Journal of Research in Science Teaching, 19,* 277-92.

White, R. T. (1988). *Learning science.* Oxford: Blackwell.

STEPHEN P. NORRIS[1]

7

Practical Reasoning in the Production of Scientific Knowledge

OUTLINE

I. Introduction
II. Aspects of scientific knowledge production
   A. Choosing standard conditions
   B. Testing theories
   C. Deriving equations
   D. Reporting observations
III. Aspects of scientific knowledge acquisition
   A. Frames of understanding and misconception
   B. Knowledge, belief, and understanding
   C. Justification requirements for scientific knowledge acquisition
   D. Avoiding stereotypical science
IV. Conclusion
V. Summary and implications for research

ABSTRACT

This paper argues that practical reasoning based on values about what ought to be done is at the root of the production of scientific knowledge and, therefore, must be at the root of the acquisition of scientific knowledge by students. Four aspects of scientific knowledge production are examined (choosing standard conditions, testing theories, deriving equations, and reporting observations), and the role of practical reasoning based on values is illustrated in each. Four aspects of scientific knowledge acquisition are then considered (the content, problem-solving, epistemic, and inquiry frames of understanding), and it is argued that a focus on practical reasoning is central to the epistemic and inquiry frames. These latter two frames are more basic than the factual content of science because they define what science is and tell how it is possible. Furthermore, once science curricula portray more accurately the practical reasoning involved in the production of scientific knowledge, then the damaging view that science is radically different from other intellectual pursuits will be undermined. Undermining this view will pave the way for a science education suitable to the wider audience that science educators intend for it.

Practical reasoning is reasoning about what ought to be done (Coombs 1987). Such reasoning is central to managing every aspect of our lives. Which, if any, retirement savings plan should I join? To which journal should I send the article I have just finished? Am I too tired to run today, or will the run do me good? Should I vote for or against a strike? Ought I complain about my niece's mathematics teacher, or ought I recommend to my niece's parents that they complain? Reasoning about these and other practical matters requires choice based on values.

Practical reasoning in the production of scientific knowledge is reasoning by scientists about what ought to be done at particular junctures in the course of their research. Dealing with such issues is central to scientific practice and it, too, requires choice based on values. Which instrument should be used to collect the data? What experimental design will best suit the questions to be answered? Should the data be taken as correct and the theory rejected, or was there an error in the data collection? With what species ought this animal be classified? Would it be better to do Experiment A first, or might doing Experiment B first save time and money?

Many models of scientific reasoning (Braithwaite 1968; Hempel 1966; Hull 1974; Popper 1959), and consequently the many science curricula that presuppose these models, do not take into account the practical reasoning required in scientific knowledge production. Instead, the models describe in what are often called "rational reconstructions' the logical relationships between scientific conclusions and scientific evidence. I shall argue that such models and the curricula based on them distort scientific knowledge production and thereby create mis-understandings of scientific knowledge. One of the most profound and disturbing of these misunderstandings is the view that science is radically different from other intellectual pursuits and, as such, should be distinguished from them.

For at least a hundred years, from the middle of the nineteenth to the middle of the twentieth century, many of the most influential philosophers of science advocated, or at least presupposed in their writings, the view that science represents the supreme intellectual activity and, as such, ought to be demarcated from other intellectual endeavours (Ayer 1952; Mill 1865; Popper 1959). In the search for demarcation criteria, science's language and its method were features often contemplated and debated. The language and method of science are different, it was surmised, so different that they justify putting science in a class by itself, set apart from the other disciplines. More specifically, science's language was thought to be characterized by a rigid distinction between observational and theoretical terms and by precise definition (Carnap 1955, 1956; Kaplan 1964, pp. 54-62; Nagel 1971); its method was taken to involve reasoning constrained by the deductive tightness of mathematics, the gathering of objective data, and the rule-governed acceptance and rejection of hypotheses on the basis of such data alone (Braithwaite 1968; Hempel 1966). These descriptions of science do not acknowledge the role in science of reasoning based on values about what ought to be done.

While most philosophers of science, and indeed much of the academy, would now reject such a view of science, the view (or significant aspects of it) still holds sway in some quarters, sometimes quite implicitly. It is not uncommon, for example, to hear the general public, educators, and academics talk of individuals' aptitudes for science as opposed to other subjects. That one could have or not have an aptitude for science, meaning that one could have or not have a special ability (as opposed to, say, an interest) to learn and understand science, presupposes that science is different in some fundamental respects from other disciplines. More explicit examples can be found in the early pages of many science texts that discuss how science differs from other pursuits, how it has a special method for solving problems, and how becoming a scientist requires being a particular sort of person.

Thus, philosophical theses, even after they are renounced, can have powerful legacies. One legacy of the view that science should be demarcated from other intellectual pursuits is the widespread belief that practical reasoning is not involved in scientific knowledge production and, consequently, that scientific reasoning is value free. The purpose of this chapter is to argue that these beliefs represent a profoundly mistaken view of science and that science teaching must evade their grasp and, in fact, do more to challenge them.

Science educators have recognized for some time that practical reasoning and value judgements must be made at the interface between science, technology, and society (Aikenhead 1985; National Science Teachers Association 1971, 1982). The need for practical reasoning based on value judgements in deciding to use basic research findings (e.g., about the structure of the DNA molecule) in order to pursue the development of a new technology (e.g., the techniques and apparatus for synthesizing DNA molecules) is typical of the examples used in science texts to show how practical reasoning is relevant to science. However, such treatment of the relationship between science and practical reasoning, while necessary, leaves unscathed the view that the production itself of basic scientific knowledge does not require practical reasoning. The treatment fails in this latter respect for at least three reasons: (a) it focuses on the application of scientific knowledge and not on its production; (b) it deals only with moral issues in the application of science, and moral issues are only one category of the value issues that must be addressed using practical reasoning; and (c) the treatment does nothing to challenge the fact that the lists of scientific processes used to help guide curriculum development and instruction rarely make explicit reference to a process essential to all scientific knowledge production—deciding what ought to be done.

From the point of view of science education, how science is compared to the other disciplines is crucial to how science teachers conceive of themselves and to how the role of science within the school curriculum is conceived. For instance, arguments over the importance of science and over the time that it should be allocated in the school schedule are based in part on how science is viewed with respect to the other subjects. But we should not wish science to be popular or to be afforded a large chunk of the school timetable on account of a false image of what science is and what can be expected from it. On the contrary, we should wish that there be a generally accurate understanding of scientific knowledge within society, and part of this understanding resides in the view of how science compares to other intellectual activities. At the same time, we must be prepared to accept that changing our collective conception of science likely will have ramifications for the place of science in the curriculum. A pair of positive ramifications would be that science courses be viewed with less trepidation and subscribed to by more students.

In this chapter, I shall examine a number of aspects of scientific knowledge production and show how in each case practical reasoning based on values is involved. The first aspect is choosing standard conditions. The choice of standard conditions in determining the referents of two natural kind terms, *water* and *yellow*, will be considered. The examples show that what scientists take to be the referents for these terms depends fundamentally upon decisions about the standard conditions under which the referents ought to be determined. The conclusion of this analysis is that the specification of the nature of 'water' and of 'yellow' involves the interaction of empirical investigation and the explicit specification of referential intentions based upon judgements of value.

The second aspect of scientific knowledge production to be considered is the testing of theories. Specifically, the focus will be upon the force of falsifying evidence. The case to be considered is the Michelson-Morley experiment and the force of its result in defeating the aether theory. The example can be used to show that any scientific statement can be held true in the face of contrary evidence, if radical enough changes are made to other beliefs or conceptual structures. The upshot is to challenge the view that there is an inherent distinction between the empirical and the conceptual aspects of science by showing that the distinction really is based upon practical reasoning about how issues ought to be classified.

The third aspect is deriving equations. The analysis will demonstrate that practical reasoning based on values is involved in deriving the fundamental equation of pendulum motion. Competing values in the decision include: having neat, easily obtainable solutions; being able to solve seemingly intractable problems; and deriving laws that do not lie about the world. These competing values must be weighed and adjudicated through practical reasoning as part and parcel of solving the equation.

The fourth aspect of scientific knowledge production to be discussed is reporting scientific observations. The argument will demonstrate the impossibility of maintaining a sharp distinction between observation and inference, a distinction that was recommended in much philosophy of science literature prior to the middle of the twentieth century and as is still advocated in many science curricula. Once this distinction disappears, much of the case for the relative objectivity of science in comparison to other disciplines falls with it. Reporting observations, it will be contended, is an activity in which scientists rely upon practical reasoning to express their values about the current state of knowledge in the area of present concern and their intentions about which propositions are to be taken for granted and which are to be tested.

The analyses of these four aspects of scientific knowledge production will be used to point to a class of misconceptions about science that have been overlooked largely in the research, namely, misconceptions about the role of practical reasoning based on values in the production of scientific knowledge. Note that my treatment of these four aspects of scientific knowledge production focuses on a slice of science that is not captured by either pole of the context-of-discovery/context-of-justification distinction. This distinction, originally proposed by Reichenbach (1938) and mentioned by Duschl, Hamilton, and Grandy (this volume), distinguishes between the psychological origin of a scientific statement in the mind of some scientist and the statement's epistemological status. According to Reichenbach, discovery was something mysterious. For example, how the idea arose in the mind of some human being that continents might drift, would be considered outside the realm of what is needed to obtain a philosophical understanding of science. Understanding justification, conceived as the relation between scientific statements and evidence, for example, between the statement that continents drift and the evidence for it, was considered central to understanding science. I shall not in this chapter focus on the context of discovery in Reichenbach's sense.

What I shall contend, however, is that understanding the context of justification requires much more than understanding evidence relationships. It requires, in addition, understanding why scientists decide to do one thing rather than another, when the evidence allows either. My focus is on both poles of the context-of-development/context-of-justification distinction used by Duschl, Hamilton, and Grandy. Their context of justification seems to square quite well with Reichenbach's. However, in their context of development they have included the practical reasoning about methods, aims, and commitments that my examples shall illustrate. As I understand the context of development as used by Duschl, Hamilton, and Grandy, it has little connection with Reichenbach's context of discovery. My thesis about knowledge production is similarly unconnected to Reichenbach's ideas about discovery.

ASPECTS OF SCIENTIFIC KNOWLEDGE PRODUCTION

Choosing Standard Conditions

Hirst (1974), who argued for years that the curriculum should be based on the structure of the disciplines, once wrote that truth in science "is determined strictly by empirical observation and experiment" (p. 167). At a recent conference, he maintained in a similar vein that the meaning of scientific terms is purely an empirical issue (Hirst 1989). Consider first the meaning of the term 'water', and then the term 'yellow', to see whether Hirst is correct.

The currently accepted scientific definition for (ordinary) water is: Water is H_2O. How was this meaning for water determined? A scientifically naive person might provide an answer something like this: Some samples of water were chosen, their underlying nature was studied scientifically (maybe using powerful microscopes or some such instruments) and discovered to consist of the molecule H_2O—two hydrogen atoms connected to an oxygen atom. The feature of this answer that is most germane to the present discussion is that it presupposes that the referent of 'water' is known, whereas the answer was supposed to respond to a question about how one would find out what water is. The presupposition is contained in the phrase "Some samples of water were chosen." But how were the samples chosen? *Scientific* water (H_2O) cannot be picked out by prescientific ostension. Our senses can be too easily fooled—the sample might be heavy water, for example. Furthermore, naturally occurring samples of water (that is, the stuff we call "water" when not wearing our scientific hats) can contain dissolved minerals, undissolved suspended substances, living organisms, nonliving organic matter, gases in solution, and contain these "impurities" in different combinations. So the idea of choosing a sample of water by, for instance, drawing a cupful from the nearest lake, and thinking that you have obtained a sample of what science might call 'water' is completely off the mark.

Nevertheless, such naturally occurring water was what science faced first, and somehow concluded that water is H_2O. How was this conclusion reached? In addition to empirical investigation, the conclusion is the result of a *choice* that depends upon the interests scientists wish to serve, that is, upon the things that scientists value. For instance, scientists value generalizability and predictability, and these values are jeopardized by including in water those things that can vary unsystematically from sample to sample, such as living organisms and dissolved minerals. In addition, scientists value parsimony, and this value is undermined by attempts to explain the properties of a substance as complex as naturally occurring water. So, as well as being an empirical issue, determining what is to count as water, that is, determining the meaning of 'water', requires practical reasoning based on values to decide what conditions ought to be held standard. Therefore, we should not interpret the scientific statement "Water is H_2O" as a statement that describes only a discovery about how the world *is*—the statement also presupposes a choice by scientists about how the world *should* be taken to be for scientific purposes (Scriven 1983). Understanding the statement entails understanding these two sides to its interpretation.

Let us turn to the second example. Think about the colour yellow, and ask when something is really yellow. Consider the statement, *"Scientific* yellow is electromagnetic radiation of wavelength 580 nanometers." Is this really yellow? Most observers would proclaim it yellow if subjected to radiation of that single wavelength. However, under the strictest controls possible, there is an infinite number of combined pairs of wavelengths of light that observers will proclaim to be yellow, and will declare none of the single members of the pairs to be yellow (Hardin 1983; Hurvich 1981). Are these pairs really yellow? There are in fact no conditions under which the phenomenal quality 'yellow' (that which observers sense) does not have a one-to-many relationship with physical magnitudes (wavelengths of electromagnetic radiation).

So the scientific method cannot supply the needed controls to say that such-and-such wavelength and no other is yellow (meaning what we sense as yellow). What do scientists do? They choose to say that specifying precisely what corresponds physically to phenomenal 'yellow', that is, specifying what is really 'yellow' in this sense, is not now an important issue for science, though it may have started out as one. In this case, the answer—yellow is defined by a one-to-one correspondence between phenomenal 'yellow' and certain physical magnitudes— was not obtained, so a different answer had to be derived. Faced with the complexity of light and color, scientists had to use practical reasoning based upon what they wanted science to achieve in order to decide what to do. This time the choice was to stop thinking that science should come to definitive answers to all questions that, without experience from science, humans might choose to ask. The choice was to judge the question, "When is something really yellow?" ill-formed from the perspective of new scientific knowledge and thus to give up trying to answer it.

Thus, we see that, contrary to Hirst, specifying the meanings of both *water* and *yellow* requires the interaction of empirical investigation and practical reasoning involving value judgments of how best to conceive the world. The meaning of *water* and of *yellow* can change as standard conditions change. What constitutes the standard conditions is under the explicit control of scientists who must choose those conditions to be standard that best promote the values for science that they hold. As Duschl, Hamilton, and Grandy (this volume) have argued, knowledge, methods, and aims are partners in the production of scientific knowledge.

Testing Theories

It is nearly universally agreed among philosophers of science that there is no scientific method, in the sense of a stepwise approach for reaching true scientific conclusions. Nevertheless, it is still common in science textbooks to find either a set of ordered steps or a flowchart that, if followed, is supposed to lead from some scientific problem, say the testing of a theory, to its solution. While the exact set of steps or the exact design of the flowchart may vary from source to source (Ennis 1979), one common feature is the injunction that the confirmation and disconfirmation of scientific conclusions are not symmetrical processes. When a conclusion is confirmed with positive evidence, the oft-found view in science textbooks goes, there is always the possibility of later finding contrary evidence which can overthrow the conclusion. Thus, confirmation is tentative. When a conclusion is disconfirmed with contrary evidence, however, the disconfirmation is final. No amount of positive evidence can salvage a disconfirmed conclusion.

The idea that confirmation and disconfirmation are asymmetrical arises from a principle of deductive logic (Hempel 1966). Suppose a scientist is testing some hypothesis, H. Suppose further that the hypothesis has certain observational implications, O. That is, O should be observed if the hypothesis is true. Or, to cast both sides of the relationship in terms of truth: if H is true, then O is also true. Suppose that the results of the scientist's tests are that O is not true. Under this circumstance, the principles of deductive logic entail that H is not true—H is disconfirmed, proven to be false. Suppose, on the other hand, that the results of the scientist's tests are that O is true. Under this circumstance, the principles of deductive logic do not allow us to conclude that H is true. To so conclude would be to commit the deductive logical fallacy of affirming the consequent. We might say that the hypothesis is supported, but we cannot say that it is proven true.

The belief that scientific confirmation is merely tentative but that disconfirmation is final was once widely held by philosophers of science on the basis of the above argument, but now has been challenged strongly by them (Duhem 1951; Quine 1953). Current thinking tends to maintain that both disconfirmation and confirmation are tentative. Suitable adjustments can always be made in scientific beliefs to save a conclusion from contrary evidence, and a conclusion with much evidence in its favor can always be rejected. The asymmetrical view of confirmation and disconfirmation described above followed from the view that statements of science could admit independently of confirmation or disconfirmation in isolation from all other statements. Duhem and Quine showed that science stands up to our experience as a single body, not as a series of separate statements. However, there is no strict method for determining what to do in particular situations when this single body of science conflicts with experience. Changes can be made anywhere. The scientific community follows practical reasoning to work through each case on its own merits, striving to take into account all the evidence, but generally preferring a conclusion that has evidence against it to no conclusion at all, and generally preferring to stay with tried-and-proven ideas rather than to venture into unknown domains (Kuhn 1970).

The scientific controversy near the turn of this century over whether or not there was an aether, a medium for transmitting light, serves to illustrate how the testing of scientific theories does not favor disconfirmation over confirmation and cannot isolate individual statements of science for examination. As postulated, the aether would need to permeate all of the otherwise empty space in the universe in order for light to travel. One consequence of the aether theory is that light would travel at different speeds, depending upon the direction of travel of the light compared to the direction of travel of the earth through the aether (see figure 7-1). If the light was directed in the direction the earth was travelling through the aether (light directed to the left in figure 7-1), then the speed of light would be diminished from its speed, were the earth stationary in the aether, because the light would have to buck (so to speak) the aether flow around the moving earth. If the light was directed in the direction opposite to the one the earth was travelling through the aether (light directed to the right in figure 7-1), then the speed of the light would increase compared to its speed, were the earth stationary in the aether, because the light would be carried along in the wake created by the earth's motion through the aether.

In 1887, two experimental physicists, Albert A. Michelson and Edward W. Morley, working at the Case School of Applied Science in Cleveland, conducted an experiment to test these implications of aether theory. The result of their measurements showed the speed of light to be the same regardless of direction. The result was highly reliable because of the care taken by the experimenters and the proven accuracy of their measurements. According to deductive logic and the views of the scientific method often found in science textbooks, this contrary evidence should have led to the rejection of the aether theory. However, in reality the issue was more complex. In 1892 H. A. Lorentz, and independently in 1893 G. F. Fitzgerald, argued, despite the evidence from the Michelson-Morley experiment, that there really was an aether and that the speed of light varied in it. Michelson and Morley detected no differ-

Figure 7-1
Speed of light as earth moves through aether

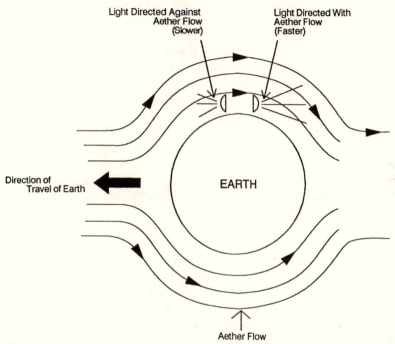

ence, Lorentz and Fitzgerald reasoned, because an implicit assumption made by Michelson and Morley and most other scientists of the day was incorrect. Michelson and Morley assumed that the length of their measuring instruments was constant throughout the experiment. Lorentz and Fitzgerald argued, however, that the length was affected by movement through the aether, decreasing or increasing by just the amounts necessary to compensate for any decreases or increases in the speed of light! Thus, the speed of light appeared by measurement to be constant in all directions, but really varied as the aether theory required. Moral: Do not underestimate the ingenuity of scientists facing threats to treasured ideas to think of auxiliary hypotheses that, if accepted, will protect the idea under threat (Duhem 1954).

Lorentz's and Fitzgerald's reasoning was not uncritical, dogmatic, or unreasonable, even though their conclusions about variation in the speed of light were finally rejected by science. In fact, their reasoning is typical of the sort of reinterpretation of seemingly incontrovertible evidence which continuously occurs in science. Since the upheaval in science marked by Einstein's proposed solution to the puzzle created by the Michelson-Morley experiment, an important implication of Einstein's solution (that the speed of light is the uppermost speed for the universe) is being challenged by some persistent anomalies in quantum mechanics (Davies & Brown 1986).

So we see that, strictly speaking, proof and disproof in science are not clear-cut. Granted, scientists often purport to prove and disprove propositions, as a brief examination of just about any scientific journal will show. However, a sophisticated understanding of proof and disproof in science interprets scientific findings under the assumptions of fallibilism, that is, the view that all scientific beliefs are subject to revision or rejection. On this understanding, proof and disproof in science means "proof and disproof beyond reasonable doubt" (Norris 1984a), and when propositions are proved or disproved beyond reasonable doubt, this does not rule out the possibility that the propositions are wrong.

More germane to this paper, the example illustrates that scientists have to decide what they ought to do in the face of uncertainty. While most definitely based upon relevant data, such decisions are also based upon the ideas that scientists find most compelling for other reasons—for example, their beauty and simplicity. Thus, the long-standing belief that data and interpretation face one another on unequal footing, the former being undeniably true and the latter being tentative, must be denied. In fact, as Hanson (1958) and others have shown, data *are* interpretation. A profound implication of this view is that theory testing is not simply a matter of squaring off data and theory against one another and following the rules of deductive logic. What is to be held true in a given context is a choice made by scientists. Sometimes the data are rejected or reinterpreted, and threatened conceptual structures held intact (e.g., the belief that it is necessary to have a medium for light transmission), through the modification of other conceptual structures (beliefs about the relationships between the length of objects and their motion). Sometimes conceptual structures are altered in order to accommodate data that are accepted. The choice is based on practical reasoning about what to do in the light of which ideas scientists find more valuable. There is no God's-eye view that gives scientists access to the truth. In the process of testing theories, aiming for the truth provides no guidance, because truth is merely an honorific that scientists apply to those beliefs they consider justified (Kaplan 1985). In real-world contexts, there is no way to distinguish something's being true from its being believed justifiably.

It is, I believe, a widespread myth that mathematics always provides straightforward solutions to scientific problems. However, consider even the rather simple problem of deriving mathematically the equation that many of us learned in high school for the period of the pendulum:

$$T = 2\pi(l/g)^{1/2}, \tag{1}$$

where T is the time for the pendulum to make one complete swing, l is the length of the pendulum string, and g is the acceleration due to gravity. We can imagine such a pendulum suspended from some horizontal surface (see figure 7-2). Its bob is displaced from the perpendicular by an angle δ and released. Neglecting air resistance, there are two forces on the bob throughout its swing, the force due to gravity (F_g), acting straight down (toward the center of the earth), and the tension on the

Figure 7-2
A simple pendulum

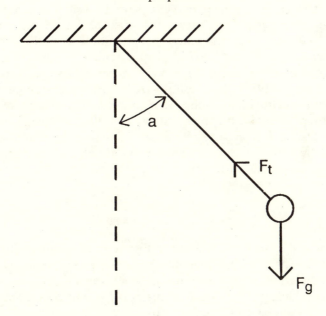

string (F_t), acting along the string in the direction of the pivot point. The fundamental law of physics governing the motion of the pendulum is given by Newton's Second Law, $a = F/m$, which says that the acceleration of the pendulum bob is calculated by dividing the force on the bob in the direction of its motion by the mass of the bob. Since the direction of motion of the bob, and hence the force in the direction of its motion change continuously as the bob swings, the equation of motion using Newton's Second Law can be written as a differential equation as follows:

$$mld^2\delta/dt^2 = -mg\sin\delta(t), \qquad (2)$$

where $\delta(t)$ is the functional relationship between the angle of displacement of the bob from the perpendicular and the time since the pendulum started swinging.

Now, getting to the point of this example, there is no simple way to solve this equation because of the sine function. The normal way to proceed is to approximate sin8(t) by an infinite series of additive terms:

$$\sin\delta(t) = \delta(t) - \delta^3(t)/3! + \delta^5(t)/5! - \ldots \qquad (3)$$

For *sufficiently* small δ, the reasoning continues, all terms beyond the first on the right hand side of equation 3 can be *considered* negligible. Having made this simplifying assumption, $\delta(t)$ can be substituted in Equation 2 for $\sin\delta(t)$, yielding an equation that is easy to solve and that leads to the formula for the period of a pendulum cited as Equation 1.

What implications for the nature of scientific knowledge production can be drawn from this example? The example shows how simplifying assumptions lead to a neat, but approximate, solution to an otherwise intractable problem. However, to adopt a form of expression from Cartwright (1983), the solution "tells lies" about pendulums, in the sense that scientists do not hold equation 1 to be a true description of pendulum motion. Practical reasoning in scientific knowledge production dictates that it is often necessary to tell lies about nature to achieve results more valued than truth. Tractability of problems and truth are thus competing values that scientists must weigh and balance when deciding what to do.

Reporting Observations

Much philosophy of science in this century has been directed towards demonstrating that scientific knowledge could be based upon a firm foundation of observation. This task was a main item on the agenda of logical positivism. Thus, the positivists first required some way to distinguish statements of observation from other scientific statements, and, second, to describe how the observation statements support the rest.

The following example from Barnes (1967) can help to illustrate how the positivist theory tried to meet these two requirements:

> The stick which looks straight in the air looks angularly bent when in water. There are good reasons for thinking that no such change

in shape takes place in the stick. Yet there *is* something straight in the one case and something bent in the other, and there is no good reason for supposing either is less or more of an existent than the other. The straight-stick appearance and the bent-stick appearance are sense-data. (p. 695)

While there might be some question of whether or not the stick actually was bent, the logical positivists thought that there could be no doubt that the stick *appeared* bent. Starting from this intuition, they built their case on three premises: (a) statements of observation are statements about how the world appears to us, about the contents of our experience, as opposed to about how the world actually is; (b) the contents of our experience are directly available for our inspection, so statements describing the contents of our experience can be believed without doubt; and (c) such indubitable statements about our experience can provide the firm foundation in observation required to justify scientific claims to knowledge, because scientific claims ultimately are translatable into the language of our experience (Vienna Circle 1929/1973). Thus, for example, a statement about an electron might be translated into statements about the appearance of pointers or lines of light against a background of numbered scales.

It may be puzzling to some that such sense-experience statements do not resemble reports of scientific observation as they appear in scientific journals. Scientists do not report observations using sense-experience statements, statements that refer to our sensations, but, rather, using statements that refer to objects in the world independent from us: statements about angles of deflection of electron beams, positions of atoms on genes, speeds of recession of galaxies from the earth, rates of growth of viruses, and the movement of the earth's plates (Achinstein 1965; Putnam 1962). The manner in which scientists actually work, therefore, casts doubt on the proposition that sense-experience statements are the observational basis of science. Furthermore, the positivists have failed to show how scientific statements about atoms, electrons, genes, viruses, and so on could be translated without loss of meaning into statements about our experience. Thus, premise (c) is undermined. In addition, premise (a), which amounts to a claim that there are theory-neutral statements that describe the contents of our experience, has also been discredited (Feyerabend 1975; Hanson 1958). Finally, psychological research (Loftus 1979) has shown that there is no privileged language that refers without the possibility of error to the contents of our experience. Thus, premise (b) is false.

Once these major positivist premises about the language of science are rejected, the distinction blurs between observable entities that are immediately accessible to human senses and theoretical entities that are inferred. Electrons, atoms, genes, galaxies, viruses, and tectonic plates are entities whose existence is inferred, yet scientists report observations in terms of them. At the same time, however, scientists turn to observational evidence to test their inferences. Thus, there seems to be a tension: on the one hand, observation seems indistinguishable from theory and inference; on the other hand, scientists turn to observation to support their theories, implying that they are able to distinguish between the two. Thus, there seems to be a stubborn intuition in science that observation has some special epistemological status. Should this intuition be challenged? Possibly it should be, but not before it is understood. Is there some way to show how science is based on observation that does not land the pitfalls encountered by positivism that I have just recounted?

On the route to answering this question, it is instructive to note that, strictly speaking, science is based not directly upon observation, but upon *reports* of observations. So, if we could understand report making, we might have a better understanding of the role of observation in science. Reports are distinguished primarily by their authors' intentions: to transmit information, usually to a fairly well-defined audience. In having such an intent, reports differ from other language uses, such as narration, which has the intent to relate a story. A theory of meaning that takes account of the intent of language uses is *speech act theory*. Hence, speech act theory may be able to shed some light on the meaning of observation reports in science. In order to assess the help it might give, I shall first provide .a brief overview of the theory.

A guiding doctrine of speech act theory is that the context of an utterance (which can be generalized to include the production of written text as well as speech) is of prime importance in determining its meaning (Austin 1962; Searle 1969). The meaning, it is postulated, is contained in the acts that have been performed in producing the utterance. Consider an example: I say to the editors of this volume, I shall have my first draft to you by January 15." In uttering this sentence, I performed at least three acts: (a) I *uttered* a particular token of an English-language sentence; (b) I *promised* the editors that I would have a manuscript to them by a certain date; and (c) I *influenced* the editors' plans for the volume. According to speech act theory, the first act, uttering a sentence in the English language, is called a "locutionary act." The second act, the promising, is called an "illocutionary act." A distinction is made between the first and the second acts because promising, unlike uttering English sentences, is not necessarily a verbal act, even though it was performed using a verbal act in the context in question. The same illocutionary act could have been performed in a different context using, for instance, a nod of the head. For example, one of the editors could have asked me at a professional meeting whether I would have my first draft to them by January 15, and I could have promised with a nod. The illocutionary act implies the intention of the speaker, in this case the intent to promise. The third act, that of affecting other people, is called "perlocutionary." In the example, the effect is to get the editors to make or retain certain plans for the production of the volume.

Now this theory can help us understand scientific observation by focusing on a category of illocutionary acts that Searle (1969) calls "assertives." When a person asserts a proposition, the person intends to send a message that he or she is committed to the truth of the proposition asserted. In this respect, reporting a scientific observation is an assertive: the scientist is committed to the report being true. Additionally, the scientist is committing himself or herself or someone else to having witnessed the event reported. Hence, the illocutionary act performed in reporting a scientific observation is twofold: (a) the scientist attests to something being the case, and (b) the scientist attests that the something was witnessed personally or by someone else.

On the basis of scientists' illocutionary acts of attesting to observations, other scientists often come to believe what has been reported. Thus, the perlocutionary act of reporting an observation is to influence the beliefs of others.

A consequence of this analysis of the meaning of scientific observation is that for science to survive, it must abide by a moral order (Harré 1986, pp. 164-66). The need for a moral order arises from the fact that, in reporting observations, scientists attest to their truth and thereby put themselves in a position to influence the beliefs of other scientists. In a community where ideas are shared and where it is necessary for each individual to rely upon the work of others, individuals will take others to be forthright and honest in their dealings and will thus tend to believe them. There is considerable opportunity to deceive in such an atmosphere. Therefore, in making observations, scientists should be aware of any interferences from their emotions, conflicts of interests, or equipment limitations, take such interferences fairly into account, and report them along with their observations. Similarly, in making observations, scientists should be careful and alert; in reporting their observations, they should report only with a precision that is justified by the techniques that they used (Norris 1984b). These are moral injunctions, not merely practical conveniences.

Thus, making the distinction between science based on observation and science based on observation reports marks the difference between portraying observation as free from human action and observation as essentially a human activity, *answerable to the same moral and ethical standards as any human action*. This is so because reports are actions performed by human beings in a social context and, given this, must adhere to the moral principles guiding all human action. In contrast to this view, scientific observation traditionally has been examined from the perspective of an outsider examining a finished product, divorced from the context of its production. The philosophers doing the examination seemed to believe that observation statements could be understood without knowledge of the producers and consumers of the statements, their motivations, and the intentions they were trying to satisfy.

Of course, scientists can, at least in the short term and sometimes for their entire careers, survive with insufficient care and alertness, by not exposing their conflicts of interest, and by reporting results not fully justified by their techniques. However, science depends upon scientists acting responsibly, so that other scientists can *trust* what they read in scientific journals. Therefore, the moral basis of scientists' behaviour is both utilitarian (science's long-term good) and principled (one should not deceive others).

What, then, of the intuition to grant scientific observation some special epistemological status? The intuition is sound, I believe, though its basis has not been described correctly by the positivist account of indubitable, theory-neutral, privileged-access statements. The special status resides in the practical reasoning of knowledgeable scientists that, in the context and for the purposes at hand, certain statements ought to be trusted on the basis of their having been witnessed and their having support in a large body of experience that demonstrates their trustworthiness. Their *relative* trustworthiness means that they can serve as the basis for testing other statements (Norris 1985, 1987). Always, however, the practical reasoning of knowledgeable scientists is evaluated by the practical reasoning of others. The special status of scientific observation is its relative reliability, not its indubitability; observation, like all of science, is fallible and, on this characteristic, cannot be sharply distinguished from interpretation.

Interim Conclusions

Return for a moment to the issue of demarcating science from other intellectual activities on the basis of language and method. The examples illustrate that the meaning of scientific terms is characterized by considerable flexibility, and sometimes vagueness, and is determined by scientists who must weigh and balance competing values. In addition, the examples show that the language of scientific observation does not provide some privileged access to the nature of the world. Language attaches to the world through experience, and all the methods available for making this connection are fallible. Thus, the issues of language and method are really the same, a fact revealed by comparing the analyses of scientific observation and theory testing. A particular observation possesses no epistemological privilege over some theory, unless scientists grant it. So the testing of theory against observation is mediated by scientists' practical reasoning judgements of what is to be taken for granted in the context, and what ideas are most valuable to preserve.

Thus, whatever the difference between science and other intellectual endeavours, it cannot be based on science's having some privileged language or method or being an enterprise devoid of values. In fact, practical reasoning based on values is at the root of science, and, as I shall argue in the following section, must therefore be at the root of the acquisition of scientific knowledge by students.

ASPECTS OF SCIENTIFIC KNOWLEDGE ACQUISITION

Frames of Understanding and Misconception

Science educators are generally and properly concerned with students' misconceptions of science. Usually, however, the concern is with misconceptions of scientific theories and concepts. For instance, naive physics students may have the false belief that objects must have a net force applied to them to remain in motion, or that an object dropped from a moving airplane will fall straight down. However, there are categories of misconceptions, and hence understandings, that do not refer directly to scientific content knowledge.

At least four frames for understanding science can be identified (Perkins & Simmons 1988), and students can have misconceptions in all four. The *content* frame "contains the facts, definitions, and algorithms associated with the 'content' of a subject matter" (p. 305). It is on understanding within this frame that much research into students' misconceptions has been done. The *problem-solving* frame "contains domain specific and general problem solving strategies, beliefs about problem solving, and autoregulative processes to keep oneself organized during problem solving" (p. 305). Much of the research on misconceptions within this frame of understanding has been done outside science, especially in the field of reading. The *epistemic* frame "focuses on general norms having to do with the grounding of the concepts and constraints in a domain" (p. 311), and the *inquiry* frame contains the knowledge and attitudes necessary for challenging and extending the knowledge in a given domain (p. 313). Both the epistemic and inquiry frames have received considerable attention from science educators, but with less impact on the curriculum than the attention paid to the content and the problem-solving frames.

If students are to understand science, in the sense of "understand" that is presupposed by educational goals, then misconceptions within each of these four frames must be avoided. However, misconceptions within the inquiry and epistemic frames are most crucial. A student who has a factual misconception about, say, freely falling objects may be said not to understand that particular phenomenon. However, a student who has epistemic or inquiry misconceptions may be said not to understand science at all. The reason that understanding within these latter two frames is so crucial is that it defines what scientific knowledge is and describes how it is possible.

It seems to me that focusing on the practical reasoning involved in scientific knowledge production is an ideal way to promote an understanding of the epistemic and inquiry frames of science. Practical reasoning about what ought to be done is extremely prevalent in scientific knowledge production. In addition, practical reasoning reveals the basic nature of the scientific endeavour, because its primary aim is to make choices based on the most fundamental values presupposed by scientists. Thus, unless students are aware of the role of practical reasoning in scientific knowledge production, their understanding of the epistemic and inquiry frames of science will be limited.

Knowledge, Belief, and Understanding

Before exploring how a focus on practical reasoning in scientific knowledge production can promote understanding of science, however, we have to deal directly with differences in linguistic intuitions about the concepts of knowledge, belief, and understanding. For instance, when psychologists speak about propositional knowledge (knowledge that such-and-such), they are often speaking about what philosophers call "true belief." Thus, on the psychological account, one would have knowledge of the true proposition "Mercury is the planet nearest the sun," as long as one believed it. According to standard philosophical accounts, knowledge requires *justification* as well as belief and truth. According to such philosophical accounts, the person who has no justification for the proposition that Mercury is the planet nearest the sun could at most believe, or *think* that he or she knows, the proposition.

In the philosophical sense, acquiring knowledge is constrained by factors both internal and external to the knower. For example, even though some proposition might be known to be true in the world at large, it would be no more than true belief in the mind of someone who does not have justification for the proposition. The person might believe the proposition; the proposition might be true; but the person could not *know* the proposition unless he or she knows why it is true. In contrast, a person could know something that no other person knows. For example, maybe only I know when I got up this morning. However, external factors apply even in this case. If others *had been* present when I got up and they *would have* reached a conclusion different from me about my rising time, then I probably do not know when I got up, even though I think I do and no one is in a position to challenge me. That is, knowledge cannot be wholly idiosyncratic—I may be the only person to have a particular piece of knowledge, but it must be possible in principle that others would have acquired this knowledge had they been in suitable circumstances.

Thus, whereas psychologists tend not to distinguish sharply between belief and knowledge, the distinction is central to certain philosophical arguments. The philosophical sense of knowledge may seem somewhat strict, but it is not foreign to educational thought. For instance, it would seem to be behind the complaint that students often learn the facts by rote and do not understand what they are learning. Learning facts by rote seems akin to acquiring true beliefs without knowing the justification for them. People complain about rote learning, because the mere acquisition of true beliefs falls short of their ideal of education. Education requires understanding, and understanding requires reasons for the truth of beliefs. That is, the philosophical notion of knowledge is close to, if not synonymous with, the notion of understanding that traditionally has underlain educational goals.

Nevertheless, the philosophical notion of knowledge does seem too strict to be followed rigidly in educational practice. In fact, there seems to be a dilemma created by the philosophical notion of knowledge and the desire by schools to teach a large amount of scientific knowledge. If we promote anything less than knowledge in the philosophical sense, we risk endorsing the rote learning of facts without understanding. If, on the other hand, we want students to learn the justification for all the science that we teach them, then it is clear that they will not have the time to understand a good deal of what we would like them to understand.

However, lack of time is not the only constraint on what knowledge can be acquired. Indeed, Hardwig (1985) has argued that we all are inevitably epistemically dependent, in that we must depend on others for virtually everything that we know. Looking at science in particular, no one person has performed the research that would provide the evidence for most of the scientific knowledge that schools teach; most people are not competent, and never will be competent, to carry out the research; most people would not be able to assess the evidence for much of the science they are taught, even if they were presented with it; and most people would not be able even to see the evidence as such were it available to them. Furthermore, no matter how expert we become, Hardwig argues, the dependency remains. Even within highly technical fields, he demonstrates, experts must trust other experts because they cannot know enough (in the philosophical sense) even to do their own work! It seems, then, that the philosophical account of knowledge that requires individuals to be able to justify statements before they can be said to know them, is too strict for more than science students. How, then, given such profound epistemic dependence, should we conceive of the acquisition of scientific knowledge for school students?

Justification Requirements for Scientific Knowledge Acquisition

The educational response to the fact of epistemic dependence must be, first, to help students understand the nature of the dependence, and, second, to help them understand the nature of the trust that they should confer on account of this dependence. Specifically, students should be taught to acquire scientific knowledge on the basis of *rational trust*. Rational trust is based on two elements: (a) a recognition of expertise (Siegel 1988); and (b) knowledge of the general shape that a justification would have to take, of the general sorts of considerations that scientists would count as justification, not knowledge of the justification's actual details. In this paper, I cannot provide a full account of the notion of rational trust. I refer to Siegel (1988) for an account of the first element, the factors that enable the recognition of expertise. I shall describe briefly some of the factors that create the second element.

The general sorts of considerations needed to justify scientific truths are available from the epistemic and inquiry frames of understanding. Here is where lessons from the study of practical reasoning in scientific knowledge production enter the picture. Under my proposal, students would be said to be able to understand and rationally to trust some scientific truth only if they could provide some accurate portrayal of a probable justificatory process for the truth under consideration.

Discussions of the practical reasoning involved in such examples as the four examined earlier provide a sense of the sort of portrayal I have in mind.

Consider how study of the previous examples could help a student understand a new scientific fact that, for example, existing species have evolved from now extinct species by a process of mutation and natural selection. When should we be satisfied that a student understands this statement? In addition to giving examples and translating the statement into his or her own words, we should expect the student to be able to imagine both context-specific and context-general considerations that might have been involved in the scientific process leading to this statement. We should not necessarily demand that the student be able to say which considerations actually were made, only that they are the sort that could have been made because they make sense in the situation.

For instance, based on previous study of theory testing in science, the student should be aware of such context-general considerations as the following: when this idea was first introduced, there likely was disagreement among scientists over how evidence should be interpreted, and there may still be some disagreement; the evidence is probably not sufficient for settling the disagreements; and, however strongly believed now, the statement might be shown wrong in the future. Based on previous study of the way in which standard conditions are chosen in science, the student should know that at the root of any disagreement over the truth of the statement there may be disagreement over the scientific meanings of some of the terms, for example, *species* and *natural selection*. From the study of observation in other contexts, the student should know that the statement is likely based upon observation that is both inaccurate in some respects, open to alternative interpretations, and subject to value judgements about its reliability.

In addition, it would be desirable if the student recognized some context-specific considerations. From a previous study of observation, the student should surmise that evolution probably is not considered a directly observable process but one that is inferred and hence judged by scientists to be less reliably known than, say, characteristics of extant species are known. From learning previously that scientists often make simplifying assumptions (as when deriving equations), the student should surmise that scientists must have made simplifying assumptions to close the gaps in the data between existing species and extinct species. The student should also realize that scientists often.dispute such simplifications and that the simplifications often result in theories that do not truly represent nature.

Being unable to think of such considerations, the student does not really understand and cannot really rationally trust the statement that species have evolved from other species. The student may believe it, and may remember it for reproduction on a test. But the student does not know it or understand it. Being able to think of such considerations, the student can be said to understand and rationally to trust, because the student is not blind to the workings of science. The student sees the reasoning and the interplay among the conceptual, empirical, and normative that goes into the production of scientific knowledge.

Avoiding Stereotypical Science

Instead of using an approach that promotes circumspection regarding the process by which scientific knowledge is produced, science curricula often stereotype scientific knowledge production by portraying it as some sort of algorithmic method that circumvents practical reasoning. More specifically, many science curricula give a false image of the justificatory process in science. Scientific justification is based upon neither once-and-for-all disproof, nor indubitable observation, nor precisely clear definition, nor perfect mathematical precision. While tightness of deductive logic, reliability of observation, clarity of definition, and precision of mathematics are crucial elements in scientific reasoning, there is a considerable and central role in the justification of scientific knowledge played by practical reasoning. Since knowledge of the justificatory process is central to achieving understanding of and rational trust for any discipline, then science students must learn about the role of practical reasoning in scientific knowledge production.

In failing to discuss the practical reasoning in scientific knowledge production, science educators have not given students an accurate portrait of science. As Duschl, Hamilton, and Grandy (this volume) have argued, knowledge production is tentative, full of fits and starts, and full of decisions that could have been made otherwise, leading to different outcomes. However, some people might believe that an accurate portrayal of science that displayed its tentativeness may be disenchanting to students. I have no doubt that it would be disenchanting for some students, because it would reduce the aura that has been created around science. I contend for a number of reasons, however, that reducing the aura of science is justified, nevertheless, on a number of grounds.

First, it is not fair to students to stereotype science, because they have a right as citizens in a democratic society to learn the workings of one of the most influential of society's institutions—science. Second, teaching based on a scientific stereotype has not worked in averting disenchantment over science in any case. Most students speak with their feet when they avoid science courses and science degrees and say that science is not for them. At the same time, our society calls out for better educated scientists and a public more informed of science. Third, the stereotyped image of science is not interesting. There is little interesting about a "rhetoric of conclusions" (Schwab 1960), and algorithmic methods become boring after they are followed a few times.

Fourth, what is in fact interesting about science is that there are far more questions than answers and an enormous choice of methods, none of which may seem exactly suited to a particular task at hand. The practical reasoning involved in the production of scientific knowledge has strong appeal. From my experience, science students find the story surrounding the Michelson-Morley experiment an incredibly interesting tale. It has intrigue, humour, interesting characters, and, if followed with a discussion of some experiments conducted during the last twenty or so years, can make one wonder whether indeed the Fitzgerald and Lorentz solution is not viable. Students are also interested in whether "Water is H_2O" is an empirical statement. They come to the question taking for granted that it is empirical—science, after all, is an empirical endeavour. When, however, they realize that to call something an empirical statement is really to presuppose for practical purposes that the normative and conceptual issues (e.g., whether predictive power ought to be considered more important than truth, and whether liquids and solids ought to be taken as distinct categories) that could arise in a thorough evaluation are being taken as settled, then an entirely different picture of scientific knowledge production is drawn. It is a more interesting picture, too, because students see that scientists do more than follow routines. Thus, telling a more accurate story of science is not disenchanting.

Telling a more accurate story of science does take considerable time, however, that traditionally would be spent covering more topics. This brings us to the fifth point. Science teachers, indeed teachers in general, tend to place considerable emphasis on covering the curriculum. Combine this emphasis with a curriculum that includes large numbers of topics and the inevitable result is superficiality. On the other hand, as Linn (1987) has pointed out, covering a smaller number of topics in greater depth has distinct advantages. A goal of greater depth allows teachers to emphasize critical thinking, enables students to gain more ownership of the problems in science, and is more likely to have lasting impact. Furthermore, consistent with what I have argued above, students find in-depth coverage more satisfying. So, both the evidence and the philosophical arguments support the contention that time spent telling the story of science more accurately pays dividends that are well worth the effort. Now what is needed is an educational atmosphere where teachers find it legitimate to sacrifice coverage for greater depth.

CONCLUSION

Many of my recommendations for science teaching are not new ideas. In 1950, James Conant argued that failure to grasp the essentials of a scientific discussion results "not because of the . . . [layperson's] lack of scientific knowledge or . . . failure to comprehend the technical jargon of the scientist [but] . . . because of . . . [the person's] fundamental igno-rance of what science can or cannot accomplish . . . [the person] has no 'feel' for what we may call 'the tactics and strategy of science'" (p. 1).

Despite their persuasiveness, Conant's ideas have had trouble finding acceptance in practice. It remains more popular to teach lots of scientific content that students will never understand or remember than to teach less content, with the prospect of teaching the transcendent and enduring lessons about science that, in turn, will enable students to understand the content that they do remember.

Students should be taught that science is a community bound together by a moral and ethical code of behaviour that, in part, defines the discipline. They should be taught that the set of propositions that make up what is called "the body of scientific knowledge" is not epis-temologically monolithic. Rather, it is comprised of propositions having varying degrees of justification, from those that are surmised but widely believed, to those that are surmised by only a subset of the scientific community and are doubted elsewhere, to those that are founded on such strong evidence that it would be hard to imagine their being false. Students should be taught how to adjust appropriately their epistemo-logical attitudes (e.g., uncertainty, weak belief, strong belief, doubt) to suit each of these types of propositions (Norris 1981a), and science edu-cators should be aware that the appropriateness of holding different epistemological attitudes towards different scientific propositions has implications for the acquisition of scientific knowledge. Finally, in order for students to grasp fully the meaning of scientific knowledge, they need to be taught the role of practical reasoning based on values in the production of scientific knowledge. Through such an approach, I would hope that the damaging view that science is radically different from other intellectual pursuits will no longer be taken for granted.

SUMMARY AND IMPLICATIONS FOR RESEARCH

I have advanced the thesis that practical reasoning that involves choice based on values is central to the production of scientific knowledge, but that its role is not sufficiently emphasized in the school curriculum. I have argued that this underemphasis has created in the minds of many of our citizens a stereotypical and thus distorted image of science that casts it as a distinctly different from other intellectual pursuits. This distortion affects how science is taught, how its importance is perceived with respect to other subjects, and how students understand science.

I examined four aspects of scientific knowledge production and showed how practical reasoning based on values is involved in each. The aspects were: choosing standard conditions, testing theories, deriving equations, and reporting scientific observations. The lessons from these examples square with the description by Duschl, Hamilton, and Grandy (this volume) of the context of development in science, in which reasoning about methods, aims, and commitments influence what knowledge is produced. The examples show that, contrary to widely held views, neither the language nor the method of science demarcates it sharply from other intellectual pursuits.

Thence, I introduced four frames for understanding science, the content, problem-solving, epistemic, and inquiry frames. Science students can have misconceptions in each of these frames, although it is the first two that are generally studied. I argued that misconceptions in the latter two frames cut to the heart of science. If students do not know what scientific knowledge is or how it comes to be, then accumulating bodies of scientific facts and problem-solving procedures is likely to have little lasting effect. It is through a nonstereotyped study of practical reasoning in the production of scientific knowledge that I suggest students' understanding of the epistemic and inquiry frames can be increased.

The motivation for teaching science, as I suggest, is to create a new and more accurate image of science in the eyes of society in general. If such a new image is created, people will have a more realistic view of what science is and what it can achieve. One implication I would expect is that new audiences of students would be attracted to the study of science.

However, there are at least three areas of substantial research that must be addressed before any of my proposals could be effected. First, there must be research into misconceptions that fall within all four frames of understanding. In particular, there must be more research into the epistemic and inquiry frames that tries to characterize what students know about scientific knowledge and its production, what reasonably can be expected of students to grasp in these areas, and what instructional approaches work best. One recent example of the research I am proposing has been conducted by Carey et al. (1988).

Second, we need more examples of practical reasoning in the production of scientific knowledge. We need examples that describe the nitty-gritty, day-to-day work of scientists. Something is needed that goes beyond the rational reconstructions of science that have typified philosophizing about science and early attempts to portray science more accurately (e.g., Conant 1950). It should be clear that rational reconstructions cannot work, because of the unreliability of the inference needed to reconstruct why scientists acted as they did in some circumstances. A better tactic would be to use ethnographic approaches that study in detail individual scientists in their everyday activities.

Finally, there must be research into the level of specific understanding that science students can be expected to acquire, given the reality of their epistemic dependence. For instance, can examples of episodes of practical reasoning by scientists be generalized by students to other contexts so that their knowledge in those contexts is more than rote? That is, can generalizations from the epistemic and inquiry frames inform understanding in the content and problem-solving frames? If we wish students to have greater understanding of what they are expected to learn in the content and methods of science, then we should hope for an affirmative answer to the previous question.

NOTES

1. I thank Linda Phillips, James Ryan, and the editors of this volume for helpful comments.

REFERENCES

Achinstein, P. (1965). The problem of theoretical terms. *American Philosophical Quarterly, 2,* 193-203.

Aikenhead, G. S. (1985). Collective decision making in the social context of science. *Science Education, 69,* 453-75.

Austin, J. L. (1962). *How to do things with words.* Cambridge, MA: Harvard University Press.

Ayer, A. J. (1952). *Language, truth and logic.* New York: Dover (Original work published in 1936).

Barnes, W. H. F. (1967). There are no sense data. In W. P. Alston & R. B. Brandt (Eds.), *The problems of philosophy* (pp. 693-702). Boston: Allyn and Bacon .

Braithwaite, R. B. (1968). *Scientific explanation*. Cambridge: Cambridge University Press.

Carey, S., Evans, R., Honda, M., Jay, E., & Unger, C. (1988). *"An experiment is when you try it and see if it works": A study of junior high school students' understanding of the construction of scientific knowledge.* (Report No. ETC-TR-88-19). Cambridge, MA: Educational Technology Center. (ERIC Document Reproduction Service No. ED 303 366)

Carnap, R. (1956). The methodological character of theoretical concepts. In H. Feigl & M. Scriven (Eds.), *Minnesota studies in the philosophy of science: Vol. 1 The foundations of science and the concepts of psychology and psychoanalysis.* (pp. 1-74). Minneapolis, MN: University of Minnesota Press.

Carnap, R. (1955). Testability and meaning. In H. Feigl & M. Brodbeck (Eds.), *Readings in the philosophy of science* (pp. 49-92). New York: Appleton-Century-Crofts.

Cartwright, N. (1983). *How the laws of physics lie.* Oxford: Oxford University Press.

Conant, J. B. (Ed.) (1950). *Harvard case histories in experimental science.* Cambridge, MA: Harvard University Press.

Coombs, J. R. (1987). Education and practical rationality. In N. C. Burbules (Ed.), *Philosophy of education 1986* (pp. 3-20). Normal, IL: Philosophy of Education Society.

Davies, P. C. W. & Brown, J. R. (Eds.). (1986). *The ghost in the atom.* Cambridge: Cambridge University Press.

Duhem, P. (1954). *The aim and structure of physical theory* (P. P. Wiener, Trans.). Princeton, NJ: Princeton University Press. (Original work published 1906)

Ennig, R. H. (1979). Research in the philosophy of science and science education. In P. Asquith and H. Kyburg (Eds.), *Current research in the philosophy of science* (pp. 138-78). East Lansing, MI: Philosophy of Science Association.

Feyerabend, P. (1975). *Against method.* London: Humanities.

Hanson, N. R. (1958). *Patterns of discovery.* Cambridge: Cambridge University Press.

Hardin, C. L. (1983). Colors, normal observers, and standard conditions. *The Journal of Philosophy, 80,* 806-13.

Hardwig, J. (1985). Epistemic dependence. *The Journal of Philosophy, 82,* 335-49.

Harré, R. (1986). *Varieties of realism*. Oxford: Blackwell.

Hempel, C. G. (1966). *Philosophy of natural science*. Englewood Cliffs, NJ: Prentice-Hall.

Hirst, P. H. (1989, June). *Epistemology and the curriculum*. Paper presented at the annual meeting of the Canadian Society for the Study of Education, Quebec City.

Hirst, P. H. (1974). *Knowledge and the curriculum*. London: Routledge & Kegan Paul.

Hull, D. (1974). *Philosophy of biological science*. Englewood Cliffs, NJ: Prentice-Hall.

Hurvich, L. M. (1981). *Color vision*. Sunderland, MA: Sinauer.

Kaplan, A. (1964). *The conduct of inquiry*. Scranton, PA: Chandler.

Kaplan, M. (1985). It's not what you know that counts. *The Journal of Philosophy, 82*, 350-63.

Kuhn, T. S. (1970). *The structure of scientific revolutions* (2nd. ed.). Chicago: University of Chicago Press.

Linn, M. C. (1987). Establishing a research base for science education: Challenges, trends, and recommendations. *Journal of Research in Science Teaching, 24*, 191-216.

Loftus, E. F. (1979). *Eyewitness testimony*. Cambridge, MA: Harvard University Press.

Mill, J. S. (1865). *A system of logic* (6th ed.). London: Longmans, Green. (Original work published 1843)

Nagel, E. (1971). Theory and observation. In E. Nagel, S. Bromberger, & A. Grunbaum (Eds.), *Observation and theory in science* (pp. 15-43). Baltimore, MD: Johns Hopkins University Press.

National Science Teachers Association (1982). *Science-technology-society: Science education for the 1980s*. Washington, DC: Author.

National Science Teachers Association (1971). School science education for the 70s. *The Science Teacher, 38*(8).

Norris, S. P. (1987). The roles of observation in science: A response to Willson. *Journal of Research in Science Teaching, 24*, 773-80.

Norris, S. P. (1984a). Cynicism, dogmatism, relativism, and scepticism: Can all these be avoided? *School Science and Mathematics, 84*, 484-95.

Norris, S. P. (1984b). Defining observational competence. *Science Education, 68*, 129-42.

Norris, S. P. (1985). The philosophical basis of observation in science and science education. *Journal of Research in Science Teaching, 22,* 817-33.

Perkins, D. N. & Simmons, R. (1988). Patterns of misunderstanding: An integrative model for science, math, and programming. *Review of Educational Research, 58*(3), 303-26.

Popper, K. R. (1959). *The logic of scientific discovery.* New York: Basic Books.

Putnam, H. (1962). What theories are not. In E. Nagel, P. Suppes, & A. Tarski (Eds.), *Logic, methodology and philosophy of science.* Stanford, CA: Stanford University Press.

Quine, W. V. O. (1953). *From a logical point of view.* Cambridge, MA: Harvard University Press.

Reichenbach, H. (1938). *Experience and prediction.* Chicago: University of Chicago Press.

Schwab, J. J. (1960). Enquiry, the science teacher, and the educator. *The Science Teacher.* October, 6-11.

Scriven, M. (1983). The evaluation taboo. In E. R. House (Ed.), *Philosophy of evaluation.* San Francisco: Jossey-Bass.

Searle, J. R. (1969). *Speech acts.* Cambridge: Cambridge University Press.

Siegel, H. (1988). Rationality and epistemic dependence. *Educational Philosophy and Theory, 20*(1), 1-6.

Vienna Circle (1973). The scientific conception of the world. In M. Neurath & R. S. Cohen (Eds.), *Otto Neurath: Empiricism and sociology.* Dordrecht, The Netherlands: Reidel. (Original work published 1929)

8

Knowledge and Thought:
Mental Models that Support Scientific Reasoning

OUTLINE

ABSTRACT

In this chapter, I examine three questions concerning scientific understanding from the standpoint of cognitive psychology. In addressing the philosophical question "What is a scientific explanation?" I review research on simulation of mechanical models supporting the view that invention of models of how systems work holds the key to scientific explanation. In addressing the psychological question "Which knowledge is needed for scientific understanding?" I review research on prose processing showing that explanative knowledge (as measured by tests of recall for information about how a system works) is related to scientific understanding (as measured by tests of problem-solving transfer) but non explanative knowledge (as measured by tests of recall for arbitrary facts) is not. In addressing the educational question "How can we help students to understand scientific explanations?" I review research on aids to prose processing showing that illustrations of models (i.e., emphasizing explanative information) can help students acquire the explanative knowledge they need to achieve scientific understanding.

What does it mean to produce a scientific explanation? What does someone have to know in order to understand a scientific explanation? How can we help a person to acquire the knowledge that enables understanding? As summarized in table 8-1, these are the questions that have motivated my research program for the past decade and that

Table 8-1
Three Questions about Scientific Explanation

Type	Question	Research Source
Philosophical	What is a scientific explanation?	Simulation of mechanical models
Psychological	Which knowledge is needed for understanding scientific explanations?	Prose processing
Educational	How can we help students to understand scientific explanations?	Aids to prose processing

motivate this chapter. In line with the theme of this volume, these questions represent three threads—the philosophical, the psychological, and the educational.For example, figure 8-1 presents a passage, adapted from *The World Book Encyclopedia*, on how a bicycle tire pump works. First, I pose a philosophical question concerning the nature of scientific explanation: what constitutes a good explanation of how a pump works? Second, I pose a psychological question concerning human

Figure 8-1
Excerpt from "How Pumps Work"

Reciprocating pumps consist of a piston that moves back and forth within a cyclinder. One end of the cylinder has an opening through which the connecting rod of the piston passes. The other end of the cylinder, called the closed end, has an inlet valve or an outlet valve or both, depending on the type of pump. In some reciprocating pumps, the inlet valve or outlet valve is on the piston. Common reciprocating pumps include lift pumps, force pumps, and bicycle tire pumps.

Bicycle tire pumps vary in the number and location of the valves they have and in the way air enters the cylinder. Some simple bicycle tire pumps have the inlet valve on the piston and the outlet valve at the closed end of the cylinder.   Air enters the pump near the point where the connecting rod passes through the cylinder.   As the handle is pulled up, air passes through the inlet valve on the piston and fills the bottom of the cylinder between the piston and the outlet valve.   As the handle is pushed in, the inlet valve closes and the piston forces air through the oulet valve to the hose.

Pumping devices have been an important means of moving fluids for thousands of years.   In the 200's B.C., Ctesibius, a Greek inventor, made the first reciprocating pump for pumping water.   About the same time, Archimedes, a Greek mathematician, invented the screw pump that consisted of a screw rotating in a cyclinder.   This type of pump was used to irrigate the Nile Valley.

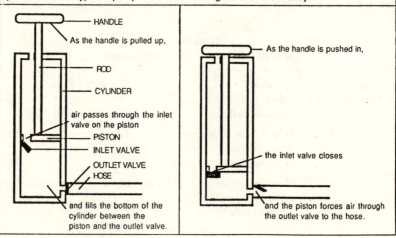

knowledge: what does someone have to know in order to understand how the pump works. Third, I pose an educational question concerning instructional methods: how can we help a learner to acquire the knowledge needed for understanding how a pump works? In the remainder of this chapter, I explore these three questions from the perspective of a cognitive psychologist.

THE PHILOSOPHICAL QUESTION:
WHAT IS A SCIENTIFIC EXPLANATION?

Definitions

The first question is philosophical: what constitutes a scientific explanation? Although a review of philosophy of science is beyond the scope of this chapter, I briefly review three theories of explanation related to cognitive psychology and then focus on one of them in this section (Bunge 1979; Craik 1943; Giere 1979, 1988; Hempel 1965; Hesse 1966; Kuhn 1962; Popper 1959; Thagard 1978). As summarized in table 8-2, scientific explanation may be viewed as description of phenomena, as induction of rules, or as invention of models.

Table 8-2
Three Views of Scientific Explanation

View	Input	Output
Description of phenomena	Observations of events	Descriptions
Induction of rules	Descriptions of relations among events	Rules
Invention of models	Descriptions and rules	Models

Description of phenomena refers to stating the relation between one observable event and another observable event. The form of the explanation may be, *a* leads to *b*. For example, a partial description of how the pump in figure 8-1 works is: "when you press down on the pump handle, air comes out of the hose." According to this view of scientific explanation, the appropriate answer to the question "Why did air come out of the hose?" is to say, "Because you pressed down on the handle."

Induction of rules refers to a process in which a rule is inferred that accounts for a collection of observations of events. Several cognitive psychologists have argued that rule induction is at the heart of scientific explanation (Anderson 1983; Holland et al. 1989; Klahr, Dunbar & Fay, in press; Langley et al. 1987). For example, if we have observed that a_1 leads to b_1, a_2 leads to b_2, and a_3 leads to b_3, then we may infer a broader rule, that A (which consists of a_1 through a_n) leads to B (which consists of b_1 through b_n). For example, in the pump example, we may notice that when we push down only slightly on the handle, only a little air comes out of the hose; when we push the handle down most of the way, a greater amount of air comes out of the hose; when we push down all the way on the handle, the most amount of air comes out of the hose. From these observations, we may induce a more general rule: the amount of pushing down on the handle is proportional to the amount of air coming out of the hose.

Invention of models involves the envisionment of a principle-based mechanism with interacting components that represents the operation of a portion of the natural world. A model may also concretize phenomena that are not directly observable. The components of the model may not be directly observable, and the relations between a change of state in one component and change of state in another component are constrained by basic principles. For example, the illustration in figure 8-1 shows a model of the pump that includes internal mechanisms such as valves and pistons, and general principles such as the idea that air moves from a space with higher pressure to a space with lower pressure. In answer to the question "Why did air come out of the hose?" a person could point out that as the piston moves down it "squeezes" the air within the the bottom of the cylinder, thus increasing the air pressure, which exerts force to open the outlet valve, and allows air to move to a space of lower pressure.

In summary, in description, we begin with observations of events as the primary data and end by describing the temporal and/or spatial contiguity between two events. In induction, we begin with a collection of descriptions of the relations between events as the primary data and end with a general rule under which these descriptions may be subsumed. In invention, we begin with descriptions and rules and end with a model consisting of components that interact in accordance with general principles to produce the observed phenomenon. Given the potential power of mechanical models as explanative devices in cognitive science, I focus on them as a basis for scientific explanation in this chapter (Bobrow 1985; Gentner & Stevens 1983; Vosniadou & Ortony 1989).

Research on Mechanical Models

A primary way of studying the validity of mechanical models is to build computer simulations of mechanical models including buzzers (de Kleer & Brown 1983), pressure regulators (de Kleer & Brown 1984), fluid flow systems (Forbus 1983, 1984), electrical circuits (Gentner 1983, 1989; White & Fredericksen 1987), and gas flow systems (Kuipers 1985). These simulations typically entail two major steps (de Kleer & Brown 1983): *envisioning* the system, including a device typology of the components of the system, possible states of each component, and the structural relations among components; and *running* the system based on basic operational rules and general scientific principles. Based on a simulation of physical devices, Forbus (1984) emphasizes the importance of envisionment by noting that "causality requires some notion of mechanism" (p. 154) and the importance of runnability by concluding that "to be useful a representation must support deductions" (p. 111).

Research on simulating models[1] of physical systems (Bobrow 1985; Vosniadou & Ortony 1989) suggests at least four features of a model of how a system works:

> *components*—the key parts of the system and their structural relation to other parts,
> *states of components*—the possible states of each component,
> *relations between state changes*—the "if-then" relations between a state change in one component and a state change in another component, and
> *principles*—fundamental natural laws that apply to the relations between state changes.

Components and states make up the device model required for envisioning a system, whereas relations and principles form the operating rules required for running a system.

Research on the simulation of physical systems validates the idea that a model can constitute an explanation—that is, a model provides information that supports scientific reasoning. Running a model of a physical system allows for problem-solving transfer including explanation, prediction, and control. These findings encourage the idea that models work as scientific explanations.

For example, table 8-3 presents the major components, possible states, relations, and principles involved in the operation of the bicycle tire pump. I refer to table 8-3 as an explanative analysis of the how pumps work and propose to use explanative analysis as the basis for answering the next two questions posed in this chapter.

THE PSYCHOLOGICAL QUESTION: WHICH KNOWLEDGE IS NEEDED FOR UNDERSTANDING?

Definitions

The second question is psychological: what does someone have to know in order to understand a scientific explanation? In order to answer

Table 8-3
An Explanative Analysis of How a Bicycle Tire Pump Works

Device model	
Key components	*Possible states*
Handle and rod	up/down
Piston	up/down
Inlet valve	open/closed
Outlet valve	open/closed
Cylinder (below piston)	high/low pressure
Hose	high/low pressure

Operating rules	
Basic relations	*Basic principles*
IF handle is pulled up THEN piston moves up	Physical connection via rod
IF piston moves up THEN inlet valve opens	Valve only opens inward; pressure exerted inward
IF inlet valve opens THEN air enters cylinder	Air travels from higher (outside) to lower pressure (inside)
IF inlet valve opens THEN outlet valve closes	Valve only opens outward/pressure exerted inward
IF handle is pushed down THEN piston moves down	Physical connection via rod
IF piston moves down THEN inlet valve closes	Valve only opens inward; pressure exerted outward
IF inlet valve closes THEN outlet valve opens	Valve only opens outward; pressure exerted outward
IF outlet valve opens THEN air escapes via hose	Air travels from higher (inside) to lower pressure (outside)

this question, I must first specify how to measure a person's *understanding and knowledge.*

Consistent with classic research on human problem solving (Mayer 1983), I propose to measure understanding through tests of problem-solving transfer. Problem-solving transfer involves applying learned information to solve problems that are different from those one was taught to solve. Because my focus is on scientific understanding, I propose to focus on problem-solving transfer tests that emphasize explanation, prediction, or control.

For example, table 8-4 lists three problem-solving transfer ques-

Table 8-4
Three Problem-Solving Transfer Questions for "How Pumps Work"

Type	Example
Explanation	Why does air enter the pump when you pull up on the handle?
Prediction	Suppose you pull and push the handle, but no air comes out. What could be wrong?
Control	How could you modify the pump so that it pumps air more rapidly?

tions concerning how pumps work. Each question requires that the learner possess and use a runnable mental model of how a pump works. The first question presents a situation and asks for an explanation; the second question asks the learner to troubleshoot a pumping system; and the third question asks the learner to modify the system to meet a specified functional requirement. In summary, the most straightforward way to measure understanding is through tests of problem-solving transfer.

Consistent with the theories of mental models (Bobrow 1985; Gentner & Stevens 1983; Vosniadou & Ortony 1989), I propose to evaluate knowledge through recall tests of explanative information. *Explanative knowledge* consists of a runnable mental model of a system, including each of the main components, the possible states of each component, the causal relations among state changes in the components, and the principles underlying the causal relations. In contrast, *nonexplanative knowledge* includes arbitrary facts and verbatim wording.

For example, table 8-5 lists some explanative information and nonexplanative information that students recalled from the pump passage

Table 8-5
Examples of Explanative and Nonexplanative Information
Recalled from "How Pumps Work"

Explanative information	Nonexplanative information
"When you pull up on the handle, air comes in."	"A bicycle tire pump is a reciprocating pump."
"Then, the piston moves down and squeezes out the air."	"The first reciprocating pump was invented in 200 B.C."
"As the handle goes down, inlet valve closes."	"Pumps can be used to irrigate land."

in figure 8-1. As you can see, each piece of explanative information focuses on a causal relation between a change in state in one component and a change in state in another component. In contrast, each piece of nonexplanative information focuses on a fact that is not essential for building a runnable mental model of a pumping system.

Research on Prose Processing

Research on text processing can pinpoint the kinds of knowledge that support scientific problem-solving performance. Consider the following scenario: students read a passage that explains how some scientific system works (such as a camera, braking system, or pumping system) and then are asked to recall the passage and solve some transfer problems. We select students who perform well on the problem-solving transfer test (high understanding group) and students who perform poorly on the problem-solving transfer test (low understanding group). Finally, in analyzing the results we ask: "What kinds of information did the high understanding group recall that the low understanding group did not recall?" Based on a philosophy of scientific explanation derived in the previous section, we can predict that high understanders should recall more explanative information but not more nonexplanative information than the low understanders.

To test this prediction, I reanalyzed the data in several experiments conducted in our lab at Santa Barbara. For example, Bromage & Mayer (1981, experiment 1) asked students to read a passage on how to operate a 35-mm camera and then asked the students to recall the passage and to solve problems based on the passage. For example, a typical problem-solving question asked the student to specify the camera settings for taking a picture of a pole-vaulter on a cloudy day. Students who scored high in problem-solving performance recalled different kinds of information from the passage than students who scored low in problem-solving performance. In particular, high understanders were more likely than low understanders to remember causal relations among variables within the internal mechanisms of the camera, such as the idea that turning the focus knob adjusts the distance between the lens elements and the film; in contrast, high and low understanders remembered equivalent amounts of information about relations that did not involve the internal workings of the camera, such as the idea that turning the focus knob affects the clarity of resultant picture.

In another set of studies, students read a passage about how braking systems work and then recalled the passage and solved transfer problems based on the passage (Mayer 1989a, experiments 1 and 2;

Mayer & Gallini, in press, experiment 1). For example, a typical problem was to describe how to make braking systems more reliable. As in the camera study, students who performed well on problem solving outperformed the poor problem solvers on recall of information about the causal relations within the braking system (such as the idea that the piston in the master cylinder moves forward when you step on the brake pedal) but not on recall of arbitrary facts (such as fact that disk brakes are used on the rear wheels of most automobiles).

Finally, Mayer and Gallini (in press, experiment 2) asked students to read a passage on how pumping systems work, to recall the passage, and to solve problems based on the passage. For example, a typical problem was to determine what might be wrong if no water came out of a pump after the handle had been pushed and pulled several times. Consistent with the camera and brakes studies, students who scored high on problem solving tended to remember more explanative information (such as what happens to the inlet valve on the piston when one pulls up on the handle of a bicycle tire pump) but not more nonexplanative information (such as the date that pumps were invented) than students who scored low on problem solving.

For each of these exemplary studies, table 8-6 summarizes the proportion of explanative and nonexplanative information retained by students who performed well or poorly on tests of problem-solving transfer. In each case, students who scored high in scientific understanding (as measured by problem-solving transfer) outperformed stu-

Table 8-6
Proportion Correct on Recall of Explanative and
Nonexplanative Information by Two Groups

Group	Explanative	Nonexplanative
Cameras (Bromage & Mayer, 1981. Expt. 1)		
Low problem-solving score (n = 8)	.23	.61
High problem-solving score (n = 7)	.58	.63
Brakes (Mayer, 1989a. Expts. 1 & 2; Mayer & Gallini, Expt. 1		
Low problem-solving score (n = 27)	.16	.20
High problem-solving score (n = 28)	.28	.24
Pumps (Mayer & Gallini, submitted, Expt. 2)		
Low problem-solving score (n = 14)	.03	.15
High problem-solving score (n = 11)	.17	.19

dents who scored low on scientific understanding on recall of explanative information but not on recall of nonexplanative information: for
the camera passage, high problem-solving students remembered 58 percent of the explanative information compared to 23 percent for the low
problem-solving students; for the brakes passage the corresponding
rates of explanative recall were 28 percent versus 16 percent; and for the
pumps passage the rates of explanative recall were 17 percent versus 3
percent. Apparently, understanding of scientific explanations is related
to one kind of knowledge (i.e., explanative) but not other kinds of
knowledge. How can we characterize the kind of knowledge that seems
to support scientific understanding? Successful problem-solvers are
more likely to remember causal relations between a state change in one
component and a state change in another component within the system.
Acquisition of this explanative knowledge involves building a mental
model of the system that can be mentally run by a learner. Our philosophical analysis of scientific explanation yielded the proposal that a
model includes key components, possible states of each component,
causal relations among state changes, and principles underlying these
relations. The results of studies involving cameras, brakes, and pumps
(as summarized in table 8-6) pinpoint knowledge of causal relations
among state changes as a factor that discriminates high from low scientific understanding.

THE EDUCATIONAL QUESTION: HOW CAN WE HELP
STUDENTS TO UNDERSTAND SCIENTIFIC EXPLANATIONS?

Definitions

The third question is educational: how can we help students to
acquire knowledge that supports scientific understanding? In a recent
review, I defined *education* as the creation of "environments that promote and nurture change in human beings" (Mayer 1987, p. vii). In the
present context, the *change* involves acquiring explanative knowledge
that supports improved scientific reasoning, and the created *environment* involves the use of words and pictures that emphasize explanation
of how systems work. Unfortunately, research on students' preconceptions indicates that many students enter the science classroom with
incorrect intuitions about how the physical world works (Champagne,
Klopfer & Anderson 1980; Clement 1982; McCloskey 1983; McCloskey,
Caramazza & Green 1980; West & Pines 1985).

One way to emphasize explanations is to use explanative illustrations as adjuncts to scientific text. *Explanative illustrations* (see also

Levin & Mayer in press; Mayer in press) present the components of a system, clarify the possible states of each component, and highlight relations among state changes. For example, figure 8-1 includes an explanative illustration for a how a bicycle tire pump works. The illustration shows each of the main components: handle, rod, piston, inlet valve, cylinder, outlet valve, and hose. The frame-by-frame presentation allows the student to see the possible states of each key component: the handle and the piston can be up or down; the input valve and outlet valve can be either open or closed; air pressure in the cyclinder can either high or low. The shading and arrows in the illustration help the student to visualize the flow of events: the direct of the arrows shows which way the air flows, and the amount of the shading represents the amount of air pressure.

Research on Aids to Prose Processing

In the previous section, I reported three examples of research showing that good scientific reasoners tended to possess more explanative knowledge than poor scientific reasoners. An instructional implication of these findings is that direct instruction that emphasizes explanative knowledge would be effective in promoting scientific understanding (as measured by problem-solving transfer).

To test this prediction, I reanalyzed the data from experiments I have conducted on students' learning and reasoning about cameras, brakes, and pumps, corresponding to those reviewed in the previous section. For example, as a follow-up to the camera study reported in the previous section, Bromage & Mayer (1981, experiment 2) asked students to read a passage on how to operate a 35-mm camera that emphasized the underlying mechanical causal relations through illustrations and signaling (explanative group) or did not emphasize mechanical causal relations (control group) and then answer eight problem-solving questions. For example, the explanative version of the passage included an illustration showing how turning the focus knob affected the distance of the film from the lens, whereas the control version did not emphasize the internal operation of the camera. As predicted, students in the explanative group generated an average of 28 percent more good solutions to problems than control students. Also consistent with the previous section, explanative students recalled more explanative information but not more nonexplanative information than control students.

Similarly, Mayer (1989a, experiment 1) and Mayer and Gallini (in press, experiment 1) asked students to read a passage on braking systems that either included explanative illustrations (explanative group) or did not (control group). For example, the illustration for disk brakes showed the state of braking system before and after the brake pedal is pushed. As predicted, the explanative students generated 71 percent more good solutions to problems than control students. Also consistent with the previous section, the explanative students recalled more explanative information but not more nonexplanative information than control students.

Finally, Mayer and Gallini (in press, experiment 2) asked students to read a passage on pumps that either included explanative illustrations (explanative group) or did not (control group). An example of an explanative illustration is given in bottom of figure 8-1. As predicted, the explanative students generated 60 percent more successful solutions to problems than control students. Consistent with the results described in the previous section, explanative students recalled more explanative information but not more nonexplanative information than control students.

For each of these exemplary studies, table 8-7 summarizes the proportion correct on problem solving, explanative recall, and nonexplanative recall for the explanative and control groups. In each case, instruction that emphasized explanations (mainly through the use of explanative illustrations) resulted in improved problem-solving transfer and explanative recall but not in improved nonexplanative recall.

Table 8-7
Proportion Correct on Problem-Solving Transfer and Recall of Explanative and Nonexplanative Information

Group	Problem-Solving	Explanative	Nonexplanative
Cameras (Bromage & Mayer, 1981. Expt. 2)			
Control (*n* = 22)	.60	.08	.56
Explanative (*n* = 23)	.77	.56	.56
Brakes (Mayer, 1989a. Expt. 1; Mayer & Gallini. Expt. 1)			
Control (*n* = 29)	.28	.18	.20
Explanative (*n* = 29)	.48	.31	.18
Pumps (Mayer & Gallini, submitted. Expt. 2)			
Control (*n* = 12)	.30	.01	.17
Explanative (*n* = 12)	.48	.25	.10

These three examples provide consistent support for the prediction that instruction that emphasizes scientific explanation tends to improve students' scientific problem-solving performance. In all, I have evaluated this prediction in a series of twenty-one experiments (summarized by Mayer 1989b) in which students read scientific text that was accompanied by explanative illustrations (experimental group) or not (control group). In each study—including comparisons of explanative illustrations versus no illustrations in texts on cameras, brakes, and pumps—the results were consistent: in twenty-one out of twenty-one tests, students given passages that included explanative illustrations performed better on problem-solving transfer than students given passages without explanative illustrations. The consistency of the effect was matched by its strength: students given explanative illustrations generated a median 67 percent more correct solutions on tests of problem-solving transfer than students who were given scientific text without explanative illustrations. These results are consistent with the idea that explanative knowledge supports scientific reasoning. When students are encouraged to build mental models of scientific systems, their scientific reasoning is improved.

As a validity check, I also tallied the performance of experimental and control students on recall of explanative and nonexplanative information in each study that these factors were measured. If explanative illustrations encourage students to build mental models, then experimental students should recall more explanative but not more nonexplanative information than control students. As predicted, experimental students recalled more than 50 percent more explanative information (across thirteen studies) and more than 10 percent less nonexplanative information (across eight studies) than control students. In addition, recent research suggests that the power of explanative illustrations to improve scientific reasoning may be extended through computer-based visual simulations of scientific systems (White in press; Williams, Hollan & Stevens 1983).

SUMMARY: IMPLEMENTATION AND RESEARCH

I explored three questions in this chapter. First, in response to the philosophical question "What does it mean to give a scientific explanation?" I proposed that a runnable model is the best explanation of how a system works. A runnable model consists of the main components, states, causal relations among state changes, and principles underlying the relations, as summarized in table 8-3 for the pump example.

Second, in response to the psychological question "What does someone have to know in order to understand a scientific explanation?" I proposed that explanative knowledge is needed to support scientific reasoning. Explanative knowledge is the learner's mental representation of a model of a scientific system. In support of my proposal, I summarized exemplary research showing that good scientific problem solvers tend to possess a better store of explanative knowledge (but not other kinds of knowledge) than poor problem solvers.

Third, in response to the educational question "How can we help a person to acquire the knowledge that enables understanding?" I proposed proving less-skilled learners with direct instruction in appropriate models underlying scientific events. My proposal is based on the idea that conceptual change is supported by a student's prior knowledge; when a student lacks useful prior knowledge, direct instruction is a reasonable remedy. In support of my proposal, I summarized a program of research showing that explanative illustrations serve to improve students' scientific problem-solving performance.

In summary, there is a persistent relationship between knowledge, such as a student's mental model, and thought, such as a student's problem-solving transfer performance. This review encourages viewing scientific explanation as the invention of models, scientific learning as the acquisition of useful mental models, and a major goal of science education as the fostering of learners' constructions of useful mental models.

Finally, this line of inquiry leads to implications for teacher training, student learning, and educational research. A major implication for teacher training is that teachers should view their academic goals for science students to include not only the acquisition of knowledge but also the construction of mental models. A major implication for student learning is that when scientific problem-solving performance is an instructional goal, students need to be taught in a way that fosters the construction a mental model of the to-be-understood system. Major implications for educational research are that subject matter in science includes knowledge of how systems work and that additional research is needed to determine how best to help students construct useful mental models.

NOTE

1. I distinguish between simulation models and mental models: simulation models refer to the *information* needed to build a runnable simulation of a system, whereas mental models refer to a person's *knowledge* of how a system works.

REFERENCES

Anderson, J. R. (1983). *The architecture of cognition.* Cambridge, MA: Harvard University Press.

Bobrow, D. G. (Ed.). (1985). *Qualitative reasoning about physical systems.* Cambridge, MA: MIT Press.

Bromage, B. K., & Mayer, R. E. (1981). Relationship between what is remembered and creative problem-solving performance in science learning. *Journal of Educational Psychology, 73,* 451-561.

Bunge, M. (1979). *Causality and modern science.* New York: Dover.

Champagne, A. B., Klopfer, L. E., & Anderson, J. H. (1980). Factors influencing the learning of classical mechanics. *American Journal of Physics, 48,* 1074-79.

Clement, J. (1982). Students' preconceptions in introductory mechanics. *American Journal of Physics, 50,* 66-71.

Craik, K. (1943). *The nature of explanation.* Cambridge: Cambridge University Press.

de Kleer, J., & Brown, J. S. (1984). A qualitative physics based on confluences. In D. G. Bobrow (Ed.), *Qualitative reasoning about physical systems* (pp. 7-84). Cambridge, MA: MIT Press.

de Kleer, J., & Brown, J. S. (1983). Assumptions and ambiguities in mechanistic mental models. In D. Gentner & A. L. Stevens (Eds.), *Mental models* (pp. 155-90). Hillsdale, NJ: Lawrence Erlbaum.

Forbus, K. D. (1984). Qualitative process theory. In D. G. Bobrow (Ed.), *Qualitative reasoning about physical systems* (pp. 85-168). Cambridge, MA: MIT Press.

Forbus, K. D. (1983). Qualitative reasoning about space and motion. In D. Gentner & A. L. Stevens (Eds.), *Mental models* (pp. 53-74). Hillsdale, NJ: Lawrence Erlbaum.

Gentner, D. (1989). The mechanisms of analogical transfer. In S. Vosniadou & A. Ortony (Eds.), *Similarity and analogical reasoning* (pp. 199-241). New York: Cambridge University Press.

Gentner, D. (1983). Structure-mapping: A theoretical framework for analogy. *Cognitive Science, 7,* 155-70.

Gentner, D., & Gentner, D. R. (1983). Flowing waters or teeming crowds: Mental models of electricity. In D. Gentner & A. L. Stevens (Eds.), *Mental models* (pp. 99-130). Hillsdale, NJ: Lawrence Erlbaum.

Gentner, D., & Stevens, A. L. (Eds.). (1983). *Mental models*. Hillsdale, NJ: Lawrence Erlbaum.

Giere, R. N. (1988). *Explaining science: A cognitive approach*. Chicago: University of Chicago Press.

Giere, R. N. (1979). *Understanding scientific reasoning*. New York: Holt, Rinehart and Winston.

Hempel, C. G. (Ed.). (1965). *Aspects of scientific explanation*. New York: Free Press.

Hesse, M. B. (1966). *Models and analogies in science*. South Bend, IN: University of Notre Dame Press.

Holland, J. H., Holyoak, K. J., Nisbett, R. E.,& Thagard, P. R. (1989). *Induction: Processes of inference, learning and discovery*. Cambridge, MA: MIT Press.

Klahr, D., Dunbar, K., & Fay, A. L. (in press). Designing good experiments to test bad hypotheses. In J. Shrager & P. Langley (Eds.), *Computational models of discovery and theory formation*. Hillsdale, NJ: Erlbaum.

Kuhn, T. S. (1962). *The structure of scientific revolutions*. Chicago: University of Chicago Press.

Kuipers, B. (1985). Commonsense reasoning about causality: Deriving behavior from structure. In D. G. Bobrow (Ed.), *Qualitative reasoning about physical systems* (pp. 169-203). Cambridge, MA: MIT Press.

Langley, P., Simon, H. A., Bradshaw, G. L. & Zytkow, J. M. (1987). *Scientific discovery*. Cambridge, MA: MIT Press.

Levin, J. R. & Mayer, R. E. (in press). Understanding illustrations in text. In M. Binkley & A. Woodward (Eds.), *Learning from textbooks: Theory and practice*. Hillsdale, NJ: Lawrence Erlbaum.

Mayer, R. E. (in press). Illustrations that instruct. In R. Glaser (Ed.), *Advances in instructional psychology*. Hillsdale, NJ: Lawrence Erlbaum.

Mayer, R. E. (1989a). Systematic thinking fostered by illustrations in scientific text. *Journal of Educational Psychology, 81*, 240-46.

Mayer, R. E. (1989b). Models for understanding. *Review of Educational Research, 59*, 43-64.

Mayer, R. E. (1987). *Educational psychology: A cognitive approach*. Glenview, IL: Scott, Foresman and Company.

Mayer, R. E. (1983). *Thinking, problem solving, cognition*. New York: Freeman.

Mayer, R. E. & Gallini, J. (in press). When is a picture worth a thousand words? *Journal of Educational Psychology*.

McCloskey, M. (1983). Intuitive physics. *Scientific American, 248*(4), 122-30.

McCloskey, M., Caramazza, A. & Green, B. (1980). Curvilinear motion in the absence of external forces: Naive beliefs about the motion of objects. *Science, 210,* 1139-41.

Popper, K. (1959). *The logic of scientific discovery.* London: Hutchinson.

Thagard, P. (1978). The best explanation: Criteria for theory choice. *Journal of Philosophy, 75,* 76-92.

Vosniadou, S. & Ortony, A. (eds.), (1989). *Similarity and analogical reasoning.* New York: Cambridge University Press.

West, L. H. T., & Pines, A. L. (Eds.). (1985). *Cognitive structure and conceptual change.* New York: Academic Press.

White, B. Y. (in press). ThinkerTools: Causal models, conceptual change and science education. *Cognition and instruction.*

White, B. Y. & Frederiksen, J. R. (1987). Qualitative models and intelligent learning environments. In R. W. Lawler & M. Yazdani (Eds.), *Artificial intelligence and education, Volume 1* (pp. 281-306). Norwood, NJ: ABLEX.

Williams, M. D., Hollan, J. D., & Stevens, A. L. (1983). Human reasoning about a simple physical system. In D. Gentner & A. L. Stevens (eds.), *Mental models* (pp. 131-54). Hillsdale, NJ: Lawrence Erlbaum.

9

Anchored Instruction in Science and Mathematics: Theoretical Basis, Developmental Projects, and Initial Research Findings[1]

OUTLINE

ABSTRACT

Over the past several years, the authors of this paper have been developing the concept of 'anchored instruction.' Anchored instruction provides a way to recreate some of the advantages of apprenticeship training in formal educational settings involving groups of students. In addition, some of the principles of anchored instruction may make it possible to create learning experiences that are more effective than many that occur in traditional apprenticeship training.

This chapter will: (1) outline the theoretical basis for anchored instruction, (2) relate it to other recent conceptual frameworks such as situated cognition, (3) give examples of developmental activities using the anchored instruction model, especially as related to mathematics and science instruction, (4) summarize first sets of research results conducted in these developmental environments, and (5) discuss future developmental and research questions.

Our goal in this chapter is to discuss an approach to instruction that we have been developing at Vanderbilt's Learning Technology Center (e.g., Bransford, Sherwood, Hasselbring, Kinzer & Williams in press; Cognition and Technology Group at Vanderbilt in press; Sherwood, Kinzer, Hasselbring & Bransford 1987). Our approach, which is based on the concept of 'anchored instruction', represents an attempt to help students become actively engaged in learning by situating or anchoring instruction in interesting and realistic problem-solving environments. These environments are designed to invite the kinds of thinking that help students develop *general* skills and attitudes that contribute to effective problem solving, plus acquire *specific* concepts and principles that allow them to think effectively about particular domains (e.g., Bransford, Vye, Kinzer & Risko 1990; Bransford, Sherwood, Vye & Rieser 1986).

Our work on anchored instruction is designed to be relevant to instruction in all content areas, including reading, writing, history, mathematics and science (e.g., Bransford, Kinzer, Risko, Rowe & Vye 1989; Cognition and Technology Group at Vanderbilt in press). We believe that there are some instructional problems that are common to all these areas, although each area also requires specific instructional techniques that mesh with domain-specific goals. In the first part of this chapter we discuss some of the general principles of anchored instruction and provide some specific examples that are not primarily science related. In the second part of the chapter we specifically address the issue of what an anchored approach to science instruction might mean.

Our discussion in the first section of this paper borrows heavily from a recently completed paper by our group that will appear in *Educational Researcher* (Cognitive and Technology Group at Vanderbilt, in press). Our goal in that paper was to explain our concept of anchored instruction and relate it to the work of Brown, Collins and Duguid (1989) on situated cognition and authentic tasks. In the second section of the present paper we go beyond our *Educational Researcher* article and consider some implications of anchored instruction for science instruction. The major focus of our discussion will be on the design of problem-solving environments that engage students in authentic, scientific tasks.

THE CONCEPT OF ANCHORED INSTRUCTION

Like many researchers (e.g., Brown, Collins & Duguid 1989; Scardamalia & Bereiter 1985; Porter 1989), our thoughts about problems with traditional approaches to instruction have been influenced by Whitehead's (1929) discussion of what he called the "inert knowledge problem." Inert knowledge is knowledge that can usually be recalled when people are explicitly asked to do so but that is not used spontaneously in problem-solving contexts even though it is relevant. Whitehead was instrumental in calling attention to the phenomenon of inert knowledge. He also made the provocative claim that, in schools, information was particularly likely to be presented in ways that make it inert (see also Gragg 1940; Simon 1980).

Bereiter (1984) provides an informative illustration of the inert knowledge problem. He describes a situation in which a teacher of educational psychology gave her students a long, difficult article and told them they had ten minutes to learn as much as they could about it. Almost without exception, the students began with the first sentence of the article and read as far as they could until the time was up. Later, when discussing their strategies, the students acknowledged that they knew better than to simply begin reading. They had all had classes that taught them to skim for main ideas, consult section headings and so forth. But they did not spontaneously use this knowledge when it would have helped.

In Sherwood, Kinzer, Bransford, & Franks (1987), we discuss an additional illustration of inert knowledge. We asked entering college students to explain how knowledge of logarithms might make it easier to solve problems. Why were they invented and what good do they do? The vast majority of the students had no idea of the uses for logarithms. They remembered learning them in school but they thought of them only as math exercises that one did in order to find answers to logarithm problems. They treated them as difficult ends to be tolerated rather than as exciting inventions (tools) that allowed a variety of problems to be solved. Imagine that our students had entered a contest that required them to multiply as many sets of large numbers as possible within one hour of time. The students could use anything they wanted to help them except a calculator or a computer. It is doubtful that they would have asked for tables of logarithms even though the tables could serve as extremely helpful tools.[2]

It is useful to contrast the "mechanical procedure" knowledge of logarithms that we found with entering college students to the understanding suggested by the following quotation from Henry Briggs (1624), an astronomer who lived in the 1600s:

> Logarithms are numbers invented for the more easy working of questions in arithmetic and geometry. By them all troublesome multiplications are avoided and performed only by addition . . . In a word, all questions not only in arithmetic and geometry but in astronomy also are thereby most plainly and easily answered.

For Briggs and his fellow astronomers, logarithms were understood to be powerful tools that greatly simplified their lives.

We are indebted to theorists such as Dewey (1933) for helping us understand the importance of viewing knowledge as tools (e.g., see Bransford & McCarrell 1974). As Dewey (1933) noted, when people learn about a tool they learn what it is and when and how to use it. When people learn new information in the context of meaningful activities (e.g., when Briggs and colleagues learned how logarithms helped them do their astronomy better), they are more likely to perceive the new information as tools rather than arbitrary sets of procedures or facts. In several demonstration studies, we have shown that one of the advantages of learning in problem-solving contexts is that students acquire information about the conditions under which it is useful to know various concepts and facts (e.g., Bransford, Goin, Hasselbring, Kinzer, Sherwood & Williams 1988). We also discuss how the learning successes of young children depend strongly on their opportunities to learn in meaningful, socially organized contexts (Sherwood, Kinzer, Bransford, & Franks 1987; Bransford & Heldmeyer 1983), and we discuss laboratory studies that indicate that meaningful, problem-oriented approaches to learning are more likely than fact-oriented approaches to overcome inert knowledge problems (e.g., see Adams et al. 1988; Lockhart, Lamon, and Gick 1988).

Of course, the idea that one needs to "make information meaningful and useful to students" is hardly new. Teachers usually try to provide examples of how information is useful. When teaching logarithms, for example, a teacher or textbook author might discuss how logarithms make it easier to solve computational problems. But statements about one or two potential applications of concepts are still a long way from the situation characteristic of the seventeenth-century astronomers who were discussed earlier. The astronomers were intimately familiar with the kinds of problems that they confronted when trying to do their astronomy. They lived with these problems and had to spend a large portion of their time with tedious calculations. For them, logarithms did not represent a specialized tool that was useful for only one or two textbook-like problems. Logarithms represented a tool that could be used every day.

One of the major goals of anchored instruction is to create shared environments that permit sustained exploration by students and teachers and enable them to understand the kinds of problems and opportunities that experts in various areas encounter and the knowledge that these experts use as tools. A related goal is to help students experience the value of exploring the same setting from multiple perspectives (e.g., as a scientist, historian, etc.). The general principles of anchored instruction are discussed next.

Anchoring Instruction in Meaningful Contexts

As discussed above, a major goal of anchored instruction is to allow students and teachers to experience the kinds of problems and opportunities that experts in various areas encounter. Theorists such as Dewey (1933), Schwab (1960), and N. R. Hanson (1970) emphasize that experts in an area have been immersed in phenomena and are familiar with how they have been thinking about them. When introduced to new theories, concepts, and principles that are relevant to their areas of interest, the experts can experience the changes in their own thinking that these ideas afford. For novices, however, the introduction of concepts and theories often seem like the mere introduction of new facts or mechanical procedures to be memorized. Because the novices have not been immersed in the phenomena being investigated, they are unable to experience the effects of the new information on their own noticing and understanding.

The general idea of anchored instruction has a long history. Dewey discussed the advantages of theme-based learning. In the 1940s, Gragg (1940) argued for the advantages of case-based approaches to instruction. One variation of case-based instruction is to use a variety of mini-cases that serve as *micro*-contexts. Our contexts are usually complex and revisited from many perspectives over periods of weeks and months, hence we refer to them as *macro*-contexts. The purpose of these contexts is to serve as environments for cooperative learning and teacher directed mediation (e.g., Feuerstein, Rand, Hoffman & Miller 1980; Vygotsky 1978). Our contexts are meant to be explored and discussed rather than simply read or watched.

Anchored instruction environments also share some of the characteristics of inquiry environments which have been suggested as a model, especially for science instruction, since Schwab (1962). They are similar in that the anchored instruction environments, as well as inquiry environments, do not propose to "directly" instruct students but provide a situation where learning can take place. As will be noted in the descriptions of the development projects, the anchored instructional environments provide a context for other instructional environments which many times will include inquiry activities.

We prefer our contexts to be in visual rather than text formats and to be on videodisc rather than videotape (see also Spiro, Vispoel, Schmitz, Samarapungavan & Boerger 1987; Miller & Gildea 1987). We selected the videodisc medium for several reasons. One is that it allows students to develop pattern recognition skills. (A major disadvantage of text is that it represents the output of the writer's pattern recognition processes; see Bransford, Franks, Vye, & Sherwood 1989). Second, video allows a more veridical representation of events than text; it is dynamic, visual, and spatial. We think that one advantage of this is that students can more easily form rich mental models of the problem situations (e.g., Johnson-Laird 1985; McNamara, Miller & Bransford in press). The ease with which mental models can be formed from video is particularly important for lower-achieving students and for students with low knowledge in the domain of interest (Bransford, Kinzer, Risko, Rowe & Vye 1989; Johnson, 1987). A third reason for using videodisc technology is that it has random-access capabilities. Random access is advantageous from an instructional viewpoint because it allows teachers to almost instantly access information for discussion (see Sherwood, Kinzer, Hasslebring, & Bransford 1987). Since one of our primary goals is to help students explore the same domain from multiple perspectives, the random-access capabilities are particularly useful for our work.

The Adventures of Jasper Woodbury Series:
An Illustration of Anchored Instruction

An example of anchored instruction is a project being conducted by the Learning Technology Center and sponsored by the James S. McDonnell Foundation. It is designed to develop and evaluate a series of videodisc adventures whose primary focus is on mathematical problem formulation and problem solving. However, we are also developing secondary applications that will enable students to learn science, history, and literature concepts.

The videodiscs that we are developing involve the adventures of a person named Jasper Woodbury. We have completed two discs, are currently finishing a third one, and envision a series comprising six to ten discs. The discs are designed for use with middle school students, although we have worked with students as young as fourth graders and as old as college freshmen. We have been fortunate to develop these discs in conjunction with Tom Sturdeant, our lead writer and the director and producer of the first two videos.

The first Jasper disc poses a very complex mathematical problem that involves more than fifteen steps. Its complexity was intentional. Students are not routinely provided with the opportunity to engage in this kind of sustained mathematical thinking (e.g., Bransford, Hasselbring, Barron, Kulewicz, Littlefield, & Goin 1988; Porter 1989; Sternberg 1986). We are convinced that a major reason for the lack of emphasis on problem solving is the difficulties teachers face in communicating problem contexts that are motivating and complex yet ultimately solvable by students.

An important design feature of the Jasper Woodbury Series disc is what we have called "embedded data design."This involves a multistep problem which is not explicitly presented as, for example, word problems are presented in textbooks. In the Jasper Woodbury Series, students have to generate the problems to be solved, and they have to find mathematical information that was presented throughout the story that will enable them to perform computations. Many researchers argue that problem generation and information finding are particularly important aspects of problem solving (e.g., Bransford & Stein 1984; Porter 1989).

Here is a brief overview of the first disc. In the first scene we meet Jasper and learn that he is going to *Journey to Cedar Creek* to look at an old cruiser that he is interested in buying. He sets out for *Journey to Cedar Creek* in his little motorboat. On the video, Jasper is shown consulting a map of the area, listening to his marine radio, and so forth. As the story continues, Jasper stops for gas at Larry's dock. He leaves Larry's after buying gas with his only cash—a twenty-dollar bill—and sets out up river. He runs into a bit of trouble when he hits something in the water and breaks the shear pin of his propeller. Jasper rows to a repair shop where he pays to have his shear pin replaced. He finally reaches *Journey to Cedar Creek* boat dock where he locates Sal, the cruiser's owner. He and Sal test drive the cruiser and find out the boat's cruising speed. They return to the dock where they fill the cruiser's gas tank (it is an old cruiser and the tank is a small, temporary tank that is being used until the real ones are fixed). Jasper decides to buy the cruiser, and he and Sal conclude the transaction.

At the end of the video we see Jasper asking himself when he needs to leave and whether he can make it home without running out of gasoline. At this point students are challenged to engage in the problem-solving activities that were mentioned earlier. Students must identify Jasper's major goal (to get home before sunset without running out of gas), formulate the subproblems that represent obstacles to this goal (e.g., running out of gasoline), and devise strategies to deal with various subproblems.

It is at this point that the embedded data design of the Jasper Woodbury Series becomes important. Throughout the story, students have been exposed to information that now becomes relevant for Jasper's decision. For example, Jasper must decide if he can pilot the boat home before dark without running out of fuel. The map from a scene shown early in the movie becomes useful for calculating the distance between *Journey to Cedar Creek* and Jasper's home dock. Also, the voice on Jasper's marine radio gave the time of sunset which is one piece of information that is needed to determine the time available for Jasper's return trip (time of sunset is routinely broadcast on the weather channel of marine radios). Many other facts are embedded throughout the video. The embedded data design allows teachers to help students to try to generate what they need to know, attempt to retrieve this information from memory, and then scan back on the disc to see if they were accurate.

Initial Findings. As noted earlier, we designed the Jasper Woodbury Series to provide students with the experience of formulating as well as solving problems. We also designed it to give them experience with a very complex problem that involved a number of interdependent steps. Our assumption was that students cannot be expected to deal with complex problems unless they have the opportunity to work with complexity.

The need to provide experiences with complex examples of problem formulation is illustrated by our data with sixth graders. Although these students had scored above average on standard mathematics achievement tests (Vye et al. 1989, April), they were extremely poor at problem identification and formulation (we expected these findings, since students have few experiences like this). However, our data also indicate that fifth-grade students can become very good at complex problem formulation on tasks similar to those Jasper dealt with after working with the Jasper Woodbury Series in cooperative learning groups for four to five class sessions (Van Haneghan et al. in press).[3] We also find that teachers have been extremely enthusiastic about the Jasper Woodbury Series, mainly because their students seem to be challenged to solve the problems and because even students who normally are not good at math can contribute to problem solving; for example, they may have noticed information on the disc that is relevant for solving Jasper's problem.

Facilitating Broad Transfer. We assume that spontaneous transfer would be limited if students worked only in the *Journey to Cedar Creek* boating context (e.g., Bransford, Sherwood, Vye & Rieser 1986; Brown, Bransford, Ferrera & Campione 1983; Gick & Holyoak 1980; Nitsch 1977; Perkins & Salomon 1989). Our current goal is to create a series of six to ten Jasper Woodbury Series discs that can provide a foundation for using key mathematics concepts in a variety of realistic settings. A second disc in the series has recently been completed and tests with it have begun. This second adventure involves an ultra-light airplane flight undertaken in order to save a wounded eagle. Students must determine the fastest way to get to the eagle and transport it to a veterinarian without running out of gasoline and without exceeding the weight limitations of the ultra-light. The problems to be formulated and solved are similar to the basic problem in *Journey to Cedar Creek*; this allows students to discuss the analogies between the first and second episode and experience the fact that it becomes much easier to solve these types of problems the second time around. Evidence from other research projects suggests that an explicit emphasis on analyzing similarities and differences among problem situations, and on bridging to new areas of application, facilitates the degree to which spontaneous transfer occurs (e.g., Bransford, Stein, Delclos & Littlefield 1986; Littlefield et al. 1988; Perkins & Salomon 1989).

We are in the process of creating computer data bases to accompany the discs in the The Adventures of Jasper Woodbury Series. These provide an opportunity to add new problems that students can work on and to integrate subject matter areas. The data base can help students learn history, science, geography, and other subject matters while also continuing to use quantitative reasoning in order to better understand the information being explored.

As a simple illustration, a data base being developed for the *Journey to Cedar Creek* includes historical information, including information relevant to life during the times of Mark Twain. When studying Mark Twain's world, it is very instructive for students to see how plans to go certain distances by water in episode 1 of The Adventures of Jasper Woodbury Series would have to be very different if the only mode of travel were by raft. A three hour trip for Jasper by motorboat would have taken the better part of a day on Huckleberry's raft. This means that drinking water, food, and other necessities would need to be included in one's plans.

As another illustration of data base problems, consider water current problems for boats, and headwind and tailwind problems for airplanes. We purposely keep details about these types of situations simple in episodes 1 and 2 of The Adventures of Jasper Woodbury Series. Nevertheless, it is an easy matter to get students to imagine that weather or water conditions were slightly different than shown in the video. Instead of the calm day shown in episode 2 of The Adventures of Jasper Woodbury Series, there could be a tailwind of twenty miles an hour on a flight from *A* to *B* which would become a headwind on the return flight. Does the wind's effect on flight time cancel itself out for the entire trip? With a slight twist, winds can also be imagined as coming from an angle (rather than pure headwinds or tailwinds). This variation can help students understand the value of new types of mathematics such as trigonometry.[4]

Anchored Instruction and Situated Cognition

An important set of principles that we believe should shape the development of anchored instruction environments derives from the situated cognition framework discussed by Brown, Collins, and Dugid (1989). Brown and colleagues emphasize the importance of looking carefully at what we know about everyday cognition and of creating apprenticeships composed of authentic tasks. They note that authentic activities are most simply defined as the "ordinary practices of the culture" (p. 34).

Many school tasks lack genuine authenticity. This is often the case in "story problems" given to students in mathematics classes. Some problems contain settings that are authentic (going to a store, etc.), but the problems are often contrived and do not represent situations in which students would normally find themselves. One of our favorite examples derives from a commercial set of curriculum materials on word problems. One of them involved an interesting context; exploring a haunted house. However, the problem posed was "If there are 3 cobwebs on the first floor and 2 on the second, how many are there altogether?" This is hardly an issue that one would care about when exploring a haunted house.

The situated cognition framework also reminds us that novices who enter into a particular apprenticeship have a reasonable chance to develop expertise. Apprentices have the opportunity for sustained thinking about specific sets of problem types over long periods of time. One of our goals in anchored instruction is to use "macro-contexts" (in contrast to "micro-contexts") that can be explored for sustained periods of time.

Authenticity and Jasper

Consider how the situated cognition framework relates to the Jasper Woodbury Series context. The degree to which our instruction involves authenticity can be analyzed from several points of view. A first level of authenticity involves the objects and data in the setting. We considered this factual level of authenticity when designing episodes 1 and 2 of The Adventures of Jasper Woodbury Series. For example, in the boat setting we had Jasper get a weather report from the marine radio (which is where boaters get such information), we used speeds and miles per gallon figures that were realistic for the boats in the video, we used formats for river maps that, though somewhat oversimplified compared to real boating charts, were true to life (e.g., they showed "mile markers" and other appropriate symbols). The airplane adventure is also factually authentic. Speeds, fuel consumption, required distances for takeoff of the ultra-light, weight limits, and so forth are all very similar to actual values in everyday life.

A second level of authenticity—the one emphasized by Brown and colleagues (Brown, Collins & Duguid 1989; Pea 1989)—involves the degree to which the tasks that students are asked to perform are authentic. Each of the details in a setting could be authentic but the tasks given to students could be contrived. For example, the problems posed by the Jasper Woodbury Series could be arbitrary problems like "If Jane had two marine radios and Mark had three, how many would they have altogether?"

In both episodes of The Adventures of Jasper Woodbury Series, the tasks to be performed require students to make and evaluate decisions that seem quite authentic; namely, decisions about when to leave in order to ensure getting somewhere before a specific deadline (episode 1) and decisions about the fastest way to get somewhere and return (episode 2). It is also authentic to be exposed to information (e.g., about weather predictions, gasoline consumption, etc.) and only later have it become relevant when specific needs arise and specific goals are formulated. And it is authentic to have to plan by *generating* sets of subproblems to be solved (e.g., "I have to see if I have enough money to buy gas"), rather than simply having specific word problems presented by someone else (e.g., Lesh 1985; Porter 1989).

But for whom are these tasks authentic? We designed the Jasper Woodbury Series discs to help students learn to "think mathematically," but our instruction does not focus on the kinds of experiences one might expect from the opportunity to be apprenticed to a true mathematician (indeed, many mathematicians we know would not be our first choice to model everyday planning tasks like those in the Jasper Woodbury Series). The focus of episodes 1 and 2 of this series is on the kinds of apprenticeship that one might hope to get from a well-informed parent or "mediator" (Feuerstein, Rand & Hoffman 1979; Feuerstein et al. 1980) who helps his or her children reflect on the types of skills and concepts necessary to deal with problems that can occur in everyday life.

A focus on everyday cognition also raises the question of whether it is reasonable to assume that novices who enter into a particular apprenticeship have a chance to develop expertise. In the Jasper Woodbury Series, the development of six to ten discs makes it reasonable to believe that students will have the opportunity to acquire expertise in solving a variety of planning problems. Without the opportunity for extended practice on a similar set of problem types, we would not expect the opportunity to work with the Jasper Woodbury Series to have much of an overall impact on students' knowledge and skills. Equally important, analyses of cognition in everyday settings reveal the use of a number of labor-saving inventions that reduce or eliminate the need for time consuming computations and hence "distribute" intelligence across the environment (Bransford & Stein 1984; Brown, Collins & Duguid 1989; Lave 1988; Pea 1988; NCTM 1989). For example, many cars now have trip-planning computers that make it easy to estimate fuel consumption and arrival time. Thanks to suggestions from the situated cognition perspective (especially Pea 1989), one of the major goals of the Jasper Woodbury Series is to provide settings that motivate students to select and invent appropriate "intelligence-enhancing" tools.

A third level of authenticity regards the process of "doing" mathematics. What is the nature of mathematics for those in the mathematical community? In essence, what do "real" mathematicians do and how do these activities compare to what students do in classrooms? Lampert (1990) recently pointed out the disjuncture between authentic mathematics and school mathematics:

> Knowing mathematics in school therefore comes to mean having a set of unexamined beliefs, whereas Lakatos and Polya suggest that the knower of mathematics needs to be able to stand back from his or her own knowledge, evaluate its antecedent assumptions, argue about the foundations of its legitimacy, and be willing to have others do the same (pg. 32).

Furthermore, the process by which mathematicians come to "know" mathematics is masked to the outsider. Lampert (1990) summarizes Lakatos's argument on this point:

> . . . mathematics develops as process of "conscious guessing" about relationships among quantities and shapes, with proof following a "zig-zag" path starting from conjectures and moving to the examination of premises through the use of counterexamples or "refutations . . . Naive conjecture and counterexamples do not appear in the fully fledged deductive structure: The zig-zag of discovery cannot be discerned in the end product" (Lakatos, 1976, p. 42). (p. 30)

In exemplary work, Lampert has demonstrated that it is indeed possible to establish classroom contexts in which authentic mathematical discourse occurs among students. Such contexts involve students in arguing from data, in proposing, testing, and revising hypotheses, and in accepting criticisms and counterarguments from their peers (Lampert 1990). As we extend the Jasper Woodbury Series into content areas such as geometry, statistics, and probability, the adventures will provide opportunities for students to engage in authentic mathematical discourse.

AN ANCHORED APPROACH TO SCIENCE INSTRUCTION

Our goal in this second section of the paper is to consider how the general concept of anchored instruction, including the emphasis on authenticity and apprenticeships found in the situated cognition perspective (e.g., Brown, Collins & Duguid 1989), might be used to guide the design of science instruction. We begin by discussing some of our earlier videodisc-based work on science instruction and consider how it is evolving into a project that, hopefully, will be exciting and useful to students and teachers. The overall goal of this new project is to use videodisc and computer technology to re-create many of the kinds of experiences that would be available to students if they apprenticed themselves to real scientists as they work on problems important to us all.

Earlier Work That Anchored Science Instruction in the Context of Indiana Jones's Quest for the Golden Idol

Much of our earlier work on anchored instruction and science involved the use of commercially available movies to create problem solving environments that helped students understand the importance of science information. In one experiment (Sherwood, Kinzer, Bransford, & Franks 1987), we explored the effects of learning science information in the context of the movie *Raiders of the Lost Ark*. The materials for this experiment involved thirteen short passages about topics that might be encountered in middle school and high school science classes. Examples included topics such as (a) the kinds of high-carbohydrate foods that are healthful versus less healthful; (b) the use of water as a standard for the density of liquids considered with the fact that, on earth, a pint of water weighs approximately one pound; (c) the possibility of solar-powered airplanes; (d) ways to make a bronze-age lamp using clay and olive oil.

College students in one condition simply read about each of thirteen topics with the intent to remember the information. Those in a second condition read the same information, but in the context of problems that might be encountered during Indiana Jones's trip to the South American jungle. For example, students in this second condition were first asked to consider the kinds of foods one should bring on a trip and then asked to read the passage about different types of high-carbohydrate foods. Similarly, the passage about the density and weight of water was read in the context of attempts to estimate the weight of fresh water needed for four people for three days; the possibility of solar-powered airplanes was discussed in the context of finding transportation in areas where fuel was difficult to obtain, and so forth. The goal of this type of presentation was to help students understand some of the kinds of problems that the science information could help them solve.

Following acquisition, all participants received one of two types of tests. One half of the students in each group were simply asked to recall the topics of the passages that they had just read. As expected, students who learned in the context of the trip to South America were able to remember a greater number of topics than were students in the no-context group.

The remaining half of the students in each group received a test designed to assess whether they would spontaneously use information that they had just read to solve a new problem. The test they received was disguised as a filler task to be completed before memory questions would be asked about the previously read topics. Students were asked to imagine that they were planning a journey to a desert area in the western part of the U.S. in order to search for relics in Pueblo caves. They were to suggest at least ten areas of information—more if possible—that would be important for planning and survival. The students were also asked to be as explicit as possible. For example, rather than say "you would need food and supplies," they were asked to describe the kinds of food and supplies needed.

The results indicated large differences in students' spontaneous use of information. Students who had simply read facts about high-carbohydrate foods, the weight of water, and so on almost never mentioned this information when providing their answers. Instead, their answers tended to be quite general, such as "take food and take fresh water to drink." In contrast, students in the second acquisition condition made excellent use of the information they had just read. When discussing food, for example, most of them focused on the importance of its nutritional contents. When discussing water they emphasized the importance of calculating its weight. Similarly, constraints on the availability of gasoline versus solar energy were discussed when the importance of transportation (e.g., airplane, car) was recalled. Overall, students who received information in the context of problem solving were much more likely to remember what they read and to spontaneously use it as a basis for creating new sets of plans. Similar effects on recall of science information were found with seventh- and eighth-grade students (Sherwood, Kinzer, Bransford, & Franks 1987).

Uses of Jasper in Science Instruction

Our experiments with the use of Indiana Jones to teach science information had important effects on the design of the Jasper Woodbury problem-solving series that we discussed earlier. At the time of script writing, we asked several groups of science experts to help us enrich the

Jasper Woodbury stories by suggesting ideas and scenes that could be used to teach important science concepts. These scenes were included in our script.

Several situations exist within the two current Jasper Woodbury episodes that are designed to provide specific anchors to science instruction. For example, in *Journey to Cedar Creek* we embedded information about simple machines and flotation. Simple machines are seen throughout the video (e.g., oars on boats, screws on propellers, etc.). One pilot study teacher used an interesting method to exploit these resources on the disc. He asked the students to watch the video and raise their hand when they saw a simple machine. The student then had to describe the machine and what it did for the person using it. In this manner, the student sees that the machine is not just an illustration on a page of text but a useful tool.

The flotation concept is seen often in the story as it is tied to the floating of various objects (boats, barges, docks) on the water. On the other hand, when Jasper drops a little sheer pin that weighs hundreds of pounds less than the boats, barges, etc., the sheer pin sinks. Situations where light objects sink and heavy objects float provide instructors with examples that can be used to extend various types of traditional instruction in the area of flotation. In the text-based materials being developed to accompany the Jasper Woodbury videodiscs, various "teaching suggestions" will be included to exploit these areas. Additional topics will be included for the remainder of the adventures in the Jasper Woodbury Series. For example, in *Rescue at Boone's Meadow*, the topics of aerodynamics and endangered species are two major areas to be explored.

The Golden Statuette

In our work with *Raiders of the Lost Ark* and other commercially available movies, we had to retrofit our instruction to fit the movie context. In our science work with the Jasper Woodbury Series we could be proactive to some extent, but the science concepts were still secondary to the math concepts. In recent years we have had the luxury of asking ourselves what we would do if we had the opportunity to design a videodisc-based series whose primary purpose was to help students learn about and appreciate science.

In 1989 we produced a short prototype video entitled *The Golden Statuette*. This video has as its primary content area the concept of measuring weight and volume (especially of irregular objects) in order to determine an objects' density. While less developed than the Jasper

Woodbury Series materials, it provides an example of how similar design principles might be used in science education.

As in the Jasper Woodbury Series, *The Golden Statuette* uses a story rather than a lecture format. Briefly, the story line is one of a young man who needs some money to buy a guitar and gets the idea to spray paint a small statue gold to try and sell it. He takes the statue to a "trading company" where a young woman examines it. She weighs it, uses water displacement to check its volume, does some calculations, and consults tables. She then offers him twenty cents for his "treasure."

As with the Jasper Woodbury Series, the viewer is never told that this is a video about density, no terminology such as mass or volume is mentioned and no formulas are presented. Instead the viewer sees a situation where a person has collected some data, completed some calculations, and answered an important question—all within five minutes. The challenge to the students is to figure out how the woman knew that the statue was not gold and how she determined how much the fake was worth.

To date field testing of *The Golden Statuette* has occurred only on a limited basis and with a small number of students. In several informal studies we asked groups of three to five students (grades 6, 7, and 8) to retell the story and then describe how the young woman in the trading company knew the statue was not real gold. All of the students seemed to enjoy the story and the challenge to explain the woman's insights. Nevertheless, unless they were provided with extra reading materials, none were able to understand the purpose of the displacement measurements nor to explain how the woman used the concept of density to determine the metallic content of the statuette. Overall, our informal findings are consistent with studies which indicate that, despite the fact that students study density multiple times in school (all our students had been exposed to density and displacement at least once), their ability to use the concept to solve problems is generally poor (Hewson 1986; Frenette 1988).

A study conducted by Barnes, Barnes, and Andriesse (1990, April) provides further evidence of the fact that students often fail to understand the usefulness of concepts such as density. The researchers used *The Golden Statuette* with preservice elementary school teachers. Their study was designed to give some indication of the knowledge level of these students about density as well as pilot some ideas on how the video could be used to teach the density concept to both preservice teachers and school-age children. Their results on the knowledge level, as measured by responses to a question asking students to explain how the young woman knew the statue was not gold, were consistent with the expected results. Over 90 percent of the preservice teachers could not explain, using density concept ideas, how the woman knew the statue was a fake.

Barnes, Barnes, and Andriesse (1990) also discussed some preliminary ideas on the use of the video for instruction, including possible placement of it within a sequence of instruction that included laboratory activities and textual materials. We strongly agree with the idea of emphasizing the importance of active, hands-on experimentation, plus the opportunity to read about information that others have discovered about an area. The goal of our anchors is to set the stage for further inquiry (including reading, discussion, and active experimentation), rather than to replace these activities. This point is explored in more detail in the discussion below.

The Scientists In-Action Series

We have discussed three projects that anchor scientific information in meaningful settings for students (i.e., *Raiders of the Lost Ark*, Science in The Jasper Woodbury Series, and *The Golden Statuette*). The work to date achieves the first two levels of authenticity discussed previously for the case of mathematics. However, just as for mathematics, there is a third level of authenticity to consider for science: Engaging students in the "real" doing of science, as scientists do it. It seems to us that Lakatos's (1976) description of mathematics applies equally well to science, and that a similar disjunction exists in considering authentic science and school science. All too often, students are faced with a body of "established" facts to learn rather than with a problem, inconsistency, or contradiction to resolve. When faced with such problems, they seem unable to engage in the scientific reasoning necessary to establish credibility in the scientific community. We are currently designing our Scientists-in-Action Series to provide macrocontexts for anchoring the discourse of authentic scientific reasoning.

Simulations of Apprenticeships. The Scientists-in-Action Series is based on the assumption that students need to see, experience, and participate in the "zig-zag"of real science. One of the ways to help students learn to engage in such scientific inquiry would be to have them work with actual scientists as they work on real issues. Most graduate training is based on apprenticeships. Similarly, innovative teachers have linked students with professional scientists through the use of telecommunications and other media (e.g., Brand 1989; Curlitz 1989; Kurshan 1990). These types of opportunities are excellent for students, but it is also seems clear that it can be very difficult to provide sustained opportunities for apprenticeship experience for all students enrolled in college, high school, or middle school; there are usually too many students and too few scientists. Our plan is to use video technology to simulate a series of opportunities to work with professional scientists on a variety of issues. We do not want to replace the opportunity for actual apprenticeships; we want to supplement them so that apprenticeship-like experiences can be more frequent for all.

Each episode in our proposed series will allow the viewers (students) to sit in on working meetings involving multidisciplinary teams of scientists who are attempting to solve important problems. The episodes will involve problems that are real rather than imaginary and/or over simplified. This means that we will need to work closely with experts in the areas relevant to each episode. For the pilot episode discussed below, our team of experts included A. B. Bond (Professor of Engineering), David Wilson (Professor of Chemistry and Engineering), and Hubert Dixon, Kaday Gray, Robert Maglievaz and staff, and members of the Vanderbilt Student Environmental Health Project. All of these individuals have been directly involved in the kinds of issues that our pilot video portrays. We are also fortunate to be working with Beth Leopold, who has an extensive background in video production and health-science issues.

Like the Jasper Woodbury Series discussed earlier, the Scientists-in-Action Series is designed to invite thinking, rather than simply present facts in a documentary fashion. The viewers participate in the problem solving and later get to compare their ideas with the other experts. All participants (the students as well as the scientists) have access to written materials about existing theories and data that allow them to take systematic approaches to hypothesis formation and testing, rather than simply be restricted to a trial and error approach to problem solving. The major emphasis is on helping students learn to use theory, data, and experimental procedures to generate and evaluate theories and make arguments about the plausibility or feasibility of specific viewpoints. We say more about the rationale for the series after discussing a sample episode.

A Sample Episode. As an illustration of a possible episode (we have not yet determined the exact problem that we shall use for the pilot video for our series), imagine that four scientists are gathered in a room. One thanks the others for coming on such short notice and presents a problem. As a doctor at the city's General Hospital, she has begun to notice a number of children who are displaying a troublesome set of symptoms. Many are extremely sick. The doctor shows videos of some of the children and their symptoms. Something is causing these symptoms but it's not clear what it is.

On the computer screen in the room the doctor displays some of the symptoms. These include elevated temperatures and the results of several tests including blood tests. The doctor says: "I think that these symptoms speak for themselves, but I want to be sure. This problem is too important for me to be wrong. What's you opinion about what they mean?"

The doctor turns to the viewers (us) and remarks that she would like our opinion too. She realizes that we don't know as much about biology and chemistry as the others in the room, so she shows a book that can help students track down basic concepts. The book she shows in the video is available in the classroom to students viewing the film. The doctor gives the viewers some time to think about the symptoms and come up with a diagnosis on their own.

After the question asked by the doctor, the videodisc stops automatically (through a built-in pause mechanism. For videotape, the teacher can select pause. This stopping point provides an opportunity for students to think about the problem given the existing data. Some of the data will be meaningful to them (e.g., elevated body temperature). Other data will purposely be presented in a form such that, without specific knowledge, will not be interpretable by the students. For example, specific data from the blood tests will be displayed on the computer screen but there will be no interpretations of these data. This allows the students to begin to experience the important role of knowledge in hypothesis formation. By referring to the book that accompanies the video (it will not provide direct answers, but instead will be something like an abridged encyclopedia of important knowledge about biology), students can eventually formulate interpretations of the test results. The most important interpretation for the present scenario will be that the blood tests on all of these children indicate an abnormal level of lead in the body.

Once the students feel that they can interpret the symptoms that were presented, the video begins again. The head doctor asks the other scientists in the room to provide their diagnosis and explain why. All emphasize lead poisoning. This provides the students an opportunity to compare their diagnosis with the experts'.

Following the diagnosis a new phase of the problem begins. What is responsible for the lead poisoning? One of the members of the group, a chemist, is asked to summarize how lead enters the body. This gives the students a framework for thinking about possible causes.

The head doctor mentions that her assistant is busy summarizing the data from over fifty cases in the city and will bring it in soon. In the meantime, she encourages members of the group to consider possible causes for lead poisoning. Examples include lead from cars, which may be especially concentrated in the inner city; toxic chemicals used on some foods, lead from burning old batteries for fuel. Hypotheses considered will be those that have actually been considered by scientists. The purpose of mentioning hypothesis is to give the students some possibilities to think about.

After considering possible hypotheses, the head doctor's assistant will arrive with the data on the fifty cases. Summaries provided by the assistant will include where the victims tend to live (most are in the inner city), their age ranges (in this cases from about one to five years of age), the incidence by gender, and so forth. Both the scientists and the students who are viewers will be asked to consider the original hypotheses (plus others that may be relevant) in light of the data. They will be asked to reconvene tomorrow to provide their views. At this point the disc will again stop and students can work on the problem and consult their "encyclopedia" of relevant ideas and facts. The book will include more information about possible causes of lead poisoning (e.g., from leaded paint), information about how to test paint for lead, and so on. Again, the book will not be laid out in a way to provide direct answers. Instead, it provides "embedded data" analogous to Jasper that students can use to generate and test their own ideas.

The challenge for the students will be to (a) come up with a good argument for the cause of lead poisoning, given the patterns of data presented, and (b) determine a way to test their hypothesis. (In this case the cause will be poisoning due to paint chips; other hypotheses are ruled out due to various patterns such as the age ranges at which children seem to get sick). Students can compare their ideas with the experts on the video by watching the "next day's" meeting where the experts present their arguments and suggest next steps. After working with the tape, the students might then be encouraged to collect data in their own community (e.g., on paint chips) and to test them to see if they contain lead. Articles about others' work on this problem (and about its recurring nature) can also be made available to the students.

Designing the Scientists-in-Action Series: A Thought Experiment. We reiterate that our plans for the Scientists-in-Action Series are in the formative stages. But the process of designing the series is an experiment in itself—an experiment in thinking about the nature of authentic science. By thinking about the series, we are prompted to consider ways to situate science instruction so that it more closely represents the kinds of "ideal" apprenticeship situations that we would like our students to have.

As we indicated above, much of our rationale for the Scientists-in-Action Series stems from a concern that students have the kinds of experiences that enable them to appreciate what it is like to be a "real" scientist. Students need to experience the actual "doing" of science and not just the finished, polished product of that process. However, in the philosophy of science, the view we advocate is a relatively recent one, one that may not be universally accepted, and one that may undergo further change. In an informative paper on changes in the philosophy of science, Cleminson (1990) argues that, until the 1950s, science instruction was primarily concerned with the transmission of factual knowledge about science. We noted earlier that a documentary about discoveries such as lead poisoning from paint could provide such factual knowledge, but that this was not what we wanted to achieve. By the same token, we want students to realize that it can be very useful to read about the products of others discoveries (hence we include our little book with the video).

Cleminson (1990) notes that during the 1960s and 1970s, science education tended to swing toward discovery learning. The idea of developing general discovery skills such as "observational skills" was stressed in many curricula, but students were not helped to see that observations are not theory free. Our Scientists-in-Action Series is designed to let students participate in the process of observation and discovery (e.g., the students are not told directly but rather need to discover that certain patterns of age ranges in the data are very relevant to sorting out hypotheses about possible causes of lead poisoning). By the same token, the series is designed to allow students to simultaneously experience the powerful effect of knowledge (e.g., relevant theory) on the observational or noticing processes. For example, theories of how lead enters the body plays an important role in thinking about the pilot scenario described above. As in our other projects that are anchored instruction (e.g., Jasper) we will attempt to design our Scientists-in-Action Series so that students are able to compare their thoughts (e.g., about various hypotheses) both prior to and after they are introduced to relevant theories about the domain being explored.

In addition to the importance of letting students experience the interplay between knowledge (e.g., theories) and processes (e.g., observation; hypothesis formation and testing), a major goal of the series is to give students a glimpse of science that often differs from their preconceptions (e.g., Linn 1986) about what scientists do. In our experience, many students in middle school and high school assume that scientists work in isolation from one another—often in labs filled with test tubes. There is rarely an appreciation of the multidisciplinary, collaborative nature of science and the excitement this generates. In addition, the idea that scientists often function as detectives is not a view that, in our experience, many students hold.

Our choices of topics to be explored will be designed to capture students' interests. Additional examples might include a search for the cause of rocky mountain spotted fever or lyme disease (both transmitted by ticks) an attempt by an interdisciplinary team to identify the nature of a chemical spill from on overturned tanker truck (the driver has been knocked unconscious) and to contain the spill and protect the population; work by a citizens group to find the causes of a polluted stream, gather data to back their claims, and convince officials that action must be taken. We will attempt to choose topics that allow students to see that the problems being tackled are important at a human level and that time is of the essence in solving them. We also want to use problems that students can expand upon and explore through laboratory experiments and through work in their own communities (e.g., Ramsey 1989) or in conjunction with collaborators who—often through the use of telecommunication—can help collect data and compare results.

Measures of Successful Science Education. Useful as our thought experiment might be to designing effective and authentic science instruction, we recognize that we have multiple criteria for judging whether the instruction is successful, many of which are not the traditional criteria for judging the success of instruction. Our thought experiment convinces us of the need to widen the range of evaluative measures that are examined. Essentially, we have asked ourselves to consider what students will think about science if they experience authentic science. Many of these perceptions hold equally for mathematics.

First, students will see science (and mathematics) as important, vital, and integral to their everyday lives. Students will be prompted to pay attention to "scientists in action" in their own communities. Ideally, students will want to contact some of these local individuals and begin to work with them. Out of these interactions might come (a) a new awareness of important scientific issues and sometimes (b) new student-generated scripts that revolve around the kinds of problems that the "local scientists" engage on a daily basis.

A second measure of success is to increase students' abilities to solve the kinds of problems presented in the videos. In order to do so, students will need an in-depth understanding of relationships between data and theory. Many students understand such relationships at only a very vague level; our series is designed to help students become more sophisticated about these relationships. Each episode will include an emphasis on the need to consider *patterns* of data in order to support and reject hypotheses; for example, patterns such as the age ranges of people who are primarily affected by lead poisoning. In short, our intent is to steep students in theory building, observation and data gathering, revision and refutation in the service of discovering new scientific knowledge.

Related to the second point above is the goal of helping students increase their understanding of the nature of science. Essentially important is the fact that students often fail to understand how theory affects their observations and interpretations (e.g., Carey, Evans, Honda, Jay & Unger 1989; Hodson 1988). One of the design features of our series involves *initial* opportunities for students to use data to make inferences and generate hypotheses followed by *subsequent attempts to use the same data* after being introduced to a new way of thinking about the data (e.g., after being introduced to a new theory). The goal here is to allow students to experience the changes in their own observation and noticing as they try on new theories. (The idea of experiencing changes in noticing and understanding is a major goal of anchored instruction in general.) In conjunction with these experiences, teaching materials to accompany the series will help students see how these relate to current ideas about the philosophy of science (e.g., Carey, Evans, Honda, Jay & Unger 1989; Cleminson 1990; Hodson 1988).

Finally, an especially important measure of success for us is to increase students' interest in careers in science and engineering—especially for women and minorities. We believe that interests in science and engineering will be increased due to our choice of problems to be explored (ones of obvious importance) and our portrayal of methods of exploration (highly collaborative and collegial). In addition, as in our Jasper Woodbury Series, we will include powerful role models of both genders and a variety of ethnic groups.

SUMMARY

Our goal in this paper was twofold. In the first part we borrowed from our Technology Center's article in the Educational Researcher in order to discuss our general approach to instruction—anchored instruction. The goal of our approach is to anchor or situate instruction in semantically rich and interesting problem-solving environments that invite sustained thinking on the part of students. Students explore the environments from their current perspectives (complete with their cur-

268 *Anchored Instruction*

rent preconceptions) and are then able to experience changes in their own noticing and understanding as they are introduced to new information generated by peers, experts, and others. By situating instruction in meaningful contexts, we hope to help students acquire knowledge of general strategies and specific concepts and theories that are non-inert.

In the second part of this paper we discussed how our approach to anchored instruction relates to issues-of science instruction. Several studies were presented that invited thinking about science concepts—studies involving contexts such as *Raiders of the Lost Ark* (a commercially available video) and *The Golden Statuette* (a prototype video developed by our Learning Technology Center). We concluded the paper by discussing our proposed Scientists-in-Action Series that is designed to provide a context for meaningful problem solving as well as follow-on experimentation plus community involvement. We noted that this series is still in the formative stages and that the pilot video is still being planned. We argued that plans for such a series provide an informative thought experiment that can help us begin to clarify assumptions about the nature of effective science instruction.

NOTES

1. Preparation of this paper was supported in part by a grant from the James S. McDonnell Foundation and grants No. G008730072 and No. G008710018 from OERI/RIE. We thank Faapio Po'e for her excellent editorial help.

2. Logarithm computations using tables and interpolation have been given less emphasis in recent years because of the availability of calculators. Logarithms, however, still serve useful computational purposes, for example, calculation of an approximation of the factorial of large numbers, a calculation important in mathematical statistics. More importantly, they provide powerful tools for mathematical modeling. Students often do not understand these uses of logarithms.

3. The following graduate students have been instrumental in our work on mathematics and anchored instruction: Paulo Alcantara, Brigid Barron, Laurie Furman, and Betsy Montavon.

4. We thank Joe B. Wyatt for bringing these possibilities to our attention.

REFERENCES

Adams, L., Kasserman, J., Yearwood, A., Perfetto, G., Bransford, J., & Franks, J. (1988). The effects of facts versus problem-oriented acquisition. *Memory & Cognition, 16,* 167-75.

Barnes, M., Barnes, L., & Andriesse, C. (1990, April). *Profiling preservice elementary teachers' knowledge of density using three assessment techniques.* A paper presented at the annual meeting of the National Association for Research in Science Teaching, Atlanta, GA.

Bereiter, C. (1984). How to keep thinking skills from going the way of all frills. *Educational Leadership, 42,* 75-77.

Brand, S. (1989). Science by mail. *The Online Journal of Distance Education and Communication, 3*(1), Item #5.

Bransford, J. D., Franks, J. J., & Vye, N. J., & Sherwood, R. D. (1989). New approaches to instruction: Because wisdom can't be told. In S. Vosniadou and A. Ortony (Eds.), *Similarity and analogical reasoning* (pp. 470-97). NY: Cambridge University Press.

Bransford, J. D., Goin, L. I., Hasselbring, T. S., Kinzer, C. Z., Sherwood, R. D., & Williams, S. M. (1988). Learning with technology: Theoretical and empirical perspectives. *Peabody Journal of Education, 64*(1), 5-26.

Bransford, J. D., Hasselbring, T., Barron, B., Kulewicz, S., Littlefield, J., & Goin, L. (1988). Uses of macro-contexts to facilitate mathematical thinking. In R. Charles & E. A. Silver (Eds.), *The teaching and assessment of mathematical problem solving* (pp. 125-47). Hillsdale, NJ: Lawrence Erlbaum, and National Council of Teachers of Mathematics.

Bransford, J. D., & Heldmeyer, K (1983). Learning from children learning. In J. Bisanz, G. Bisanz, & R. Kail (Eds.), *Learning in children: Progress in cognitive development research* (pp. 171-90). New York: Springer-Verlag.

Bransford, J., Kinzer C., Risko, V., Rowe, D., & Vye, N (1989). Designing invitations to thinking: Some initial thoughts. In S. McCormick & J. Zutell (Eds.), *Cognitive and social perspectives for literacy research and instruction* (pp. 35-54). Chicago, IL: The National Reading Conference.

Bransford, J. D., & McCarrell, N. S. (1974). A sketch of cognitive approach to comprehension. In W. B. Weimer & D. S. Palermo (Eds.), *Cognition and the symbolic processes* (299-303). Hillsdale, NJ: Lawrence Erlbaum.

Bransford, J. D., Sherwood, R. S., Hasselbring, T. S., Kinzer, C. K, & Williams, S. M. (in press). Anchored Instruction: Why we need it and how technology can help. In D. Nix & R. Spiro (Eds.), *Advances in computer-video technology, computers, cognition, and multi-media: Explorations in high technology.* Hillsdale, NJ: Lawrence Erlbaum.

Bransford, J. D., Sherwood, R., Vye, N. J., & Rieser, J. (1986). Teaching thinking and problem solving: Research foundations. *American Psychologist, 41*(10), 1078-89.

Bransford, J. D., & Stein, B. S. (1984). *The IDEAL problem solver*. New York: Freeman.

Bransford, J. D., Stein, B. S., Delclos, V., & Littlefield, J. (1986). Computers and problem solving. In C. Kinzer, R. Sherwood, & J. Bransford (Eds.), *Computers strategies for education: Foundations and content-area applications*. Columbus, OH: Merrill.

Bransford, J. D., Vye, N., Kinzer, C., & Risko, V. (1990). Teaching thinking and content knowledge: Toward an integrated approach. In B. F. Jones & L. Idol (Eds.), *Dimensions of thinking and cognitive instruction*. Hillsdale, NJ: Lawrence Erlbaum.

Brown, A. L., Bransford, J. D., Ferrara, R. A., & Campione, J. C. (1983). Learning, remembering and understanding. In J. H. Flavell & E. M. Markman (Eds.), *Carmichael's manual of child psychology Vol. 1* (pp. 77-166). New York: Wiley.

Brown, J. S., Collins, A., & Duguid, P. (1989). Situated cognition and the culture of learning. *Educational Researcher, 17,* 32-41.

Carey, I., Flower, L., Hayes, J. R., Schriver, K A., & Hass, C. (1989). Establishing an epistemological base for science teaching in the light of contemporary notions of the nature of science and how children learn science. *Journal of Research in Science Teaching, 26,* 429-47

Carey, S., Evans, R., Honda, M., Jay, E., & Unger, C. (1989). An experiment is when you try it and see if it works: a study of grade 7 students' understanding of the construction of scientific knowledge. *International Journal of Science Education, 11,* 514-29.

Cleminson, A. (1990). Establishing an epistemological base for science teaching in the light of contemporary notions of the nature of science and how children learn science. *Journal of Research in Science Teaching, 27,* 429-47.

Cognition and Technology Group at Vanderbilt. (in press). Anchored instruction and its relationship to situated cognition, *Educational Researcher*.

Curlitz, R. D. (1989). A global network for children: second installment. *The Online Journal of Distance Education and Communication, 3*(1), Item #1.

Dewey, J. 1933. *How we think* (rev. ed.) Boston: Heath.

Frenette, M. (1988). Promoting changes in children's predictive rules about natural phenomena: The role of computer-based modelling strategies. [Technical Report]. Cambridge, MA: Educational Technology Center.

Feuerstein, R., Rand, Y., & Hoffman, M. (1979). *The dynamic assessment of retarded performers: The learning potential assessment device: Theory, instruments, and techniques*. Baltimore, MD: University Park Press.

Feuerstein, R., Rand, Y., Hoffman, M. B., & Miller, R. (1980). *Instrumental enrichment*. Baltimore, MD: University Park Press.

Gick, M. L. & Holyoak, K J. (1980). Analogical problem solving. *Cognitive Psychology, 12,* 306-65.

Gragg, C. I. (1940). Because wisdom can't be told. *Harvard Alumni Bulletin,* 78-84.

Hanson, N. R. (1970). A picture theory of theory meaning. In R. G. Colodny (Ed.), *The nature and function of scientific theories* (pp. 233-74). Pittsburgh, PA: University of Pittsburgh Press.

Hewson, M. G. (1986). The acquisition of scientific knowledge: Analysis and representation of student conceptions concerning density. *Science Education, 70*(2), 159-70.

Hodson, D. (1988). Toward a philosophically more valid science curriculum. *Science Education, 72*(1), 19-40.

Johnson, R. (1987). *The ability to retell a story: Effects of adult mediation in a videodisc context on children's story recall and comprehension.* Unpublished doctoral dissertation, Vanderbilt University, Nashville, TN.

Johnson-Laird, P. N. (1985). Deductive reasoning ability. In R. J. Sternberg (Ed.), *Human abilities: An information-processing approach.* New York: Freeman.

Kurshan, B. (1990). Educational telecommunications connections for the classroom—Part 1. *The Computing Teacher, 17*(6), 30-35.

Lakatos, I. (1976). *Proofs and refutations: Logic of mathematical discovery.* New York: Cambridge University Press.

Lampert, M. (1990). When the problem is not the question and the solution is not the answer: Mathematical knowing and teaching. *American Educational Research Journal, 27,* 29-63.

Lave, J. (1988). *Cognition in practice.* New York: Cambridge University Press.

Lesh, R. (1985). Processes and abilities needed to use mathematics in everyday situations. *Education and Urban Society, 17,* 330-36.

Linn, M. C. (1986). *Establishing a research base for science education: Challenges, trends, and recommendations.* Report of a National Science Foundation national conference. Berkeley, CA: University of California.

Littlefield, J., Delclos, V., Lever, S., Clayton, K., Bransford, J., & Franks, J. (1988) Learning logo: Method of teaching, transfer of general skills and attitude toward school and computers. In R. E. Mayer (Ed.), *Teaching and learning computer programming.* Hillsdale, NJ: Lawrence Erlbaum.

Lockhart, R. S., Lamon, M., & Gick, M. L. (1988). Conceptual transfer in simple insight problems. *Memory & Cognition, 16*, 36-44.

McNamara, T. P., Miller, D. L., & Bransford, J. D. (in press). *Mental models and reading comprehension.* In T. D. Pearson, R. Barr, M. Kamil, & P. Mosenthal. (Eds.), *Handbook of Reading Research, Vol 2.* New York: Longman.

Miller, G. A., & Gildea, P. M. (1987). How children learn words. *Scientific American, 275*(3), 94-99.

National Council of Teachers of Mathematics. (1989). *Curriculum and evaluation standards for school mathematics.* Reston, VA: Author.

Nitsch, K E. (1977). Structuring decontextualized forms of knowledge. *Dissertation Abstracts International, 38B*, 3935.

Pea, R. D. (1989). Personal communication. February 23, 1989.

Pea, R. D. (1988, August). *Distributed intelligence in learning and reasoning processes.* Paper presented at the meeting of the Cognitive Science Society, Montreal.

Perkins, D. N, & Salomon, G. (1989). Are cognitive skills context-bound? *Educational Researcher, 18*(1),16-25.

Porter, A. (1989). A curriculum out of Balance: The case of elementary school mathematics. *Educational Researcher, 18*(5), 9-15.

Ramsey, J. M. (1989). A curricular framework for community-based sts issue instruction, *Education and Urban Society, 22*(1), 40-53.

Scardamalia, M., & Bereiter, C. (1985). Fostering the development of self-regulation in children's knowledge processing. In S. F. Chipman, J. W. Segal, & R. Glaser (Eds.), *Thinking and learning skills: Vol. 2. Research and open questions.* (pp. 563-78). Hillsdale, NJ: Lawrence Erlbaum.

Schwab, J. J. (1960). What do scientists do? *Behavioral Science, 5*, 1-27.

Schwab, J. J. (1962). The teaching of science as enquiry. In J. Schwab & P. Brandwein, *The Teaching of Science.* Cambridge, MA: Harvard University Press, 3-103.

Sherwood, R., Kinzer, C., Hasselbring, T., & Bransford, J. (1987). Macro-contexts for learning: Initial findings and issues. *Journal of Applied Cognition, 1*, 93-108.

Sherwood, R. D., Kinzer, C. K, Bransford, J. D., & Franks, J. J. (1987). Some benefits of creating macro-contexts for science instruction: Initial findings. *Journal of Research in Science Teaching, 24*(5), 417-35.

Simon, H. A. (1980). Problem solving and education. In D. T. Tuma & R. Reif

(Eds.), *Problem solving and education: Issues in teaching and research* (pp. 81-96). Hillsdale, NJ: Lawrence Erlbaum.

Spiro, R. J., Vispoel, W. L, Schmitz, J., Samarapungavan, A., & Boerger, A. (1987). Knowledge acquisition for application: Cognitive Flexibility and transfer in complex content domains. In B. C. Britton & S. Glynn (Eds.), *Executive Control Processess*. Hillsdale, NJ: Lawrence Erlbaum.

Sternberg, R. J. (1986). *Intelligence applied*. San Diego, CA: Harcourt Brace Jovanovich.

Van Haneghan, J., Barron, L., Young, M., Williams, S., Vye, N., & Bransford, J. (in press). The Jasper Series: An experiment with new ways to enhance mathematical thinking. In D. Halpern (Ed.) *Concerning: The development of thinking skills in the sciences and mathematics*. American Association for the Advancement of Science.

Vye, N., Bransford, J., Furman, L, Barron, B., Montavon, E., Young, M., Van Haneghan, J., & Barron, L (1989, April). *An analysis of students' mathematical problem solving in real world settings*. Paper presented at the meeting of the American Educational Research Association, San Fransisco, CA.

Vygotsky, L. S. (1978). *Mind in society*. Cambridge, MA: Harvard University Press.

Whitehead, A. N. (1929). *The aims of education*. New York: Macmillan.

Contributors

Nancy J. Nersessian is assistant professor in the Program in History Department of History at Princeton University. She is also an associate member of the Department of Philosophy and a member of the Program in Cognitive Studies. Her publications include: *Faraday to Einstein: Constructing Meaning in Scientific Theories* and the edited volumes *The Process of Science: Contemporary Philosophical Approaches to Understanding Scientific Practice* and *Selected Works of H. A. Lorentz.* She is series editor of the Science and Philosophy book series, published by Kluwer Academic Publishers.

Stephen P. Norris is a professor of Educational Research and Philosophy of Education at Memorial University of Newfoundland, where he has been since 1980. He has bachelor's degrees in physics and education, a masters degree in science education from Memorial University of Newfoundland, and a Ph.D. in philosophy of education from the University of Illinois in Urbana-Champagne. He publishes in the areas of science education, philosophy of education, and educational testing and measurement.

Gregory Nowak is a graduate student in the Program in History of Science at Princeton University. His interests include the philosophy of science and mathematics and the history of modern mathematics. He is currently completing a dissertation on the algebraic topology of Henri Poincaré.

George Posner is a professor of Education at Cornell University specializing in science education, curriculum development, and school improvement. He is the author of five books, including *Course Design* (Longman); *Field Experience* (Longman); and *Analyzing the Curriculum* (McGraw-Hill), as well as over twenty-five articles and book chapters. A former science teacher, he most recently has served as consultant to school districts and as a school board member.

Kenneth A. Strike is a professor of Philosophy of Education at Cornell University. His principal interests are professional ethics and educational policy. His recent works include *The Ethics of Teaching* (with Jonas Soltis, Teacher's College Press), *The Ethics of School Administration* (with Jonas Soltis and Emil Haller, Teacher's College Press), and *Liberal Justice and the Marxist Critique of Schooling*.

Paul Thagard is senior research cognitive scientist at the Princeton University Cognitive Science Laboratory. He is coauthor of *Induction: Processes of Inference, Learning, and Discovery* (MIT Press, 1986), author of *Computational Philosophy of Science*, (MIT Press, 1988), and author of *Conceptual Revolutions* (forthcoming).

Cognition and Technology Group at Vanderbilt is a multidisciplinary team of researchers located at the Learning Technology Center, Vanderbilt University, Nashville, Tennessee 37203. Contributors to this chapter are: Linda Barron, John Bransford, Bill Corbin, Laura Goin, Elizabeth Goldman, Susan Goldman, Ted Hasselbring, Cliff Hofwolt, Charles Kinzer, Tim McNamara, Ann Michael, Diana Miller, Jim Pellegrino, Vicki Risko, Dan Rock, Robert Sherwood, Salvatore Soraci, James Van Haneghan, Nancy Vye, Susan Williams, and Michael Young.

Jeffrey Bloom is an assistant professor of Science Education at Queen's University in Kingston, Ontario. After working at a marine biology laboratory, he taught in the classroom for six years. Upon completing his doctoral degree at the University of Houston in 1987, he joined the faculty at Queen's. His research interests focus primarily on how children construct meaning around science topics and how teachers can create learning environments that encourage contextually rich learning.

Richard A. Duschl is associate professor of Science Education and Cognitive Studies at the University of Pittsburgh. He also holds a secondary appointment to the University's Center for Philosophy of Science. A Ph.D. was earned at the University of Maryland-College Park in 1983 following three years of employment as an earth science teacher. Richard's interests include history of modern science, theory development, and the relationship between epistemological and cognitive psychological tenets of knowledge growth. These interests and how they relate to science education are developed in his book *Restructuring Science Education: The Importance of Theories and Their Development* (Teachers' College Press; Columbia University, 1990).

Richard E. Grandy currently is a professor of Philosophy and chair of the Cognitive Sciences Program at Rice University. He received his bachelor's degree in mathematics from the University of Pittsburgh and the Ph.D. in History and Philosophy of Science from Princeton. He has taught at Princeton and UNC-Chapel Hill. He edited *Theories and Observation in Science* and is the author of several recent papers on the significance of cognitive science for philosophy of science.

Richard J. Hamilton is an assistant professor of Educational Psychology at the University of Houston. Research interests include concept development, instructional psychology, and validation of teaching strategies for the adult learner. Recent publications are found in the *American Educational Research Journal*, the *Journal of Experimental Education*, *International Journal of Science Education*, and the *Review of Educational Research*.

Richard F. Kitchener is professor and chair of the Department of Philosophy, Colorado State University. He has an M.A. in Psychology (CSU, Los Angeles, 1987) and a Ph.D. in Philosophy (University of Minnesota, 1970) and specializes in philosophical problems of psychology. He is the author of *Piaget's Theory of Knowledge* (1986) and numerous articles on philosophy of psychology.

Richard E. Mayer is professor of Psychology at the University of California, Santa Barbara. His research interests include scientific and mathematical problem solving. He is the author of several books including *Educational Psychology: A Cognitive Approach, The Future of Cognitive Psychology,* and *Thinking, Problem Solving, Cognition.* He has served as editor of *Educational Psychologist* and coeditor of *Instructional Science;* he is the president-elect of the Division of Educational Psychology of the American Psychological Association.

Index

A

Abstraction techniques
  analogy, 9, 55, 61, 62, 64, 66
  limiting case analysis, 9, 55, 56-58
  reasoning from imagistic
    representation, 9, 55, 60, 61, 63
  thought experiment, 9, 55, 56-58,
    64
Accommodation, 148, 159
Adaptation
  see Interactionism
"Adventures of Jasper Woodbury
  Series"
  description of, 250-251
  focus on situated cognition, 254-
    256
  research on instructional effects
    of, 251-253
  science education, 258-259
  use of anchored instruction in,
    254-256
  use of embedded data design in,
    254-256
Analogy
  see Abstraction techniques,
    Maxwell; Conceptual ecology;
    Contexts of meaning
Anchored instruction
  compared with situated cognition,
    253-254
  definition of, 245
  implications for science

education, 256-265, 268
influence on problem solving, 245,
  267-268
principles of, 248
Apprenticeship
  as an example of situated
    cognition, 254
  as used in "Scientists-in-Action
    Series," 262
  description of, 261
Aristotle, 51, 55-56, 148
Artificial intelligence 96
Assimilation, 149

B

Beliefs
  additions to, 126-127
  as guiding frameworks for
    construction of knowledge,
    180, 182-183
  as carriers of knowledge, 121
  dynamics, 126
  justification of, 121
  kinematics, 126
  revisions of, 126-127
  teachers', 2

C

Carnap's theory of scientific
  confirmation, 126

standards of, 134
social aspect of, 125
strategic, 3, 6, 8
Kuhn's normal science, 6, 25, 28
Kuhn's revolutionary science, 6, 25, 28

L

Limiting case analysis
  see Abstraction techniques;
    Galileo's Theory of Motion
Logical positivism
  focus on normative guidelines, 8
  theory construction and
    evaluation, 129
  view of the nature of scientific
    observation, 208-210
Logicism, 126

M

Mathematization of nature, 55
Maxwell
  use of imagistic representation in
    kinematical analysis, 60-61, 63
  use of analogy in dynamical
    analysis, 61-62, 64
Meaning
  emotional component, of 181
  formal, 179-180
  influence of socio-cultural
    contexts on, 180-181
  personal, 181
  propositional, 179-180, 187
Meaningful learning, 179-180
Mechanical models
  computer simulations of, 230-231
  role of scientific explanation, 230-231
Mental models
  acquisition of explanative
    knowledge, 233-234, 236

as product of limiting case
  analysis, 58
influence on problem solving, 240
use in teacher training, 240
use of explanative illustrations to
  induce the development of, 239
well suited for videodisc
  presentation, 249
theories of, 233
Metaphors
process for the development of
  meaning, 183, 187, 198
Michelson-Morley experiments, 199, 204-206, 219
Micro-contexts, 249, 254
Macro-contexts, 249, 254, 261
Misconceptions
  categories of, 213
  conceptual change and, 152-153
  conceptual ecology and, 154-160
  different from scientific
    paradigms, 158
  empirical account of, 155
  epistemological account of, 153-155
  forms of representation of, 156-157
  role of practical reasoning in
    knowledge production, 200
  teachers influence on the
    development of, 4
  within frames of understanding, 213-214
  within inquiry frame of
    understanding, 214
  within epistemic frame of
    understanding, 214

N

Naturalistic epistemology
  empirical aspects of, 120
  normative aspects of,120
  reductionist approach of Quine, 120

Scientific explanation (continued)
explanative illustrations as a
vehicle for, 12, 236-239
Hempel's theory of, 126
philosophical view of, 12, 227-229,
234, 239
problem solving and, 232, 240
production of, 227
psychological view of, 12, 227-228,
231, 236, 240
Scientific confirmation, 203-204, 206
Scientific disconfirmation, 203-204,
206
Scientific knowledge acquisition
abstraction techniques for, 55-62
justification requirement for, 215
philosophical account of, 215
psychological account of, 215
science education and, 215
see also Conceptual change
Scientific knowledge production
as topic of science education, 198,
217-218, 220-221
determination of standard
conditions, 199, 201-202, 221
deriving equations, 199, 221
reporting scientific observation,
199, 208-210, 221
role of simplifying assumptions
in, 208
testing theories, 199, 203-206, 219,
221
Scientific justification 214-218
Scientific problem solving
influence of explanative
knowledge on, 237-240
research on text processing and,
234-239
Scientific reasoning
algorithmic view of, 64
constructivist view of, 64
compared with practical
reasoning, 196
influence of explanative
illustrations on, 239

influence of explanative
knowledge on, 237, 240
influence of science education on,
236-237
philosophical view of, 197
"Scientists-in-Action Series"
description of, 261-264
and apprenticeship, 262
and science education, 265, 268
Self-regulation
see Equilibration
Situated cognition
as a component of "Adventures of
Jasper Woodbury Series," 254-
256
and science education, 257
apprenticeships involving, 254
compared with anchored
instruction, 253-254
Socio-cultural context
influence on meaning, 180-181
Speech act theory, 210-211
Stages
as conceptual laws, 127
as operatory laws, 127
concrete operational, 127
domain general, 127
domain specific, 127
epistemic development, 132-133, 135
formal operational, 127

T

Teacher training
construction of mental models as
a goal of, 240
curriculum implementation and,
2, 3, 6
curriculum intent and, 3, 6
early attempts in science
education, 2
influence of psychological and
epistemological view of
knowledge on, 29, 37, 39, 41